DATE DUE

July 6, 09	
Sept 17, 2012	
April 5, 2013	

Privacy Crisis

Crisis

IDENTITY THEFT
PREVENTION PLAN
AND GUIDE TO
ANONYMOUS LIVING

Grant Hall

JAMES CLARK KING, LLC

Editing, design, and page composition by Ken McFarland

Photographs in this book are for illustrative purposes only. No
endorsement of the contents of this book is implied by the
subjects of images utilized.

James Clark King, LLC, assumes responsibility for the accuracy of
all facts and quotations as cited in this book.

Visa, MasterCard, American Express, and Discover Card are
registered ® trademarks of their respective companies.

Website, telephone, and all other contact information was current and
accurate as of publication of this book.

DISCLAIMER

The information, services, products, and suggestions in this
book—individually and collectively—are provided with the
understanding that the author is not engaged in rendering legal,
accounting, financial, or any other professional advice.
If such expert assistance is desired or required, the counsel of
a competent professional should be sought.

Library of Congress No. 2006933062

ISBN: 0-9786573-0-6
First printing October 2006
06 07 08 09 10 • 5 4 3 2 1

Contents

PART VII–BUSINESS

PART VIII–BEHAVIOR

NOTE: Readers may wish to consult the Glossary for definitions of specialized terms. All such terms are italicized where they first appear in the book.

Dedication

This book is dedicated to Victoria.

It is also dedicated to victims of identity theft everywhere and to privacy seekers who wish to limit the threats posed by the prying eyes of criminals and our own government agencies in these critical times when personal security has become a personal responsibility.

Acknowledgments

The author wishes to acknowledge the contributions of two fine attorneys—Dick and John—for providing expert counsel concerning certain issues and narratives in this book.

Also appreciated for contributing to the cover design and editing of the book is Wild Spirit West Irrevocable Trust.

Introduction

There is a Privacy Crisis in America, and it affects you and your pocketbook. Your privacy is being invaded, eroded, and destroyed by government and criminals. The Privacy Crisis is so serious that you're in danger of becoming a victim of the fastest-growing crime of the twenty-first century—identity theft. As a law-abiding citizen, you have a right to privacy and the freedoms it provides you and your family.

People in the United States of America are losing the privacy battle to those with access to their most personal and confidential information. It's time to awaken to the reality that accepted methods of dealing with the Privacy Crisis are not working. Shredding trash, checking bank and credit card statements, and keeping your mailbox locked are only band-aids—inadequate remedies to stop the hemorrhaging flow of personal freedom. It's time to realize that only through the use of proven and effective privacy principles and concepts will your most sensitive information be kept out of reach—away from those who want to rob, cheat, or harm you.

This book provides a new and effective plan for preventing identity theft. It provides the tools that enable you to live anonymously—beneath the radar of government and corporate databases. Once you learn the art of practicing low-profile living, you will no longer be threatened by anyone—not the NSA listening in on your phone calls, not those who attempt to monitor your email communications, not a stalker peeking into your bedroom window.

Forget about a divorce attorney's private investigator diving into your dumpster or a government agency garnishing your wages or seizing your assets. You can make your life as private as you wish by following the principles and examples outlined in the chapters of this book. And you can accomplish a high level of privacy legally—while sitting at your desk and enjoying the comforts of your own home.

Your author has lived a private lifestyle for many years. No one can tap into my credit reports or find any link to property or businesses under my control. I also have experienced another aspect of privacy invasion—the side of a person being investigated and hunted. I can promise you that what you read in this book will work for you, as it has for me.

Grant Hall
September 2006
North Dakota, U.S.A.

ONE

Privacy Prevents Identity Theft

"A good name, like good will, is got by many actions and lost by one."—Lord Jeffrey

PRIVACY IN CRISIS

I am going to steal everything you own today.

By tomorrow morning, your home equity will be spent, your bank and brokerage accounts will be drained, your credit cards will be maxed out, and I will be "you." Within forty-eight hours, I am going to use your name and Social Security number to get a job, buy a house, and borrow more money. I am Pedro Ortiz, the illegal alien from Mexico whom your next door neighbor picked up at the home improvement store and hired to do his yard work. I have stolen your identity.

THE COMPUTER: AN IDENTITY THEFT TOOL

Identity theft is the fastest-growing crime in the United States of America. Nearly one of every twenty people has had his or her name stolen. Subsequently, these people lost over $2,400 on average—plus their credit and reputation—to an identity thief.

Are you and your home being watched? As you drive your car, go to work, pick up the kids from school, and return home to your "private" residence, the chances are good that someone is learning all he or she can about you while attempting to become you—temporarily or permanently. Your mail may be opened without your knowledge. Your car's license plates may be run through databases to identify you and learn more about you. Your home may be cased as well.

Once someone begins to investigate you, a great deal can be learned about you in a short period of time and without much effort or expense on the part of the perpetrator. A slick operator can learn where you live, what vehicle you drive, where you bank, and where you work within just a few hours of targeting you. Unless you take special precautions to guard against someone else knowing your personal business, you risk having your life turned upside down—not to mention the danger and expense of it all.

OPEN TO THE PUBLIC

Americans are having their identities stolen at the fastest rate in history. Half of those who have their names stolen know the perpetrator. So be careful who knows your business. Those who steal identities take the information necessary to "become" someone else by accessing any or all of the "usual suspect" documents and places: your mailbox, credit reports, bank account information, driver's license, property registrations, Social Security card, credit cards, checkbooks, computer files, and your trash—wherever any personal information about you can be found.

Regardless of how the information is obtained, once you have your identity stolen, it is a time-consuming, expensive mess to fix. So take the crime of identity theft seriously. Prevention is, by far, the most inexpensive insurance policy you can buy, so insulate your identification and your identity data—literally—from everyone who does not need to know your personal business.

A reader whom I will call Anna Maria Gonzales recently wrote explaining she'd had her identity stolen. The crime caught Ms. Gonzales completely by surprise. Apparently, the culprit had assumed this woman's identity in preparation for taking full advantage of Anna's resources. First, her full name, Social Security number, date of birth, home address, and credit card and bank account numbers were stolen. Once this information was in the hands of the identity thief, she was able to access the victim's credit bureau files for even more personal financial information.

Over a period of several weeks, the identity thief left Anna deeply in debt, unable to access her own bank account or credit lines. Her bank accounts and credit lines were drained—leaving her with no emergency funds. Anna was soon inundated with official claim forms and letters of affidavit to complete and have notarized. Numerous time-consuming phone calls and trips became necessary once the crime had been committed against her.

For weeks, Anna spent most of her waking hours assisting law enforcement's efforts to catch the criminal, and the remainder of her days—what was left of them—she spent corresponding and communicating with state and federal government agencies, banks, and financial institutions, attempting to rehabilitate her credibility and her credit. As a victim of this crime, she was forced to take a second job in order to meet her living expenses. After this disaster, she had no credit available and no money. None. The identity thief had taken it all.

PERSONAL INFORMATION IS EASILY ACCESSED ON THE INTERNET.

While it is not going to solve Anna Maria Gonzales' difficulty to point out the errors she made that enabled the crook to steal from her, this case is not all that unusual and will serve as a model of how average Americans leave their lives wide open and vulnerable to identity theft. Since Mr. and Ms. Average American obviously do not understand how to handle their private affairs privately, based on the rise in identity theft, changes and preparations need to be made to prevent this crime. Knowing some of the leads Ms. Identity Thief used to track down Ms. Gonzales, steal her name, and take her money is a starting point in learning how to avoid this dastardly crime.

PERSONAL "PUBLIC" INFORMATION

Anna Maria Gonzales owns a hair salon in a large northeastern city. Her business is held in her name and registered as a solely owned business. Since she is a sole proprietor, Anna uses a checking account held in her name, with her Social Security number (SSN) as the taxpayer I.D. on the bank's records. She deposits business checks and buys supplies with checks from this account. Her salon address and her home address are both used to receive mail.

Credit card bills, bank account statements, automobile registration and insurance correspondences, association membership notices, magazine and newspaper subscriptions, medical and dental bills, statements of all types, state and federal tax correspondences, and personal and business shipments and deliveries come either to the hair salon or to Anna's home, which she owns in her own name.

Anna has her computer, land-line telephone, and cell phone listed under her name and home address. She also has her car titled in her name and her home address listed on the registration. Business associates, a few customers and friends, as well as several new acquaintances know the home address of Anna Maria Gonzales. Others who want to know it can do a property search to find out where she lives.

A Christmas party attended by thirty-five people was held at the Gonzales residence—a two-story, four-bedroom, two-bath house in a middle-class neighborhood—where Anna and her boyfriend of three years reside. Her business website provides anyone with access, to Internet information about her career experiences as a hair stylist, including her professional association memberships, the school she attended for her credentials, and her in-depth biographical sketch. Although she was unaware of it until the identification theft occurred, the life of Anna Maria Gonzales is literally an open book for all the world to read.

PREVENTION

Since key personal information is used in identity theft, the best way to prevent becoming a victim is to eliminate—or at least drastically reduce—the availability of information about you to anyone who might want to "become" you. A good foundation to prevent identity theft can be laid by following privacy rules. These rules will enable you to conduct your everyday life as an anonymous person, in order to avoid the predators who are stealing Americans' identities at an unprecedented rate. While the rules are briefly outlined here, you'll need to read and study each section of this book in order to effectively implement a plan tailored to your individual circumstances. Rules and principles to prevent identity theft include:

▸ Become invisible to those who search property databases for your home address. Whether you rent or own your home, you can accomplish this by using a *trust* to own the house or condominium or by renting in an *alternate name*. While the latter can be accomplished (and must be for home privacy), it will require special skills and diligence to do it, so prepare thoroughly by studying the "Home" section of this book.

▸ Travel anonymously by driving a trust-owned vehicle with no mention of you as *trustee* on the registration documents.

▸ Bank secretly. Utilize a trust checking account or check-cashing stores—or obtain an anonymous safe deposit box.

▸ A *Nevada Limited Partnership* is the entity preferred by many privacy seekers who wish to hold liquid assets anonymously.

▸ Freeze all credit reports and receive your credit card statements, bank account statements, brokerage statements, tax correspondences, and all other "official" and personal mail at a distant address, utilizing prescreened *nominees* to receive your mail.

▸ Hold businesses and investments in entity names unrelated to your true name. Avoid working as an employee whenever possible, and use a *Nevada Limited Liability Company* (LLC) or a trust to receive payments on your behalf

▸ Use an *"assumed name"* or "alternate name" for routine communication and make telephone calls from public phones or a cell phone registered anonymously. Use your alternate name or company name for all business and communication unless you are legally required to provide your true name.

These guidelines are the basics for structuring a necessary privacy program to protect you from becoming a victim of identity theft.

INVISIBLE ON PAPER

It's possible to become "invisible" through implementation of the privacy tactics outlined in this book. Once this is done, identity thieves who may be looking for a score will pass you by in hopes of finding more unaware prey for their crime. What choice will they have? Your home address will not be included in any searchable database, your car will have only a trust's name with a distant mailing address, and your personal bank account will be held by a trust with no mention of you as signer to the outside world.

Mail, shipments, and deliveries of all kinds will be received at a distant address by a reliable prescreened nominee. Credit cards will not be in danger, as *fraud alerts* and/or passwords will be assigned to each credit line, and your credit bureau files will be locked up—"frozen" as per new laws protecting your rights to privacy.

And you can become a "resident" of any state you choose when you learn the ropes and practice techniques that will enable you to "live" someplace far away from your physical residence while carefully concealing your actual address from everyone except the people you want to include in your circle of friends. Keeping your home location a secret is of paramount importance to prevent anyone—regardless of the motive—from placing a *keylogger* program on your computer and from bugging your phones—from a distance, as is common today. These things will not happen to you, because you will become anonymous and "invisible" on paper—and all of this can be accomplished from the comfort of your own home.

Government agencies and all of their employees who have access to your confidential driver's license, U.S. passport, Social Security and tax records, and the like need know nothing about your actual whereabouts, save whatever contact information you choose to give them. And when you do it right, the trail to you will lead nowhere, really, except to a distant residence address that is used as your "front" address in order to prevent anyone from disturbing you at home. Likewise, your phone number will lead to a voicemail somewhere in cyberspace that you rented in your alternate name, thus preventing anyone—no matter who they are—from ever finding you via National Security Agency (NSA) or other government surveillance, snoop traps, telephone records, payment receipts, phone number searches, or traces, because the real you will be carefully hidden behind a necessary alternate name.

And whenever it is necessary for you to provide your actual and true information—to the tax man or airline ticket agent, for example—you can control the risk by deciding whether you really need to make this trip by plane and choosing who you want to trust to have your confidential tax records.

Once you effectively manage your most important asset—your identity—a new freedom within you will emerge. No longer will you need to worry about thieves stealing your bank accounts or accessing your credit lines—as was the case with Anna Maria Gonzales—for you will be protected by your personal privacy plan. Private investigators, government agents, identity thieves, and stalkers will have no idea how to find the real you—when you do it right.

And even if through persistence, one of these vultures should uncover some clue as to the identity and personal business of the real you, it will become cost prohibitive for those doing the hunting—in most cases. It is very expensive to find someone who practices the high-level privacy tactics outlined in this book—if that person can be found at all. Once you master the art of becoming "invisible" on paper, you become an expensive person to find, and few, if any, will choose to target you as an identity theft victim.

IDENTITY THEFT GROWTH AND COSTS

Currently, identity theft ranks at the top of fraudulent crime growth in America. Nearly ten million people had their identities stolen during 2005. Losses to businesses totaled $47.6 billion, and consumer victims reported $5 billion in out-of-pocket expenses. Of these cases, the average loss to businesses was $10,200 per victim. Individuals incurred average losses of $2,412 per person. Among those victims reporting personal losses, forty-nine reported losses in excess of $1 million during 2005 due to identity theft crimes. Figures for 2006 are expected to be substantially higher.

The most common form of identity theft is credit card fraud, which accounts for 26 percent of all cases. Other types were bank fraud (17 percent), employment fraud (12 percent), government documents/benefits fraud (9 percent), and loan fraud (5 percent). The time required for individual victims to resolve problems related to the crime varies widely, but it's safe to say that once your identity is stolen, it will take anywhere from weeks to as long as years to restore your good name.

Identity theft is a nightmare waiting to happen. Don't let it happen to you. Guard against it by following privacy principles that will keep your name out of databases, such as *"freezing" credit bureau reports* and avoiding having your name, property records, money sources, or credit lines available for anyone to see unless you authorize it. It is imperative that you learn and practice high-level privacy tactics in order to avoid becoming just another identity theft fraud statistic.

Through proven privacy principles and concepts, the individual who recognizes the current Privacy Crisis will be able to privately and effectively manage finances, work, and travel, and be able to live beneath the radar of all who are in the business of identity theft.

SUMMARY

1. America is facing a "Privacy Crisis," and identity theft is the fastest-growing crime in the country. Unaware Americans are having their identities stolen at the greatest numbers in history.

2. Most Americans' confidential identity documents as well as property and business information can be obtained by those who have the skills and inclination to find them. Privacy principles, when utilized correctly, enable one to bank, drive, work, and live anonymously.

3. American businesses, institutions, and government agencies become the sources for obtaining personal and business information by identity thieves.

4. Prevention of identity theft is achieved by utilizing high-level privacy tactics to shield one's personal data and business from all sources that store such data.

5. By becoming "invisible" on paper, privacy seekers will have little risk of having their identities stolen.

6. The costs of identity theft to individuals, businesses and government are astronomical and continue to grow.

◆ TWO ◆

Identity Theft
Resource Guide

"Existence is identity."—Ayn Rand

Prevention of identity theft through a properly planned privacy program based on your individual needs and circumstances is the solution to the identity theft problem. If you are one of the many millions of Americans who has been victimized by those committing this fraud, this chapter is a guide to resources providing assistance once the crime has been committed against you. When you've restored your banking, property, and other financial records, your credit bureau reports, identification and other personal records—hopefully with minimal loss of time, effort, and money—you'll appreciate the value of enhancing your privacy through the practices outlined in this book.

FRAUD AGENCIES

Federal Trade Commission Identity Theft Clearinghouse *has as its mission the protection of consumers from companies that misinform or overreach with regard to the U.S. economy.*
Federal Trade Commission—Identity Theft Clearinghouse
600 Pennsylvania Avenue N.W.
Washington, D.C. 20580
Telephone: (877) 438-4338
Website: www.consumer.gov

National Fraud Information Center *has a victims' help line and website.*
National Fraud Information Center
Telephone: (800) 876-7060
Website: www.fraud.org

LEGAL CONTACTS

State Attorneys General *Specific resources are listed alphabetically by state or city.*
Website: www.findlaw.com

Federal Bureau of Investigation (FBI)
Federal Bureau of Investigation Criminal Justice Information Services Division
J. Edgar Hoover Building, 935 Pennsylvania Avenue, N.W.
Washington, D.C. 20535-0001
Telephone: (202) 324-3000
Website: www.fbi.gov

U.S. Department of Justice
U.S. Department of Justice, Identity Theft Information
Website: www.usdoj.gov

The National Center for Victims of Crime *(referral to local services)*
National Center for Victims of Crime
2000 M Street N.W., Suite 480
Washington, D.C. 20036
Telephone: 800-394-2255
Website: www.ncvc.org

BANKING AND INVESTMENTS

Federal Deposit Insurance Corporation (FDIC)
Federal Deposit Insurance Corporation Division of Compliance and Consumer Affairs
550 17th Street N.W.

Washington, D.C. 20429
Website: www.fdic.gov

National Credit Union Administration (NCUA)
National Credit Union Administration
1175 Duke Street, Suite 4206
Alexandria, Virginia 22314-3437
Website: www.ncua.gov

U.S. Securities and Exchange Commission (SEC)
U.S. Securities and Exchange Commission
450 Fifth Street N.W.
Washington, D.C. 20549-0213
Telephone: (202) 942-7040
Website: www.sec.gov

Office of Thrift Supervision (OTS)
Office of Thrift Supervision
1700 G Street N.W.
Washington, D.C. 20552
Telephone: (202) 906-6000
Website: www.ots.treas.gov

COMMUNICATIONS FRAUD

The Federal Communications Commission (FCC) *should be contacted for cellular telephone and long distance fraud.*
Federal Communications Commission—Consumer Information Bureau
445 12th Street S.W., Room 5A863
Washington D.C. 20554
Telephone: (888) 225-5322
Website: www.fcc.gov

U.S. Postal Service
U.S. Postal Service—Criminal Investigations Service Center—Mail Fraud
222 South Riverside Plaza, Suite 1250

Chicago, Illinois 60606-6100
Telephone: (800) 275-8777
Website: www.usps.com

IDENTIFICATION

U.S. Department of State
U.S. Department of State—Passport Services
Consular Lost/Stolen Passport Section
1111 19th Street N.W., Suite 500
Washington, D.C. 20036
Website: www.state.gov

State Driver's License Agency Links:
www.aamva.org

TAXES

Internal Revenue Service (IRS)
Internal Revenue Service—Office of the Privacy Advocate
Room 7050 OS:PA
1111 Constitution Avenue N.W.
Washington, D.C. 20224
Fraud Telephone: (800) 829-0433
Website: www.irs.gov

Social Security Administration (SSA)
Social Security Administration
P.O. Box 17768
Baltimore, Maryland 21235
(800) 269-0271
Website: www.socialsecurity.gov

CREDIT BUREAUS

Equifax
P.O. Box 740241
Atlanta, Georgia 30374-0241

To report fraud: (800) 525-6285
Website: www.equifax.com

Experian
Consumer Fraud Assistance
P.O. Box 9532
Allen, Texas 75013
To report fraud: (888) 397-3742
Website: www.experian.com

TransUnion
Fraud Victim Assistance Division
P.O. Box 6790
Fullerton, California 92834-6790
To report fraud: (800) 680-7289
Website: www.transunion.com

CREDIT CARDS

MasterCard
Website: www.mastercard.com

Visa Card
Website: www.visa.com

Discover Card
Website: www.discovercard.com

American Express Card
Website: www.americanexpress.com

SUMMARY

1. Victims of identity theft crimes should immediately contact the appropriate companies and agencies to file complaints and complete necessary documents.

2. Privacy in all personal and business affairs is the best insurance policy to prevent identity theft fraud.

3. The remainder of this book includes sections and chapters that provide privacy-conscious individuals with principles and concepts for anonymous living and prevention of identity theft.

THREE

Using I.D. to "Disappear"

"There comes a point in many people's lives when they can no longer play the role they have chosen for themselves. When that happens, we are like actors finding that someone has changed the play."—Brian Moore, Irish novelist

ALTERNATE IDENTITY: KEY TO PRIVACY

Walking toward the hotel front desk, Alex appeared relaxed. But beneath his cool exterior, his heart was pounding, his pulse was quickening, and he was experiencing an adrenaline rush that made him feel as if he could run five marathons. As he filled out the room registration form, he observed the clerk.

Alex Corbin was on the run. Having learned that a civil lawsuit had been filed against him, he was avoiding the process servers, as his attorney had advised him to do. And then there was the private investigator—a non-government Dick who was on retainer and paid by the hour, plus expenses. Actually, he didn't worry Alex. But the government guys did. They never run out of money.

Having completed the hotel registration form, Alex watched the clerk photocopy his *alternate identification* card—a slick plastic "official" foreign photo I.D. that claimed to give a version of Alex, wearing a wig and make-up, the right to drive. After paying cash for a one-week hotel stay and obtaining his receipt, Alex grabbed his single suitcase and headed for his suite.

"Wait," Ms. Clerk shouted as he was halfway through the elevator door. "We need your credit card on file."

Returning to the desk, Alex noticed that a supervisor had called this to her attention. He glanced at the supervisor. Reading Alex's mind, Mr. Supervisor mumbled, "We just need to make a photocopy . . . for security. No hold on funds."

Alex pulled out a MasterCard and placed it on the hotel front desk. Checking to see that the name matched his *foreign I.D.*, the supervisor entered the bank card numbers on the registration form, copied it, handed it back, and wished Alex a "pleasant stay."

Hotels are usually easy. But this one wanted a lot of information. Just a couple of days until the meeting, Alex thought. His business was nearing completion, and he looked forward to relaxing. In another city.

With sufficient nerve and confidence, the right "papers," and the knowledge that you have a right to be whomever you choose to be at the time, you too—whether being investigated or not—can pull off the challenge of convincing people in everyday life that you are someone else. And you have a right to do it.

Anyone has the right to go by whatever name he or she chooses, so long as there is no "intent to defraud." And so far as the I.D. card is concerned, so-called "novelty" I.D. cards are sold in all shapes, colors, and sizes—and for any number of reasons. Just don't try handing one over to a policeman, banker, or any "government" person. Use the real thing for them.

"ALSO KNOWN AS" (AKA)

A correspondent who has used an alternate identification to cope with the Privacy Crisis in the U.S. sent the author the following e-mail regarding the value of using an alternate name for privacy purposes:

"Dear Mr. Hall: For over four years, I was sought by my ex-boyfriend and his private investigator's team of detectives. Then I made the decision to go underground and to live under the radar to escape my tormentors, for my personal safety. During that period, I registered in hotels and motels, lived in a beach house, leased an apartment, joined gyms and clubs, received treatment from doctors, purchased high-speed Internet services and cell telephones, obtained a library card, rented mail-drop boxes and storage spaces, purchased and used pre-paid debit cards, and cashed checks—all while pretending to be someone else. Finally, I escaped this sociopath and his henchmen, and I am free of him forever. Sincerely, J.B., Utah."

In order to keep your life private while also avoiding the prying eyes of identity thieves who may attempt to steal your most precious possession—your identity—you can use an alternate name, or perhaps two or three.

Under those circumstances, when you don't want your true legal name associated with "the real you," an alternate name can be used. Privacy-conscious individuals often obtain official-looking identification documents to add credibility to their alternate identity. Although this is legal, it's a touchy subject to discuss with anyone. So don't.

When obtaining alternate identification documents, privacy seekers have found it most prudent and private not to depend on any assistance from others. Usually they do it all, or most of it, themselves.

Our fictitious character, Alex Corbin, might tell you that persistence pays off. He ordered a set of identification cards over the Internet and received nothing. But realizing that obtaining an alternate I.D. was key to becoming "invisible" to those seeking him, Alex persisted in searching for new sources for his identity documents.

He had given some thought to disappearing altogether. One author wrote a book claiming it can be done. Maybe it can. I don't know. But Alex didn't want to give up his real identity—he only wanted to create an alternate identity by using an assumed name as needed for privacy. He intended to use his true name only for anything legal and official.

Whatever your reasons for wanting to "disappear" by using an alternate name and novelty I.D. cards, it's important to keep everything legal—to work within the rule of law, so to speak. You can avoid the potential fall you might take if you listened to one of those private investigators who wrote about waltzing into a Department of Motor Vehicles (DMV) office and presenting the birth certificate of a long-passed youth who never made it into government databases. The intent, of course, is to pass off this phony paperwork as a credential for obtaining a state-issued driver's license.

In the author's opinion, it's a huge mistake to give false I.D.s of any kind to government officials. It's not necessary for privacy, and the risk of being caught and possibly being charged with a crime is high. Why do you think there is always a police officer within shouting distance of

even the smallest DMV office or other government agency that processes state-issued driver's licenses and *state-issued identification* cards?

I.D. PORTFOLIO

Back now to our fictitious and persistent friend, Alex, who continued
searching for a usable alternate I.D. He visited printing shops in parts
of the city that are not at all pretty and had identification documents
custom made while he waited. He also found an Internet source or two

that delivered. Some check-cashing
stores make their own "official" I.D.
cards, too. The best sources, however,
according to seasoned *privacy advocates,* are the real artists, found however guys like that are found. Sometimes they are discovered by calling
mail order companies, or by searching
on the Internet.

A number of privacy seekers have explained that there is no easy way
to obtain these important privacy tools. Those serious about doing it
have to just buckle down and look.

However, finding artists with the talent to make a foreign driver's license or a *novelty identification card* from another country that looks
official—and who has the ethics to ship it to you, his customer—can be
time consuming.

Debit cards by MasterCard or Visa can be purchased at some check
cashing stores. The government keeps trying to change the requirements for these prepaid little jewels, however. It used to be that someone desiring privacy could buy one of these cards in any name he or she
wished, have it shipped to a mail-drop box, pick it up, and deposit unlimited funds into the account. No questions asked.

Then the issuing banks started asking a lot more questions once activation of the card was attempted. It became necessary to supply a Social Security number or a foreign passport or driver's license number
in order to open the account. They now request a photocopy of foreign
identity documents, and the limit on stored-value U.S. bank debit card
accounts has been reduced again—usually to $5,000 or less, in most
cases.

Other worthwhile *alternate secondary I.D.s* might include an insurance card or two obtained via an alternate-identity mailing address

(from those nice folks in Omaha who want to pay you when you are sick or when you die) or a work identification card with a disguised photograph. But there's no need to go overboard. Privacy practitioners—the real ones who actually live as someone else most of the time—explain that a good-quality "novelty" foreign driver's license or other such foreign *primary identification* documents (which really aren't primary I.D. documents but will pass as such at hotels and the like), plus a bank card with a matching name is about all you will need.

REGISTERING AT HOTELS ANONYMOUSLY

With these, you can make your way through the maze of everyday life while keeping the "real you" hidden. Your true identity can be concealed from the used car sales vulture who wants to know who you are, where you live, what you drive, and what kind of credit score you have—or the doctor who treats you for a sexually transmitted disease (STD) and insists on writing a report that may be obtained by an insurance company, which may in turn provide it to the *Medical Information Bureau.*

Then there's the guy you just met at the health club who's going through a bankruptcy and could become your worst nightmare by stealing your spotless credit, if you let him, making you another victim of the most prevalent crime of the twenty-first century—identity theft.

USE OF ALTERNATE NAMES

Most people give up their private information willingly and unnecessarily to anyone who asks. But there is no need to risk compromising your privacy when conducting everyday business. Privacy seekers use an alternate name to register new computers and software programs, obtain all kinds of personal and business services, purchase telephones and telephone services, receive sensitive mail, register at hotels and motels anonymously, lease apartments, and do all other business that is not official business.

To protect your privacy you may choose to use an alternate name, or *alias*, when meeting individuals whose contact is not of an "official" nature, or whose relationship will not lead in that direction. Those desiring a high level of privacy often use an alternate name when in doubt as to whether their *true name* should be used.

In the event you want to share your true name with a person you previously met under an alternate name, a simple explanation stating that you've had privacy challenges (no matter what they were) will be sufficient. In fact, privacy practitioners—the experts, not the storyteller writers on the subject—often say that few people need to know anything about the "real you," including your true name.

When communicating by telephone with government agencies, serious privacy advocates don't use their true name unless required by law to do so. Those practicing high-level privacy have represented themselves as "clerks" calling on behalf of the entity or person whose business is the subject of the discussion.

According to one privacy-conscious attorney with whom your author has consulted, it's permissible both for privacy purposes and from a legal standpoint to operate almost entirely under the guise of other entities and company names while keeping your true name out of databases designed to compromise your privacy.

So when those who desire privacy use an alternate name when calling the Internet service provider and the cell telephone company, they are exercising their right to privacy while still operating morally and legally. No one is hurt when someone desiring privacy uses an alternate name. And people don't then run the risk of having some guy at the phone company (who, for all anyone knows, could have been just released from prison after serving time for rape or burglary) know where he can find them because they revealed their real name and residential address while making a purchase.

As you become more aware of all the potential privacy invasions in today's digital world, and if you're objective, you too will come to appreciate the importance of an alternate identity to ensure your privacy—and even your personal safety.

In the event you become the target of an aggressive stalker, an identity theft wizard, or a threatening and dissatisfied customer, you'll find that being able to "disappear" as a non-traceable you—backed up by believable alternate identity documents—is invaluable for peaceful and safe living.

Those who practice high-level privacy living are anonymous in almost everything they do—and they use alternate names and good-quality alternate identification documents to assist them in making their lives private.

SUMMARY

1. Law-abiding privacy practitioners use "alternate identification" whenever their privacy and security could be compromised—and providing it is permissible by law to do so.

2. Do not give any government or law enforcement agent an "alternate I.D" or "novelty" I.D. card.

3. Privacy seekers discreetly obtain quality "alternate identification" documents for privacy and security purposes.

4. Prepaid debit cards have been useful for those practicing privacy as an alternate, secondary identification document, as well as a means for purchasing goods and services anonymously.

5. Those living private lifestyles use alternate or assumed names for privately receiving sensitive mail—and when doing private business, making personal acquaintances, or receiving confidential medical services—as well as to prevent becoming a target of identity theft.

6. Historically, one has been able to use an alternate name throughout the Western Hemisphere as long as there is no intent to defraud. Those seeking high-level privacy should keep apprised of all pertinent laws relevant to their plan for personal and business privacy.

7. Do not attempt to obtain a forged government-issued identity document.

♦ FOUR ♦

Government Identification

"Government is not reason, it is not eloquence, it is force; like fire, a troublesome servant and a fearful master. Never for a moment should it be left to irresponsible action."
—George Washington

ESCAPE FROM THE BONDAGE

Sabihah Ziglari is a U.S. citizen who naturalized following her immigration from Pakistan to study Business Administration at the University of Southern California. But she received a real education—in privacy—when she tried to renew her expiring U.S. passport while using her real home address—a West Los Angeles apartment.

Sabihah (an alternate name) submitted her original passport, which was scheduled to expire within two months, with her renewal application, as requested on the State Department  form. An entrepreneur, Sabihah had been in the import-export business for the previous seven or eight years. And while business had been good, the normal business cycle had caused an interruption in cash flow. Hence, Sabihah's company—a California corporation of which she was an officer—was nearly bankrupt. And there was, in fact, three years' worth of back federal tax (including penalties and interest, of course) owed to the Internal Revenue Service (IRS) by the near-defunct corporation, now a mere shell of its formal self. Ditto for California state income tax.

Sabihah had been properly counseled by her attorney and CPA alike and was told that her brother, Akram, also an officer of the previous enterprise, would take the IRS fall. She was informed by counsel that she had no liability and that, in fact, her brother had scheduled a repayment plan with the tax man.

But of course, the IRS forgot to tell the State Department, whose computers went "ding" when Sabihah's personal data was entered into its massive database. It took sixteen months (during which time Sabihah was literally a woman without a country), thirty-two certified letters, about $3,600 in legal fees, and more than fifty telephone calls to "the powers that be" before the mess was straightened out. Only then could Sabihah once again prove she was legally a citizen of the United States, as evidenced by her official U.S. passport.

And let's not forget the seven unannounced home visits by the IRS agents, the bi-weekly telephone calls to her home land-line phone, and the unidentified government cars seen driving by Sabihah's home during the time her U.S. passport was in limbo.

Following this lengthy, time-consuming, and expensive ordeal, Sabihah came to believe what some privacy advocates have stated: *Never give Big Government your home address or home telephone number.*

Privacy-conscious people ensure their home privacy and security by utilizing the services of a mail nominee (one designated as a stand-in to receive mail for them at the nominee's own residence). Using a *residence mail drop,* combined with a dedicated voicemail number, as contact information on all government applications and records will prevent intrusive visits from government officials at your actual residence address.

PRIMARY IDENTITY DOCUMENTS

Identity documents in the U.S. are classified into two categories: *primary* and *secondary.* Generally, there are four forms of identification that government entities consider to be acceptable as primary I.D. These include the U.S. passport, a state-issued driver's license, a state-issued identification card, and a birth certificate. These documents are sufficient for proving one's true birth identity.

A U.S. passport is the preferred primary I.D. and is equal to a driver's license. A birth certificate, while proof of birth, can present problems and may cause many questions to be asked once a person passes his or her mid-twenties, unless it is presented along with a passport or state-issued driver's license. The state-issued I.D. card is equivalent to the state-issued driver's license for identification purposes and is used primarily by those who do not drive.

In certain states, individuals have been able to obtain a driver's license from one state while keeping a state-issued identification card from a second state. Having two primary identifications can be useful for banking in those two different states. Those who are in their mid-twenties or older are expected to have obtained a government-issued primary identification document (driver's license, state-issued I.D., or U.S. passport). So expect to have your documents carefully examined if you fall outside this norm.

All fifty U.S. states have managed to cross-reference their driver's license information, so don't believe for a moment that you can fool anyone about your driving record, especially if it is less than perfect.

THE U.S. PASSPORT

All American citizens can legally obtain U.S. passports, which are valid for ten years after they are issued. For privacy purposes, the U.S. passport is the superior form of primary identification. It is less common than the more widely used driver's license, an advantage by itself, and it contains much less available information. While the holder's full name, photo, date of birth, place of birth, and a passport number appear

on his or her passport—as well as stamped records identifying entry and exit points for most countries and dates traveled by the citizen—no Social Security number, home address, or identifying state of residence information is included on the passport itself.

And although this personal information is required on the U.S. State Department's passport application form prior to their issuance of the document, it is more difficult and time consuming to verify passports, compared to a state-issued I.D. card or driver's license. In this case, the time-consuming verification process—including long-distance telephone calls, lengthy hold time, mounds of paperwork, and difficult-to-obtain records stored in secure databases—works to the advantage of the privacy seeker. Bankers, prospective employers, and state and local officials usually will not go to all the trouble of attempting to verify the validity of a U.S. passport. Nor should they, as passports are easily recognized and nearly impossible to forge. In fact, verification of a U.S. passport cannot be done immediately, due to the fact that the State Department's database records are inaccessible to most local officials, including municipal police.

Not so with the state-issued I.D. or state-issued driver's license, as all fifty states make their DMV records available to many state and local government agencies for verifying driver's license information and the driver's identity. It is the author's opinion that the U.S. passport, rather than a state-issued I.D. or driver's license, should be used as a primary I.D. document for privacy purposes.

"INVISIBLE" CITIZEN

In order to avoid the potential abuse, inconvenience, and expense incurred by Sabihah Ziglari just to claim what was rightfully hers—citizenship—privacy advocates take the U.S. passport application process seriously and take measures to protect their privacy. Serious privacy advocates arrange (via Internet advertising) for a nominee to receive mail in another state and then pick up their primary identification

documents in person or have them forwarded to a secure location for pick up.

To prevent redundancy here, please see Chapter 12—"Mail: Creating an Illusion"—and follow the guidelines explaining how to secure a proper mailing address to receive your U.S. passport. Generally, three to four weeks are required to process and mail your passport after you submit an application. Once your new passport is in hand, you are free from dealing with the U.S. State Department for the next ten years, hopefully.

If you so choose, you could terminate the service agreement with your mail drop nominee and cancel the voicemail telephone number you used on the application, once the passport is in hand.

Congratulations. You now possess a first-class, number-one rated primary I.D. document, and *Big Bureaucrat* has no known address for you.

STATE-ISSUED DRIVER'S LICENSE

Driver's licenses are issued by the Department of Motor Vehicles (DMV) offices or other state agency that processes driver's licenses for "residents" of that state. Applicants are given their driver's licenses following proof of their date of birth, physical ability to drive, knowledge of traffic laws, and driving proficiency. Written tests, eye tests, and behind-the-wheel driving skills tests also may be required to prove an applicant's suitability to operate a motor vehicle.

The state-issued driver's license is considered the primary form of I.D. in the U.S. But while banks, businesses, and individuals ask for your driver's license as proof of your identity, it is the opinion of several veteran privacy practitioners that you should not use it unless stopped by local police or highway patrol officers while driving a vehicle.

Instead of using the driver's license as an I.D. for official business, some who have successfully practiced a privacy lifestyle suggest using your passport instead. They suggest that when not driving, you may carry your passport as a means of identification, or you can choose to carry no I.D. at all while a pedestrian.

A number of privacy advocates do not carry a driver's license but instead leave it under lock and key inside the car, along with the automobile registration and proof of insurance documents. For a privacy advantage, they suggest you should *always use your U.S. passport instead of your driver's license* for the reasons previously mentioned.

DRIVER'S LICENCE PRIVACY

It is important to keep your driver's license as private as possible. Since we have become accustomed to carrying a driver's license in our wallets and producing it whenever asked, this will take some practice. But remember that your passport contains far less available information about you and is a superior primary identification document. Using a U.S. passport offers privacy advantages when banking (except in those rare cases when banks require a valid state driver's license to open an account), when registering a trust-owned vehicle, and for all identification requirements not associated with operating a motor vehicle.

Driver's licenses are usually issued every four years, since Big Bureaucrat wants to check you out every so often, generate more money for various government spending sprees, and have an opportunity to revoke the licenses of those boys and girls who have been naughty during the prior four years. Driver's license information also can be used to locate those who have, in the opinion of the state, committed some offense—as in the case of our friend Alex in Chapter 3.

In fact, DMV database information is commonly used by investigative agencies, both public and private, to locate citizens for questioning in all matters, whether civil or criminal. Therefore, anyone desiring to be anonymous and to keep his or her private life private will choose to obtain a driver's license discreetly. For maximum security and secrecy, privacy advocates obtain their driver's licenses utilizing the same principles and methods described previously on how to obtain a U.S. passport. They choose a state other than the one in which most of their time is spent, obtain a residence mail drop by contracting with a mail nominee there, and supply all information required by that state, including their new "address."

Some states issue applicants temporary permission to drive while their computer completely checks them out and then send an actual license to them in the mail. Others issue a driver's license on the same day they show up, complete the application, and pay the license fee. A license issued by a state other than the one in which you spend most of your time, combined with an address on DMV records that is completely unrelated to your physical address, will add a substantial amount of privacy to your life.

Consider the following actual case of a man and woman, whom I will call Dean and Bertha McCoy.

CASE STUDY: DMV TARGETS "DEADBEAT DAD"

Dean and Bertha McCoy are California residents who were married for nine years before differences in money matters (as well as Bertha's nocturnal wanderings) caused their separation, divorce, and an eventual divorce settlement. California is a community property state reputed to skew the division of property in favor of women in divorce courts and to provide "annuity type" child support offerings to women based on Dad's earnings or his capacity to earn.

Dean, the father of three minor children, was taken to the proverbial cleaners in the settlement and left with a mere allowance after all the legal dust had settled. Three years after the divorce, Dean found himself laid off from his once-secure position as an engineer at an aerospace firm and attempting to make ends meet with unemployment checks. He was mandated to pay an amount exceeding $2,800 per month for child support until the eldest turned 18 or until a new and of course higher amount was carefully calculated by a Los Angeles court, based on Dean's earnings or his capacity to earn.

Five months after his company laid him off, and at that time three months in arrears in child support payments, Dean was still unable to find suitable employment that offered earnings sufficient to pay his living expenses and his court-ordered child support payments.

About this time, Dean's California driver's license was up for renewal, and in order to keep driving legally and thus be available for job interviews and work when it finally came, Dean presented himself at the local DMV office. The officials at the California Child Support Enforcement Office already had flagged his file, and once his Social Security number was entered into the Department of Motor Vehicles database, the computer went "ding," and our boy Dean returned to his tiny rented room on skid row without a valid driver's license.

Forced to use city buses and legal aid attorneys and to live like a hobo, our once-prosperous west-side L.A. engineer was now in the government's computers—in the "deadbeat dads" file.

When Dean was eight months in arrears in child support payments, the sheriff arrived at Dean's last-known address—that of the skid row room he had supplied to the California DMV office, where the computer had "dinged" and refused his license-renewal application. Dean was pulled from his bed, read his rights, arrested, and thrown in the county pokey.

Later, he was brought before a judge and told to "pay up or else." At last check, Dean was still in arrears and still unable to drive legally due to his "deadbeat dad" status. Dean learned the hard way what many practicing privacy living have emphatically stated: *Never, ever give the government your real home address.*

"PERMANENT" DRIVER'S LICENSE

Most states round up resident drivers every four years or so, reward the good guys and gals by stealing three hours of their day in completing new forms, standing in lines, paying more fees, and taking a new photograph—all for a brand-new license for four more years. While the good continue to drive with only a drain on pocketbook and time, government agencies will penalize the violators—such as Dean our "deadbeat dad"—whether for driving offenses or any alleged action going against any government grain.

Those practicing personal and business privacy prefer the least amount of government contact possible, and Arizona is their state of choice for obtaining a state-issued driver's license. Arizona issues licenses that are valid from the date of issue until the driver is 65 years of age, at which time renewal is required. So you could obtain an Arizona driver's license at age 16 and possibly never have to go into a DMV office again for 49 years!

And if you utilize privacy principles as described herein, you will never, ever (regardless of whether you are at fault or not) wind up like Dean McCoy. The smaller cities in Arizona are staffed with adequate personnel in their DMV offices to make your wait a short one. Eye tests are required for those over age 50. A simple application and the driver's license from your previous "residence" state is the only I.D. required to obtain your new license in Arizona. And the best part is that you walk out with the actual license on the day you apply for it.

STATE IDENTIFICATION

Everything written in this chapter pertaining to state-issued driver's licenses is applicable for those seeking a state-issued I.D.—the primary identification document provided for residents who need an official state-government identity document, minus the "privilege" of driving a vehicle.

As previously mentioned, certain states have allowed individuals to obtain a state I.D. while retaining their state-issued driver's license from their "previous" state of residence. However, individual policies and laws change faster than books can be accurately written. Current information is easily found online at official state Internet websites. Having both a state driver's license and a state I.D. from separate states can be an advantage in some cases, particularly when doing business in both states.

BIRTH CERTIFICATES

The problem with birth certificates is that few agencies ask to see them for identification purposes. While a birth certificate is required as a primary identification document when you apply for your first driver's license and your first U.S. passport, once you are past age 16 and begin to drive, you can put your birth certificate in a safe deposit box, because now, the driver's license will upstage it as a requested or required I.D. document.

There are those who have written that the birth certificate—the so-called "breeder document"—is the key to a new identity and sought after by so many unhappily married souls, debtors, criminals, and others attempting to flee jurisdictions and escape the long-reaching arm of government entities.

Please don't follow the advice of the private investigators who write books claiming that such capers can be pulled off successfully. Don't believe the pseudo privacy experts—those storytellers who freelance for publishing houses that print the stuff desperate people purchase to fulfill their dreams of escape.

Phony birth documents would never make it past Supervisor Number One's desk, let alone provide a bankrupted individual a new start under a different name. In fact, if you go to a DMV office wanting to use a birth certificate to reinvent yourself in the wrong way, by attempting to change your identity, the person behind the counter, the DMV supervisors, and state detectives will scrutinize that "certified birth certificate" in ways that the private investigators who write about pulling such tricks forgot to mention in their last mail order manual.

Appearing at the DMV or passport office with a birth certificate that does not belong to you, no matter how authentic, will almost certainly guarantee you jail time when you are caught, according to an attorney who fielded a hypothetical question about this type of offense. This is especially true since 9-11-01 and the terrorist events on that date that gave the federal government the fuel to feed the fire that is burning up your privacy rights.

Maybe there was a time when gutsy guys of 40-something conned Bureau of Vital Statistics clerks in some states to provide them with certified birth certificates of someone near their age and of the same race. As the story goes, they used it as a "breeder document" to then obtain a driver's license and passport under a brand-new identity. Perhaps it has happened. Discoveries are made all the time. More than three hundred phony Social Security numbers flagged an equal number of driver's licenses in New York State in 2004. Somehow, those drivers made it past the examiners and the clerks to become licensed drivers. For a while.

Please don't try to obtain a U.S. primary identity document by using a birth certificate unless it is, in fact, *your* birth certificate. And don't attempt to make one on a computer, as some have advocated. Don't hire a minister to sign a fake baptismal certificate indicating you were born as someone else, and don't claim some religious-related, silly story as the reason you are applying for your first driver's license at age 37, unless it is the truth—or you will risk becoming a felon. The importance of a forged birth certificate for obtaining valid, government-issued primary I.D. documents has been overrated by story teller authors.

COVERING YOUR TRACKS

Those who begin to practice privacy living are often counseled never to receive mail at their real home or business address. Serious privacy advocates generally agree that when one's actual physical location is known by government agencies, individuals become vulnerable to having investigators pay them a visit, no matter whether any charges or accusations made against them are true or without merit.

One high-level privacy practitioner who has successfully lived beneath the radar of government has related his belief that by far, the best defense against government abuse and irresponsible actions against innocent citizens is to "create an illusion" regarding one's home or business address. An e-mail correspondent wrote that she and her husband arranged a *"dummy sale"* of their home to another entity in order to disassociate their names from the residence address that was on DMV records. After "selling" their house, they began using a mail nominee for all correspondences and notified the DMV of their change of address.

Others have moved within a period of time, following their awareness of the necessity of keeping their home address a secret to preserve their privacy and to prevent anyone—government, identity thieves, private investigators, or stalkers—from paying them a surprise visit.

A man wrote explaining that he sold his home and moved to another address when he began practicing privacy principles. Weigh the risks and decide which privacy measures you should employ, based on your own circumstances.

SUMMARY

1. An individual can essentially "disappear" from state and federal government databases by obtaining primary identification documents, including a U.S. passport, a state-issued driver's license or a state I.D., while utilizing residence mail-drop addresses and voicemail telephone numbers.

2. Privacy-conscious people prefer using a U.S. passport for identification purposes. They advocate showing a state driver's license *only* when asked for it by law enforcement officials while driving. For primary identification, people may choose to carry the passport on their person or carry no identification at all. Your driver's license should be kept in a secure place that is accessible while driving.

3. Do not, under any circumstances, give any state or federal government agency or person your real home address, unless required by law to do so.

4. For the highest level of security, privacy seekers utilize mailing addresses in states other than the state in which they spend most of their time.

5. The State of Arizona currently offers the longest-term driver's license available in any of the fifty states.

MONUMENT VALLEY, ARIZONA

♦ FIVE ♦

Foreign and Secondary Identification

"Freedom is like birth. Till we are fully free, we are slaves."
—Gandhi

BANKING PASSPORTS

The advertisement promised "Anonymous Banking," complete with a debit card in any name desired or with no name at all on the card. This would come from an island haven country reputed to have "banking secrecy."

Scrolling down the Internet website brought to view another service listed as a *"Banking Passport."* It promised to complement the anonymous bank account by providing a passport from a country that had undergone a change of name. This "camouflage" document was recommended as a "banking passport" only—an identification piece to fool bankers but not recommended for crossing international borders. And they wanted $10,000 for the deal.

While such a promise may entice someone wanting a new identity—complete with a fake passport that supposedly will suffice as an I.D. for opening an offshore or U.S. bank account—the risk is high that such documents will never be received when ordered. To whom do you make a complaint about not receiving your fake passport? To whom do you speak about not receiving your passport from some African country whose government supposedly granted you citizenship for your "donation"?

Although obtaining a banking passport is a good idea in theory, don't approach a banker, foreign or American, with a fake identification document. Banks are quasi-government agencies in the U.S. and require you to sign an application attesting to the validity of all information provided on it, so attempts to open a bank account in another name will probably fail. You risk having the account closed just when you need it, not to mention having the money seized by you-know-who.

Likewise, foreign banks and bankers today are careful to do business only with customers who are on the up and up. Your efforts to use a "banking passport" for the very purpose for which it was intended—even if you happen to have received it from an ostensible Internet "broker" who claims to have been an African diplomat in a previous career—place your deposit at risk. Bank according to the recommendations in the "Finances" section of this book, and you will preserve your privacy without getting into trouble.

Certain individuals have used "banking passports" as "alternate" or "novelty" identification, which would be considered an alternate primary identification document.

Privacy-minded folks are cognizant of the law while using their alternate name and remember to not present these privacy tools for any official or government requests when their true names are required.

FOREIGN PASSPORTS

Passports that are real and "official" are issued by governments of countries. Anything else is a fake document. Government-issued passports are primary identity documents so long as they are real and are issued to citizens of countries who provide satisfactory identity and residence information according to that country's criteria for obtaining passports.

One may obtain a second citizenship by emigrating to a country and becoming a resident there by spending a substantial amount of time in that country—usually three to five years or longer—prior to being eligible to apply for citizenship.

There are shortcuts to becoming a citizen in several first-world countries. One may, in certain cases, make a substantial investment or start a business that provides jobs, thereby speeding up the eligibility time for a citizenship application. Canada offers such a program for those who meet the character and sponsorship requirements.

Individuals whose parents or grandparents were born in Ireland may have just won a citizenship lottery—an easy and residence-free way to become an Irish citizen. And they can keep their original U.S. passports as well. Similarly, Israel allows Americans with a Jewish heritage to obtain dual citizenship. The United Kingdom has offered second citizenships to accomplished artists who want to enjoy the benefits of holding resident status in an additional country—and other benefits a U.K. passport will provide.

In certain cases, one may be offered citizenship in a country merely by associating with those who have the influence or the right government connections to expedite a citizenship application. Money, promises, and political friendships are without question worthwhile assets for those desiring a second "mother country." Many countries provide a clear and quick pathway to second citizenship through marriage to a citizen. The residency and time requirements vary widely, and abuse of this method of obtaining citizenship runs rampant.

For those with the patience and wherewithal to obtain a second citizenship, the hard way—spending time in a foreign country, establishing residency after a period of time, and eventually applying for citizenship—is, of course, the right way to accomplish this. However, the time requirements vary greatly, from a reported twelve years for citizenship eligibility in Switzerland to as few as three years in Canada. Unfortunately, this approach simply doesn't offer one seeking anonymity a quick and easy solution to establishing a second primary identity document from a foreign country.

There are, of course, "buy out" programs offered by nations that

CANADA'S FLAG   SWITZERLAND'S FLAG

grant citizenships, for the sacrifice of money alone. These can range in cost from over $1 million U.S. in some first-world European countries to as little as $35,000 in some Caribbean nations, which may only sporadically offer such programs. Consider the value of citizenship from the country offering it before becoming a countryman, be it via the legitimate and time-consuming way—or by buying it outright.

Citizenship from Ireland, for example, will allow you to travel the world freely, while a Nevis passport may require supporting documents, visas, and an original passport as well, just to cross another border. The quality and perception of citizenship in a given country by authorities who regulate international

SOME ISLAND NATIONS OFFER CITIZENSHIPS FOR A FEE.

travel are factors you will want to consider as you make plans to acquire a second passport. Official Internet websites maintained by countries of interest are a good source for the most current information. Inquiries also can be made at foreign embassies in the U.S.

SECONDARY IDENTIFICATION

Secondary identification—to review from Chapter 4—includes all of those pieces of identification other than your primary identification (government-issued passports, state-issued driver's licenses, state-issued identification cards, and birth certificates). The preferred secondary I.D.s are a MasterCard or Visa—whether a credit card or prepaid debit card—plus an insurance card, library card, or school or work I.D.

ALTERNATE SECONDARY IDENTIFICATION

Privacy-conscious men and women obtain supporting identification to complement their alternate primary identification or novelty I.D.s —those fake foreign driver's licenses and other privately manufactured foreign identification cards, such as Alex Corbin used for his privacy in Chapter 3.

The most useful *alternate secondary identifications* for one who is living anonymously are debit cards offered by Visa and MasterCard, obtained in an alternate name. These cards can be used for private purchases without generating payment records to any of the credit bureaus. These accounts are managed online by the account holders. Only the issuing banks, the point-of-sale merchants, and the account holder will be aware of the debit card account activity.

Holders of these debit cards are able to make deposits at certain business establishments—check-cashing stores, for example—as well as to make cash withdrawals at ATM machines everywhere. Hotels and motels often require a credit or debit card for their files as a security measure, and of course the name on the card must match the resident's alternate primary identification in order for the resident to preserve his or her true name for privacy and security purposes.

Those who fly under the radar of many privacy-invasive databases have been known to take night classes under alternate names or to enroll in online classes in order to secure suitable school identification in an alternate name. Insurance cards and automobile membership cards are easily obtained by those using alternate names to receive mail.

Those who travel and live anonymously require supporting alternate identity documents, and those in the know have indicated that the best choices are a good-quality "foreign"-issued driver's license or other "foreign" photo I.D., as well as a MasterCard or Visa issued in the same alternate name. This combination, according to those experienced in living as "someone else"— at least most of the time—is about all you'll find necessary to accomplish your privacy goals, while doing it all legitimately.

SUMMARY

1. Banking passports or "camouflage" passports should not be used to attempt to pass false identification to banks for the purpose of opening U.S. or foreign bank accounts. See the "Finances" section of this book for information on anonymous business and personal banking.

2. A "camouflage" passport may serve as an alternate or novelty identification document while using an alternate or assumed name.

3. A *bona fide* foreign passport will serve as a primary identification document.

4. Foreign citizenship may be obtained through a variety of ways, including emigration, followed by the establishment of residency and applying for citizenship through birthright, marriage, business and investment contribution, artistic contribution, political recommendation, or the purchase of foreign passports.

5. Carefully consider the quality of the country's passport for international traveling purposes prior to undertaking the task of obtaining a dual citizenship.

6. Primary state-issued I.D. documents are government-issued passports and I.D. cards, driver's licenses, and birth certificates. All other sources of identification represent secondary I.D. and are used as supporting identification to primary I.D.s.

7. The most prestigious secondary identification documents include credit cards and debit cards, school or work I.D.s, insurance cards, and library cards.

home-style
percent high

Residents
plete with k
brush, stay
some due-
will be able
you require

For exan
convenient
ing, or wo
usually the
tels includ
savings ov
able, as hi
continued
longer. O
means of

The Mobile
Living in S

"A foolish consistency is the hol
—Ralph Waldo Emerso

EXTENDED-STAY HOTELS

Hotel living—by its very nature of sh are generally conscious of privacy n good choice for the privacy seeker. H ly private person, used hotels as his residen event you do not have the resources of a H consider a more cost-effective type of hote in recent years—the "extended-stay" hotel.

These residence hotels offer suites with c

PRIVATE

Once y
phone. W
location i

serve yo
Some
requirin
nation,
alternat
the trus
receivin

iving at reasonable rates—approximately 30 percent to 35
␣er than the cost of renting a comparable apartment.

␣are provided fully furnished apartment-style suites, com-
␣tchens, linens, and cooking utensils. Just bring your tooth-
␣s long as you desire, and enjoy the comforts of home. With
␣iligence research, which can be done on the Internet, you
␣to determine which extended-stay hotels offer the facilities
␣for your lifestyle needs.

␣ple, you may need high-speed Internet service, a location
␣to the airport or downtown, shuttle services, covered park-
␣kout facilities. Hotels in middle-class neighborhoods are
␣best choices. While the cost of living in extended-stay ho-
␣s all utilities—including telephone and Internet services, a
␣r apartment rentals—hotel taxes charged can be consider-
␣h as 14 percent in some cities. In some cases, taxes are dis-
␣for, or reimbursed to, hotel residents who stay one month or
␣erall, extended-stay hotels offer a cost-effective, convenient
␣iving, while providing you the ability to live privately.

REGISTRATION

␣ou choose a hotel, you may handle the reservation by tele-
␣hen calling, request information and confirm that a suitable
␣s available to satisfy your security and privacy requirements.

 A second-floor end unit, close to the rental
office, is a good choice.

When all your requirements have been
satisfied, you will be asked to reserve your
suite with a credit card. You may use your
preloaded MasterCard or Visa card, held
in your alternate name or company name
(see Chapter 15, "Anonymous Banking," and
Chapter 16, "Private Bill Payments") to re-
␣r suite—or use no card at all.

␣imes, extended-stay hotels will hold a room for you without
␣g a card to secure your reservation. Upon arrival at your desti-
␣ou may choose to pay in cash, or use your debit card with your
␣ name on it or a debit card in the name of the trust—with only
␣t's name on the card. You will be required to pay in advance of
␣g services.

The hotel will want to gather your personal and business information, and you'll be required to complete an application. Privacy-conscious travelers use an alternate name and address, furnish vague information about their employer or business, and give fictitious references and voicemail telephone numbers, if any, to hotels. When registering at the hotel, you want no links to the real you, so be prepared to eliminate any paper or electronic trail to your true name.

The hotel will request identification documents—usually a driver's license, along with a credit or debit card. But instead of using a legal driver's license, privacy advocates use a novelty foreign driver's license or identification card. Hotels almost always photocopy I.D.s for their records. So consider that the photocopy of the alternate identification will remain in the hotel database for a long time.

Some privacy seekers intentionally alter their appearance and dress in a disguise for the photographs placed on their alternate identification cards. In my extensive travels, I have never been questioned about my identification when staying at a hotel. Remember, they want your business, so as long as  you look the part of a business traveler and act professionally in both demeanor and speech, you will do fine in your dealings with hotels.

You'll be asked to provide the hotel with information about your automobile, if you have one. Some living a low-profile life have provided their license plate number, but eliminate or change one number or letter on the plate. For added security, it's a good idea to conceal the car's vehicle identification number (VIN) in order to prevent snoops from learning anything about your automobile. VINs on some cars, trucks, and SUVs are inaccessible or difficult to conceal, however.

Presumably, your car is registered in the name of a trust, you as trustee are not named on the registration, and your car's owner—the trust—has an address located far away from where you usually travel (see Chapter 10, "Driving Secretly"). When this is the case, you need not be concerned that your automobile will be traced back to your true name while staying at hotels.

HOTEL LIVING

While living at an extended-stay hotel, your utilities are furnished entirely by the hotel, so your true name will not be in any databases of utility, telephone, or Internet service providers. Also, you have the option of leaving on short notice if and when the need should arise. If you choose a hotel that is convenient to the business district, short and convenient commutes will help you efficiently manage your time.

Keep in mind that hotel suites are not entirely secure, as the hotel staff has access to rooms. Therefore, precautions should be taken while a hotel resident. Privacy advocates store all valuables, confidential paperwork, documents, sensitive items, and other private possessions off site in a rented storage facility secured in an alternate name or company name.

Take your laptop computer with you whenever you leave the hotel and keep little cash and no credit cards in the room. Also, schedule a time for hotel staff to service your suite when you are present and advise hotel management not to allow housekeeping inside your room unless you are present.

Routine maintenance and service repairs are necessary from time to time, and you can arrange to be in your suite when entrance into your room is required for these purposes. Limit maid service to once per week and be present when the housekeeping staff comes into your suite. Keep the "do not disturb" sign on the outside of the door and only allow staff inside the room as per a prearranged schedule for services.

When you are away from your suite, leave the television or radio and room lights on. Monitor any entries into your residence by placing a small piece of Scotch® tape across the door in order to determine whether an entry has been made during your absence.

The automobile you drive should be parked a distance from your hotel suite, yet be visible from your windows if possible. It is best to travel in a low-profile car, perhaps a medium-priced sedan in a neutral color. This type of car will be less in demand for theft and will not call attention to you. If you are not profiled as one who has wealth, you lessen your chances of being a target of thieves. For additional security, be sure the car is equipped with an alarm system.

HOTELS AND MOTELS

Traditional hotels and motels also offer accommodations to the privacy-seeking traveler who may not choose an extended-stay hotel.

Privacy-conscious people follow the same registration principles and guidelines described earlier in this chapter to preserve their privacy and to prevent anyone from finding them by name as a registered guest of a hotel or motel.

More exclusive hotels will be particular about having a credit card on file as a security measure against damages and will, in most cases, require one for making reservations as well. In fact, credit cards and debit cards are so valuable for travelers that all privacy seekers will want to secure such a card for those purchases that require one—and for secondary alternate identity purposes.

Be sure to keep abreast of what is available to you for purchase in an alternate name, as these companies change their policies so fast that it is difficult to make concrete recommendations about any in particular. However, you will want to obtain one in your alternate name for the convenience it provides as you travel and stay in hotels and motels. Also, obtaining a card in a company name is an option and will serve your privacy needs reasonably well.

PrivaCash offers debit cards to individuals with the Visa and MasterCard logo in no name at all, although these preloaded cards are restricted to relatively low amounts. The issuing bank, as well as Visa and MasterCard, will have access to all signers on company and trust-account credit or debit cards. Your true name must not be on a company or trust debit card if you wish to operate effectively under your alternate name.

Motels are usually the least expensive of all lodging facilities and are the least particular about registration requirements. Sometimes they don't ask for identification and readily accept cash for services, while not requiring a credit card to be placed on file. In certain locations, motels offer extended-stay rates, depending on demand and season, of course.

TELEPHONE CONSIDERATIONS

Local telephone calls are often free of charge to customers of hotels, motels, and extended-stay hotels. In order to preserve your privacy while a resident, you should use a telephone calling card when making these local calls in order to mask the location from which you are making the call. By dialing the telephone numbers on the calling card, plus the area code and number of the local telephone number, your actual telephone number and the hotel location should not appear on the receiving person's caller I.D.

Long-distance calls made from a hotel or motel telephone while using a telephone calling card should show only the telephone number associated with the company servicing the calling card. However, it is a good idea to test each card you buy by making a few calls when a new card is purchased.

Toll free "1-800" and other free calls will reveal your phone number at the hotel and sometimes the hotel name as well. Seldom will your room number be revealed to the receiving party, however. For the highest level of security, use a pay telephone when making toll-free calls instead of using the hotel telephones. Often, there are pay phones on the grounds of the hotel. Or, for highly sensitive calls, use a pay phone some distance from your hotel location, thereby preventing any potential link to you or your locale in the event the call is traced.

Do not receive any telephone messages at the hotel office and do not receive calls in your room. Do not answer your hotel room telephone. Use a cell telephone and a dedicated voicemail service and make sure both are in your alternate name. Or you may use a prepaid cell phone that requires no name at all. Tracfone and Net 10 are two brands that require no name or address for activation and may be loaded with telephone minutes through anonymously purchased calling cards.

MOTOR HOMES AND RECREATIONAL VEHICLES

Of all the choices available for those who opt for a mobile lifestyle, motor homes and other recreational vehicles may be the most private of all. First, they are mobile, and while most fifth wheels and trav-

el trailers will require some due diligence and a three-quarter-ton or one-ton truck to move them, they can be moved quickly and registered discreetly in the name of trusts. Also, RV resorts and mobile home parks generally ask few questions.

The epitome of mobile living, the self-contained motor home or trailer offers the convenience of not having to call the movers and the ease of changing your residential location on short notice—a distinct advantage in the event of an emergency. The downside is less space and fewer comforts, plus a large capital outlay for the initial purchase of the home. Fuel bills and space rents can be expensive, as is maintenance of the motor home or RV or towing vehicle when repairs are necessary.

Depending on the city in which you choose to live, space rental costs may outweigh the practicality of owning a mobile home, if you are weighing your decisions on economic considerations entirely. Some spaces at mobile home parks rent for an amount equal to the price of an apartment, depending on the neighborhood. So you will need to decide whether it is cost effective for you to buy a motor home or other RV instead of renting an apartment or a house. However, when compared to the costs of living in a more traditional home, self-contained motor homes and fifth wheels—which can be purchased at relatively low prices once they are a few years old—offer the buyer a reasonable value for living quarters.

OWNERSHIP AND REGISTRATION

All mobile living vehicles, including motor homes and towable travel trailers or fifth wheels, can be easily registered in the name of a trust. You must register them at your state department of motor vehicles office or similar agency that handles automobile registrations. Follow the registration guidelines on how to discreetly register these vehicles, as outlined in Chapter 10, "Driving Secretly." Remember, you want no personal ties to these vehicles, so be sure to handle this registration process correctly.

INSURANCE

Buying renter's insurance will compromise your residence privacy unless precautions are taken to ensure that the insurance company has no information about your actual home address. Those choosing the mobile lifestyle—the most private way to live—may want to limit their insurance coverage to the policy purchased for their off-site storage facility, offered by companies that insure the contents of rented storage spaces. Automobile policies offer some coverage for theft under the comprehensive/collision section of the policy. Also, certain specialty coverages, such as for firearms, is available through the National Rifle Association and other organizations.

Self-insurance, a disciplined approach whereby would-be premium dollars are deposited into an insurance fund account or set aside to cover property losses, is an option that can be used in lieu of buying renter's content insurance. The mobile lifestyle may prohibit holding a renter's policy, and the invasion of privacy required to be underwritten for it is a consideration as well.

Motor homes and recreational vehicles, depending on their use, may be added onto vehicle insurance policies. If they are lived in full time, however, a specialty company that insures these homes will need to be used to obtain insurance. Buy the RV policy in the name of the trust which owns the motor home, fifth wheel, or travel trailer, rather than being named individually on the insurance contract. Then only the insurance company file—not the DMV records or your policy, will show you as the named insured. But you as an individual will have to be underwritten for the policy. A few insurance companies specializing in this type of policy will write it solely in the name of the trust—a high level privacy advantage.

FINANCING OPTIONS

Traditional financing through companies that offer motor home, travel trailer, and recreational vehicle financing is not a viable option for the privacy advocate. Such a payment plan will provide a payment history to the company holding the note, which will be placed in your personal credit bureau files. You do not want this to occur, even though you would be mobile and discovery of your location by an investigator or other snoop would be difficult.

See Chapter 19, "Credit Bureaus," in this book for some ideas on how to creatively obtain money to fund your motor home or recreational vehicle. Financing the RV through a private party is one choice, although you will not want the note holder to access your credit reports under any circumstances. So be careful about obtaining money from private parties. Essentially, if you choose financing over paying cash, your goal should be to divert the loan received for the purchase into another entity under your control, while still making the cash for the purchase available to you and at an attractive interest rate.

PRIVACY PRINCIPLES FOR MOBILE LIVING

Never receive mail, home deliveries, or faxes at your place of residence. Arrange to use Office Depot, the UPS Store, or another company to

PAPER SHREDDER

receive faxes at your request. Or you may want to receive faxes on your computer, providing you can obtain a number from a far-away state and you are certain that your computer's I.P. address is not revealed through the use of this type of fax. Test it to be sure you are not sacrificing privacy for convenience.

A mail-drop nominee can also receive faxes on your behalf, then scan and e-mail them to you. When deliveries are necessary, have them sent to your mail nominee's address and instruct the nominee to forward them to you. Shred all trash papers that contain information about you. If you are careful, you will not need to be concerned with private investigators or others diving into your dumpsters looking for your trash in hopes of obtaining information about you. Without any links to your actual address, which no one will be able to obtain if you follow the principles of privacy in this book, a snoopy gumshoe or identity thief will not be able to locate a dumpster in which to dive.

Keep contacts with neighbors and others around your living vicinity on a casual and polite level. Be courteous to managers and staff personnel. Mind your own business and do not draw attention to yourself by throwing loud parties at your residence. When you want to have parties, utilize an off-site location to socialize and keep your actual physical residence location a secret to all except those very few who can be trusted with this important information.

SUMMARY

1. Mobile living offers privacy advantages, including ease of changing locations on short notice and difficulty of locating travelers or short-term residents with brief histories.

2. Extended-stay hotels provide privacy, convenience, comfort, and short- or long-term housing at cost-effective prices without ownership or lease commitments.

3. Special precautions need to be taken when providing personal and business information to hotels, in order to preserve privacy and maintain a low profile.

4. Privacy advocates use alternate I.D. and alternate name or company name debit cards while living the mobile lifestyle, to ensure their anonymity.

5. Your automobile should have no links to your true name. Register it in the name of a trust, while keeping your name off of all registration records.

6. Spare weapons and permanent documents should be stored off site in a secure storage facility—documents and valuables may be placed in a safe deposit box.

7. Hotel staff should enter your suite or room only by appointment.

8. Hotels, motels, extended-stay hotels, and RVs offer mobile living options with high-level security and the convenience of short- or long-term residence and privacy at reasonable costs. Utilities are provided by third parties for additional privacy.

9. Avoid being discovered through caller I.D. by using calling cards, pay telephones, and cell telephones held in alternate names or no name at all.

10. Recreational vehicles must be registered at the Department of Motor Vehicles or other state vehicle registration agencies. Motor homes may be owned by a trust, which has no

registration requirements. Positively make sure that only the trust's name is on the vehicle registration and title, without reference to you as the trustee.

11. Specialty insurance may be obtained to cover valuables while traveling. Off-site storage facilities offer content insurance. RVs may require specialty insurance policies.

12. *Self-insurance* is an option for mobile residents and frequent travelers.

13. Traditional financing of recreational vehicles and towing vehicles will compromise one's personal privacy. Review the "Finances" section—particularly the chapter on "Credit Bureaus"—for guidance on creative financing of large purchases. Paying cash for recreational vehicles—and private registration in a trust—assures personal privacy.

14. Never receive any mail or home deliveries at your home. Use third-party nominees to receive and forward mail.

15. Be polite as you do business with managers at hotels, motels, extended-stay hotels, and RV parks.

16. Keep a low profile while at home. Avoid noisy parties or large gatherings at your residence. Use off-site facilities for reunions and parties.

17. Be polite to your neighbors, while using your alternate name for privacy purposes.

18. Carefully file important documents. Shred all paperwork going into your trash.

♦ SEVEN ♦

The Anonymous Resident

"Where thou art, that is home."
—Emily Dickinson

LIVING BENEATH THE RADAR

The vehicle resembled a van, although it appeared somewhat larger. Maybe the term is "paddy wagon." That seems to fit. Anyway, it was white, with writing on both sides advertising its government-agency name as it slowly made its way over the speed bumps and cruised through the large apartment complex every couple of weeks or so.

The two oversized dudes up front looked "official," leaning back in their seats, gawking outside through sunglasses at license plates of cars parked throughout, occasionally stopping to jot down some numbers for reference, and then continuing on.

"They're investigators," Chip whispered, hammer in hand and an assortment of tools dangling from a belt wrapped tightly around his bib overalls, as he stood in the laundry room door. He placed four coins inside the slots, preparing to wash another load.

"Last week they kicked down a guy's door and hauled him off to jail," the maintenance man continued. "Said he was overdue a year and a half on owing the state for his kids. Me, I pay nearly a third of what I make down at the school." He stared at the hammer, thoughtfully, then looked Alex Corbin in the eye, a smile starting to form.

"They don't know about this, though. This job is paid in cash." He winked, then walked out.

Had he been careful enough? It was a decent part of town—not the best, but convenient. Close to a shopping mall, freeway accessible, within a short drive to businesses, and situated among homes and apartment buildings. An average place. Not at all fancy. And, now government investigators were a part of the traffic.

The lease had expired a few weeks back. Three months had gone by quickly—the term of the lease—negotiated down from six, with him agreeing to pay twenty bucks more each month for the shorter-term agreement. So now, he could move on if he so chose, to place distance between himself and those who wanted him.

But there was not a trace of "him" here. Not the guy named in their credit bureau reports. And he looked different than years ago. A beard on his previously clean-shaven face, his hair dyed red instead of its usual jet-black, and he wore glasses—always, even though he had 20/20 vision. The guy who was being hunted didn't live here. Not on paper anyway. Just his body—and they would never know that. At least he hoped not, and he had made carefully planned efforts to prevent anyone from knowing anything about him, including where he lived.

Finally, he had settled down again and had a permanent residence. Alex had been advised by his attorney to avoid the process server for the civil matter now pending. His ex reportedly wanted even more money for child support—never mind that his current amount was already excessive and beyond the amount required to support his family.

Alex would be penalized for receiving a capital gains windfall, no matter how much it really took to support his kids—but only if he were served, according to the lawyer. Knowing he was meeting his parental obligations and following his attorney's advice, Alex elected to avoid the court system, an unfair, skewed, punishment-oriented affair— again, according to his attorney. So he continued paying his previously ordered support payments while living beneath the radar to avoid being penalized for his success.

ADVANTAGES OF RENTING

For most who desire privacy, renting offers several advantages over owning a residence. For example, the renter has a short- to medium-term commitment to stay in the property, a time which can be as short as one month to no longer than six months. The privacy seeker should not commit to longer than a three-month or six-month lease, in order to keep relocation options available without unnecessary promises to

pay, which a long-term lease requires.

Furthermore, it is often possible and more practical to opt for a short-term rental agreement—say a month-to-month or a three-month lease, even at a higher monthly rate—in order to gain a flexibility advantage to relocate should the need arise. More personal privacy is generally assured for renters, because their sole responsibility is limited to paying the rent when due, while enjoying freedom from the time commitments associated with home ownership.

Renters generally need not retain outside repair people such as roofers, carpenters, carpet installers, carpet cleaners, and other service people. When and if these types of property repairs or maintenance are needed, the renter can decide whether he or she wants to tolerate the inconvenience, or simply move. Most repairs are completed prior to moving in, and any repairs necessary during a renter's tenancy are handled by in-house maintenance personnel or contractors retained by the property management.

Renters also avoid the cost of property taxes, which in many cities is between 1 percent and 3.75 percent of the most recent selling price of the property. Governments sometimes tax homes according to the most recent appraisal value of the property. Imagine paying the government 3.75 percent of the value of your home yearly for the privilege of "owning" it. Homeowners in a subdivision near Austin, Texas, do just that.

The government's investment return on "your" home is sometimes about the same as your money market fund pays you on your capital. Miss a payment on your property taxes, and you will quickly discover who really "owns" it, because Big Bureaucrat is ready, willing, and able to confiscate the property of those delinquent on tax bills.

Seriously weigh the advantages of renting versus owning, with property taxes as one consideration. Being without a mortgage—at least a traditional one with a bank, savings and loan, or a mortgage company—

provides a much-needed layer of privacy. As a renter, providing you handle your lease correctly, you can remain anonymous and be free from inclusion in databases containing homeowners' names derived from real estate agents' files, credit bureau files, property tax bills, or other compilations of names used to form such lists to track your whereabouts.

Furthermore, houses purchased through traditional mortgages and financed long term—thirty years, for example—are paid for multiple times, and the equity one gains from home "ownership" may not be the best way to invest capital. Insurance coverage, if one chooses to have it when renting, will be limited to "contents" coverage and liability coverage. I say, "if one chooses to have it," because, unless handled correctly, buying insurance on your rented home or apartment may require a serious invasion of your privacy.

You may be best served to self-insure rather than cover the cost of your belongings under a third-party contract. Whether you decide to cover your home's contents yourself or through an insurance policy, renting will enable you to save on the cost of structure insurance— necessary coverage to protect your physical dwelling—if you own the property.

As a renter, you are free of the expenses associated with the formation of an entity to hold your "owned" property—a trust, for example— as well as associated *"administrative trustee"* costs or other costs in order to make your dwelling private and keep it without ties to you personally.

These privacy measures are not necessary if your rent your home. While renting, your name will not be associated with any county home ownership records whatsoever, and these records are open to the public.

NEIGHBORHOOD RULES

For privacy-concerned persons who decide to rent, some due diligence is required in order to find a suitable place in which to live. The most convenient rental homes or apartments available are located in lower-middle-class neighborhoods, with the emphasis on "lower" middle class. Residences in such areas have management that is more amenable to satisfying the requirements of the privacy seeker. A renter also needs to have a flexible manager to deal with, who also has an incentive to rent a residence due to the inventory of available apartments or homes. Such requirements are best satisfied in these neighborhoods.

Drive by the areas that most interest you during the day and night-time, obtain the telephone numbers of available rentals from posted signs, and evaluate the general area by driving around and viewing nearby tenants, neighbors, and cars. You can learn a great deal even before you make your first calls to owners or property managers. Several trips touring prospective neighborhoods during the night hours, on the weekend, and during business hours can provide information on the actual living conditions of an area under consideration.

Avoid actual "skid row" areas. These areas are crawling with cops looking for the latest liquor store robbery suspect, and you will come into police view as they are casing these neighborhoods. Also, you do not want to live among the lowest of the socioeconomic classes of a given city or town but instead, fall into the middle class resident status and appear as a working person, regardless of your financial means.

A lower-middle-class neighborhood will have a substantial number of legal immigrants and "illegal aliens" who do not speak English, and while you want to be careful in picking your area to live, this mixed neighborhood—with all conceivable races, creeds, and colors—can greatly enhance your success in leasing a totally private home.

Property managers in such neighborhoods are accustomed to seeing out-of-country references and employment histories, as well as applicants' historical residences from another country. In such cases, not only will U.S. credit bureaus be impossible as sources of verification, in most cases management will have frequently heard the story of prospective renters claiming to have no credit. So your chances of success will be better as you formulate a story not at all unfamiliar to the property manager who makes decisions about rental applications.

EFFECTIVE NEGOTIATING

"Your application has been approved," stated the middle-aged manager over the telephone. Victoria knew her on a first-name basis by this time, having met her twice and having spoken to her now for the fourth time by telephone during the application process.

"You just need to come in and sign the lease and pick from the two apartments we have available, and then you can move in," the manager continued.

Could she mail the lease? Victoria asked. The manager agreed she could. Victoria reviewed the lease, made an addendum note or two, and passed the paper to her secretary nominee, who scribbled an illegible signature just invented for this purpose, having been given authorization to sign on Victoria's behalf. Once this was done, Victoria copied everything, sent the manager the copy, and prepared to return and move in within a few days.

In order to have true privacy, long term, you can lease an apartment or house in an alternate or assumed name. This practice of using an alternate name has been practiced legally in most countries in the Western Hemisphere and has been deemed a legal practice so long as there is no intent to defraud anyone. So, *don't* intend to defraud. Intend instead to make your life private, and utilize an alternate name to conceal your true identity at your place of residence.

If law enforcement ever asks who you are, however, whether you are at home or not, tell them the truth. They will nail you if you use an alias, and certainly the rules change when dealing with them, so you should provide your real identity if and when you are confronted.

Privacy seekers have lived a very low-profile lifestyle throughout their lifetimes, while using an alternate name as they follow certain steps to successfully accomplish necessary transactions. Privacy living is never as convenient or inexpensive as the ordinary way of life, but there is no comparison to the peace of mind enjoyed by living anonymously. Using methods described in this section can help you achieve your goals.

Victoria—the woman mentioned a few paragraphs earlier—was taking steps to privatize her life. Thirty-something, she intended to become an anonymous resident while renting in an alternate name. Her former husband, a stalker and abuser, motivated her to take steps to become untraceable through ordinary investigative channels.

So she met the apartment manager in person after having screened properties suitable for her needs based on location, price, and lease-length requirements. She was careful to dress in business attire and had her residential and work histories organized. Following her initial meeting, Victoria took an application and advised the manager that she would complete and return it in the event that she wanted to rent the apartment.

Privacy seekers recommend establishing a business rapport with the person leasing the property and stress the importance of dealing with the same person during the application process. Successful applicants who desire privacy establish their credibility with the manager by appearing for appointments on time, following up visits with courteous telephone calls thanking management for their time and efforts, and providing necessary information to facilitate the rental application process.

Above all, the privacy advocate who wants to become an anonymous resident wants no connection whatsoever to their true name or their home location. During the initial meeting with the manager, Victoria  was prepared to answer the questions about her previous residential history as well as her employment status and work history. That's what property managers do as they screen potential residents for their properties.

Victoria's previous abuse from her ex-husband made her determined to prepare well and take charge of her personal privacy through the use of references and income verifications, which she had prearranged. This documentation, which Victoria herself created, added credibility to her past, while preserving her much-needed privacy.

Successful privacy advocates utilize their people skills to convince property managers and owners of their reliability through effective communication, while providing to the manager background documentation that is adequate and under their control. Often, the rental applicant will have resources at his or her disposal to facilitate the process of becoming an approved applicant very soon after the initial interview with the property manager.

Employment and income-verification letters have been mailed from *offshore mail-drop addresses,* while being signed by nominee managers for the purpose of qualifying the privacy-seeking applicant for the rental unit.

A person's income and place of residence are highly confidential items of information and should be treated as such in the current Privacy Crisis. You must take responsibility for your living expenses and pay bills on time, while being as assertive as is necessary to accomplish privacy, safety, and freedom in your home.

Keep in mind that you will find individual managers who will reject you. Do not despair. Keep swinging the bat of persistence and recognize that the right fit of manager is required in order for you to have a successful tenant-property manager relationship. You will find a manager who is flexible and will take your first month's rent money with a reasonable security deposit, if any, while being impressed enough with you—despite your explanation for having no credit history with U.S. credit bureaus.

Be persistent, search the right neighborhoods for the right manager, and you will accomplish your goal of renting a home in complete privacy.

APPLICATION GUIDELINES

Victoria, the former stalking victim who was physically and emotionally abused by her ex-husband, took special care to complete the rental application to ensure that she would have the best possible chance at being approved for her apartment. She was careful to make sure that no data or information was included which would give away her true name and past history. She knew that such an error would jeopardize her privacy and place her at risk of sustaining additional personal injuries.

The examples in this book are illustrations, and the author is merely reporting on what has worked, rather than endorsing any particular privacy behavior. It should be noted, however, that he encourages all who seek privacy to take responsibility for themselves and their living expenses so that they are capable of paying for all services necessary for a privacy lifestyle—regardless of whatever name they may choose to call themselves.

Remember to opt for what works during your quest for privacy while still doing ethical business and providing a fair and agreed-upon payment for residential rental services. Privacy experts generally discourage providing a copy of an alternate identification with a long-term lease and rental application. Often, an identifying number on a novelty identification card can be provided in lieu of any photocopies—and of course, the novelty or alternate identification number cannot be traced through any databases.

Banking history and account information is often requested on an application to rent property. Can you believe that anyone would actually provide the bank's name, account number, and credit card numbers to a rental management company or property owner? Privacy-conscious renters have used banks from outside of the country, with account numbers that are not verifiable. An old, outdated, preloaded

MasterCard or Visa account number—providing the account was held in your alternate name, of course—is an option for a credit reference.

Victoria had utilized her *offshore mailing address* as she was providing necessary documentation to the property manager. Her company name, as well as her own, was on record with this western European mail-drop operator. Thus, her proper documentation for the apartment was under her full control as she advised the manager, through her own company, of her sufficient income necessary to cover her future apartment rental expenses.

In Victoria's case, she was able to use the lengthy time required to receive out-of-country verifications on previous residences and other verifications to her advantage. In this case, the apartment manager elected to take what could be obtained within a reasonable period of time, with full recognition that information from abroad travels slowly sometimes. So our previous stalking victim and abused woman was able to pass the verification test with flying colors while providing adequate—not excessive—information and without letting the entire world know her business.

Returning to the rental-application process, Victoria typed hers, completing it entirely, and made a copy, which she sent to the manager with her nominee's signature in place of her own, retaining the original for her files. It is not prudent or necessary to pay forward an arbitrary amount of money as a large rental security deposit in exchange for bypassing the normal income and credit history verification requirements. Rather than humbly approaching a property manager with hat in hand, offering to pay six months to a year of rent in advance for being able to live in a property, it is more acceptable and prudent and a better business practice to find the right manager who will accept your privacy requirements and who really wants your business, based on his impression of you and the information he obtains from you.

Some renters have found that providing a letter of recommendation from a previous manager or landlord—noting that rents there were always paid on a timely basis and referring to you by your alternate name—helps greatly in creating a favorable impression when searching for a new rental.

PRIVATE UTILITIES

While renting property in an alternate name accomplishes a high level of privacy for individuals who want to live below the radar screen of databases containing "occupant" names and U.S. credit bureau re-cords—or avoid being identified by name to investigators who make door-to-door inquiries, stalkers, and others—only half the battle is won once the property is leased. Securing and paying your new home's utili-ties must be taken seriously as you strive to maintain your privacy.

Later in this book an entire chapter (24) will focus on the topic of nominees—substitutes who agree to stand in for you in various situa-tions as you pursue your privacy goals. Here, however, I want to direct your attention briefly to the value of retaining the services of a nominee for the particular purpose of holding your utility accounts.

These accounts may include, but are not limited to, cable television, high-speed Internet, trash pickup, natural gas, electricity, and water. Nominees are important pieces of your privacy puzzle, and it is impor-tant for you to learn how to select and use them properly to assist in your home privacy objectives.

Do not recruit spouses who might use their maiden names on util-ity accounts or relatives or friends to become your nominees. Those seeking you, in the event you are ever hunted, will gravitate first to-ward those who know you or have had past relationships with you. You might be shocked to discover just how many of your friends and rela-tives would almost certainly sell you out entirely to law enforcement types and others who claim authority—or to licensed investigators, those using "pretext" names, and others.

Even in the event that Aunt Martha holds out and does not spill the proverbial beans, once Mr. Investigator searches utility company da-tabases and learns of Auntie's multiple utility accounts, a quick path will be beaten to the doors where utility services are provided under her name, and bingo—you are found. So be professional and discreet about using nominees and retain an independent businessperson, with no ties to you, to ensure your safety and personal privacy.

Do not use a nominee for utility accounts unless you are reasonably assured that the individual is of sound character and law abiding. If you make a bad choice and use the wrong person, he or she may be under investigation, be sought by law enforcement in the future, or be dragged into court at some future time. You cannot be assured that these events will not occur with even the strongest of human characters.

But you are less likely to have investigators, police, bill collectors, process servers, stalkers, and others march to your door and subject you to an investigation and home invasion, if you select a reliable busi-ness person to be your nominee and hold utility accounts. You should utilize the services of a professional independent *nominee*—one who provides these services for others—or a business person you trust in a normal business relationship. Bookkeepers, office managers, and independent secretaries are good candidates.

A few companies provide to privacy advocates, nominees who have been screened. In all nominee business relationships, form a written contractual agreement outlining the service provisions, payment schedule, and responsibilities of each party. It is important that nominee services be paid professional services. The payment you provide the nominee for his or her services will act as an incentive for professional and confidential services on your behalf.

Generally, a nominee will obtain the utility and other services necessary for your home by providing proper account information to the given utility or service company. The nominee's Social Security number or his or her spouse's Social Security number—or perhaps a company tax EIN—may be tied to the account. In some cases, monetary deposits are used in lieu of the Social Security number and verified credit report.

Nominees will require deposits to assure that they will be paid for the services they provide on your behalf. So expect to provide them with a deposit of about three months' worth of the expected cost of utilities at your residence. Also, the nominee will pay the bills as they come to their mailing address, and you will in turn pay the nominee for the utility bills, plus a service fee for handling your account. Third-party payment of utility bills at your residence provides high-level security for you as you rent your home anonymously.

MOVERS

Use movers who are carefully screened or obtain by referral the names of individuals to assist with moving. Using a company name or a non-registered *fictitious business name* for services assures that there will be no link to your alternate name or address.

Pay for moving services in cash. Move all sensitive information and items yourself while carefully inventorying the property to be moved. When long hauls are required, make sure the truck's doors are sealed, and be present when they are both sealed and re-opened. Use companies with a reasonable business history who pay their employees a salary. Use bonded movers and obtain the first and last names of the individuals who move your property.

NOMINEES FOR RENTING SERVICES

Do not, under normal circumstances, use a nominee to rent an apartment or house for you. One should avoid surprises to the property management. When a person other than the one who agreed to the lease shows up and begins living in the rental, without the manager of the property expecting it, an investigation will surely follow. And we want to avoid that type of scrutiny of you in your own home.

Most landlords and property managers have been treated poorly by some previous tenants, once they have been in the business for any period of time. That's why they are suspicious and want personal information about those who stay in their properties. Don't compound your privacy problem by having someone else rent the apartment for you. So, barring unusual cases, privacy advocates or their spouses or significant others rent their own homes or apartments while using alternate names.

BECOMING A ROOMMATE

In the event you need to disappear quickly and live privately—long term or for a brief period of time—the simplest way to accomplish this is to become a roommate. Those who have advertised for a roommate will have already signed a lease or purchased a property and usually have obtained all necessary utilities at the house, condominium, or apartment to be shared. So all the privacy-invasive legwork has been accomplished, and you need only to bring minimal possessions when moving in.

This ease of moving without the costs of using nominees makes living in a roommate situation an attractive option for privacy living, particularly when time and costs are important considerations. When compared to other options of renting residential property, renting a room in another's house or apartment offers privacy and convenience advantages for one wishing to live low profile.

First of all, in most cases, a very short application form, or none at all, will be required when you become a roommate. Rather than rely on applications, credit checks, references, and employment histories as with traditional property managers, individuals renting to roommates tend to be more lenient and subjective in making their decisions. Therefore, it's imperative to use your best people skills when speaking to those who have advertised their home for rent—and during subsequent interviews.

As always, to preserve your privacy, use an alternate name when introductions are made and explain only those parts of your life you deem necessary for strangers to know. By providing your alternate name to a prospective roommate, you are laying a foundation for a very high level of privacy, because without a true name, links to the real you become difficult to trace.

Establishing yourself under your alternate name will prevent anyone from knowing your living location, since credit bureaus and other large databases cannot follow you to your new address. In the event your alternate name is reported to a record-keeping agency or company, no association will be made with your true name. When dealing with prospective roommates, speak plainly, dress well, have your story and background prepared, and treat the interview as you would any other important meeting. It is an opportunity to sell yourself—so do it well.

Prior to finalizing a roommate deal, you should screen those with whom you will be sharing your residence in order to satisfy yourself about their character. You may investigate anyone for criminal background information, obtain an address history, civil lawsuit history, and other public information by purchasing services from any number of companies on the Internet that conduct people searches—for costs under $50 per person—or you may use a private investigator at a higher cost but with more information usually provided.

In all cases, it is recommended that you screen all prospective roommates for your own safety, security, and peace of mind. Here are three websites that can assist you in making roommate decisions:

1. www.PeopleSearch.Intelius.com
2. www.Criminalcbs.com
3. www.PrivateEye.com

ROOMMATE CASE HISTORY

Having roommates can have a downside, as an acquaintance of mine, whom we'll call Marcus, found out. Prior to agreeing to live in a shared residence, Marcus neglected to do the necessary background work on those sharing the residence and was later unpleasantly surprised. Learn from his mistakes.

Having lived in extended-stay hotels and an apartment during a portion of his very low-profile years, Marcus returned to a city on the West Coast following a long absence. Because his income was limited, and he was not sure how long he would stay in his former hometown, he considered living as a roommate.

This style of living had appeal for several reasons. First, it's always cheaper than leasing a traditional apartment—perhaps 25 percent to 35 percent less on average—and when you consider everything, it can be pleasant having another person or two nearby for company, conversation, and added house security.

Furthermore, if schedules are different, as is often the case, you may have the place to yourself for long periods of time. And of course, no extra expenses or time-consuming work need be spent finding suitable, credible, nominees for obtaining utilities when one becomes a roommate. If an additional service, such as high-speed Internet, is required once you move in, the homeowner or person leasing the room to you may be willing to put the service in his name when you agree to pay him for the service, thereby becoming the only nominee you need when you are a roommate.

With these thoughts in mind, Marcus began to look for a suitable roommate situation. After reading classified ads and making some calls, he found several prospects and narrowed his selection to a few choices based on location, property description, residents' profiles, and rental costs.

Marcus found one prospect offering a shared-living arrangement in a house near the ocean. He described himself as an executive who was away on business for extended periods of time—another plus. Marcus scheduled an appointment for the following afternoon. The man with whom he spoke said he was the owner of the property and explained that due to his frequent absences, he wanted a responsible, mature person as a roommate. In a short period of time, he offered Marcus the rental.

Another man who worked the night shift at a local business also rented a room in the same house and, much of the time, just he and Marcus would occupy the spacious home during the owner's absences. Marcus agreed to give the offer consideration.

Marcus checked the homeowner's background by paying a nominal fee to a service on the Internet and discovered nothing out of the ordinary. He did not meet the other tenant, the night shift worker, who the owner described as "a very nice man." Not knowing the other roommate's last name, Marcus could not make a routine online investigation and decided not to ask the owner for his name before agreeing to rent the property as a roommate.

Marcus moved in the following week. Several weeks passed, with the owner staying in the house infrequently and the other roommate seldom seen due to his night work schedule. While sitting at his desk one afternoon, Marcus heard voices at the front door of the house. Recognizing Mr. Night Shift's voice, he believed his roommate had visitors and continued with his work.

Minutes later, a police detective appeared at the door, stating that he had a search warrant for Mr. Night Shift's room. He asked Marcus to leave the property for several hours while the police accomplished their work. Additional plainclothes detectives came to the house as he was leaving, and Marcus' "private home" became an open book and was now under investigation. A privacy seeker's nightmare!

Mr. Night Shift, Marcus later learned, had been under investigation for some months and was charged with a serious crime on the day the police arrived at the house. Now, a search of this man's name would have revealed his name in newspaper articles some months earlier, though he was then only considered "a person of suspicion" and was not arrested or charged with any crime until the day the police arrived at the house.

So knowing this information might have swayed Marcus from moving into the house. If he had known about the ongoing investigation, however, he would not have made the choice to live at the beach house. Marcus could only blame himself for being ignorant of those sharing his living environment. Marcus moved out at the end of the month.

This incident underscores the importance of knowing all you can about those with whom you share your residence. Do a background check to obtain information about a prospective roommate's criminal history prior to making your decision.

RENTING AND PRIVACY CONSIDERATIONS

Once you believe you have found a compatible and credible room-mate, insist on a month-to-month rental agreement. Most will agree to your terms, as their motivation to rent to you is clearly to have help with the rent or mortgage, and it's not uncommon to have only a month-to-month agreement rather than a long-term lease when renting.

Under even the best of circumstances, your privacy will be compromised to some extent while you share a residence. Some restrictions will apply as you take the steps to live anonymously. Routine telephone calls to your accountant, attorney, credit card companies, some state and federal agencies, physicians, and others may require your "true name" during the conversation. As you are living under your "alternate name," be sure to make these sensitive calls off site so that your conversations are not heard by anyone in the house.

Do not have a land-line telephone installed while living as a room-mate. Use a cell telephone and public telephones for more privacy. Keep confidential paperwork, documents, permanent records, private equipment, and other information that could provide a link to your true name stored off site. Take your laptop computer and cell phone with you when you leave to prevent anyone from searching your files. Lock your bedroom door for privacy and change previously installed locks.

INSURANCE

If you rent your home under an alternate name, whether through a lease agreement or as a roommate, the physical rental structure is not your responsibility as a tenant. For the ultimate in personal privacy and as mentioned earlier, it is advisable to "self-insure" all personal property, setting aside premium dollars to cover a loss rather than buying coverage from a third party. An off-site storage facility should be used to store your most private documents and equipment as well as certain valuables. You may rent this space in a company name or in the name of a trust. Certain individuals have rented off-site storage spaces in alternate names.

HOME DELIVERIES AND MAIL

Never receive mail of any kind at your home. Do not sign for certified mail or private mail deliveries of any kind. Do not answer your door unless you are expecting a visitor. When there is a need for a home delivery—a piece of heavy furniture, for example—use the highest level of security possible. Purchase it under your alternate name and have it delivered to your off-site storage facility. This ruse delivery eliminates any trail whatsoever to your home address. Hire a different delivery crew to pick up and deliver the stored item to your home. Use a different name than your alternate name for this second delivery. Pay for all delivery services in cash.

AUTOMOBILES

Park your car in a garage or on the rental property whenever possible, while avoiding the streets. Street parking is less secure and will make you vulnerable to receiving unnecessary, costly parking tickets. An effective car alarm is a good security device that will alert you in the event that theft or a break-in is attempted. A steering wheel locking device adds security to the automobile and reduces the chances of theft.

The car you drive should be registered to a trust as described in the "Travel" section of this book to assure your identity is not discovered in the event the police, investigators, or others "run" your license plates. When they do, the trust's name, with its distant address, will come up, and you, as trustee, will not be listed on the registration if you register it with the Department of Motor Vehicles correctly. This is absolutely necessary to preserve your privacy.

Automobiles are an easy source for determining identity unless you take steps to ensure your privacy. Driving a car that is registered and titled in your true name makes it impossible to keep your life private.

SECURITY

Medeco high-security locks are a good choice for your doors as you live privately while renting. Hire a locksmith to change the locks once you move in and keep the old locks to reinstall when you move out.

Keep a spare key for yourself and do not give anyone else your secure keys. Placing your spare key in a safe place—such as in a magnetic key holder that is carefully hidden—assures you easy access to your home in the event you misplace your original key.

Do not use alarm companies for home security—they ask too many personal questions, and law enforcement will become involved when alarms are triggered in some cities. Establish security measures that you control entirely for the highest level of personal privacy.

A twelve-gauge shotgun has been recommended for home security. A handgun loaded with safety bullets to prevent dangerous, long-range travel of fired rounds is a consideration for apartment safety.

Watchdogs can be another good security choice, but for apartment living, they are not recommended. When renting a house, a well-trained dog can be effective for home security. Make your choices to secure your living quarters based on available facilities, your budget, and your property and personal requirements.

SUMMARY

1. Renting a home or apartment allows one to live privately, while having the flexibility of changing locations within a reasonable amount of time.

2. Leases should be kept to between three and six months. Month-to-month agreements are better. Security deposits should be reasonably small.

3. Renting saves on home repairs and eliminates the expense of property taxes.

4. Middle-class neighborhoods are the most suitable for finding cost-effective housing and property managers who are sensitive to privacy needs.

5. Renting in an alternate name will assure you of home living privacy.

6. Meet property managers and establish a business relationship, while providing only necessary information to lease a property. Successful privacy seekers keep their employment and income information and true names confidential, while supplying property managers only with sufficient information for application-processing requirements.

7. Consider utilizing the concept of self-insurance for possessions in your rental property. It is possible—legally and effectively—to insure contents of a home while not giving away the actual address.

8. Establish utility accounts under third-party names. Use professional nominees or business people to obtain and service your home utility accounts. Carefully select nominees who have no links to you and who will handle the utility accounts confidentially and professionally.

9. Rental property should be leased by those who will be living in the property.

10. Living as a roommate provides reasonable rent costs and eliminates the need for nominees.

11. Certain privacy compromises are made when living as a roommate.

12. Carefully screen ALL roommates prior to living with them.

13. Do not receive mail of any kind at home.

14. Make deliveries to your home private by using your off-site storage facility as the first stop and by hiring a second delivery crew to deliver items to your home.

15. Use fictitious names and company names when utilizing delivery and moving personnel.

16. Pay for all delivery and moving services in cash.

17. Use movers who are bonded and insured and obtain the first and last names of delivery persons.

18. Keep automobiles secure with sensitive, loud alarms; park cars on the property.

19. Register and hold the title of the car in the name of a trust, without any trustee or other name on the registration or title documents.

20. Locks, firearms, and guard dogs are security options for your rental home.

EIGHT

Private Home Ownership

"Mid pleasures and palaces though we may roam, be it ever so humble, there's no place like home"—John Howard Payne

SAFETY FIRST

According to author Kristin Ohlson, who wrote, *Stalking the Divine: Contemplating Faith With the Poor Clares*, one in twelve women will be stalking victims during their lifetimes. Furthermore, she found that most stalking is done by ex-husbands and previous boyfriends who refuse to let go of a relationship.

Also, more than 80 percent of women who are stalked by a current or former lover are assaulted by him, and 31 percent of these same women are sexually assaulted. Ms. Ohlson also wrote that 76 percent of the women murdered each year were previously stalked by their killers. Stalkers try to control their victims, and stalking cases typi-

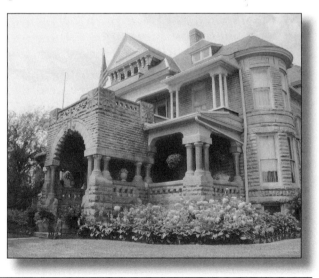

cally last from eighteen months to forty years, according to Ms. Ohlson.

Are these statistics enough to make you and your family take home privacy seriously? Read on. A Bureau of Justice statistic for 2002 states that 43 percent of murder victims were related to or acquainted with their assailants; 14 percent of victims were murdered by strangers, while 43 percent of victims had an unknown relationship with their murderer. Additional statistics by the Bureau of Justice state that in 2003, about a quarter of incidents of violent crime occurred near or at the victim's home.

How many of these crimes could have been prevented if the victims had kept their home locations a secret? Your home residence location should be kept a secret if you want to avoid becoming a statistic.

BUYING IT RIGHT

If you choose to live a private lifestyle, you must realize that the home is an extremely important part of your privacy plan and will present the most challenges, under normal circumstances. Careful attention to privacy details is necessary from the time you begin searching for a home to purchase and throughout the period of time you reside in your home.

For example, once a real estate broker is retained, a trust—in a name with no relationship to your true name—should bid on property for your benefit, with your name as trustee hidden beneath the confidentiality agreement between you and the broker you choose to represent you for purchasing real property. Or you may choose to operate entirely under an alternate name.

The rule of thumb is to work with a broker or real estate agent who respects your privacy and agrees in writing never to disclose your true name in conjunction with any real estate deal. Instead, only the trust will be named as the entity agreeing to buy property through the real estate company. Certain privacy advocates use alternate names and assign duties to nominee managers to eliminate their personal contact with brokers and real estate agents.

The selection of a title company is of paramount importance in maintaining your privacy in real estate transactions. Carefully interview the managers or upper-level management at several title companies before deciding which firm and individual you will use to accomplish the all-important tasks associated with making sure the property has a clear title, as well as other due-diligence work associated with the property. You do not have to use the title company that your broker normally uses. Choose whichever company will best serve you and your privacy concerns. All title companies are not the same, so talk to several and choose one that agrees to keep your true name out of all records during the home-buying process. Certain privacy advocates have advised that they do not provide their true name—even to title companies.

Total and complete anonymity is possible when making real property transactions. A *revocable trust* is often the preferred entity for owning a personal residence. Select a name for the trust that has no relationship whatsoever to you or your family's name. An *administrative trustee,* who could be your attorney or someone else you designate, may be given very limited power of signing on behalf of the trustee(s) on government-related documents such as county records—and may be given power to purchase insurance for the property, as per the instructions of the trustee(s).

Do not relinquish the important trustee powers. You and your spouse (if you are married) will want to remain in full control of the trust, so delegate responsibility only for "administrative duties" to the administrative trustee—not the decision-making powers. The title company will perform a search on the trust, the prospective holder of the property, for judgments entered against it in the county where the property will be purchased.

The trustee should *not* be searched. Make sure you insist on this as you retain a title company. If the title company representative will not agree to performing no searches or keeping you out of all of his company records entirely, find a title company that will.

Be sure you have no risk whatsoever of becoming a part of any real-property records anywhere. This is an extremely valuable part of utilizing trusts as owners of real property and will assure your privacy in virtually all circumstances, regardless of any problems your previous dealings may have caused.

While using a trust to do your bidding, you as an individual escape any mention whatsoever—your name as trustee will never appear anywhere on county real estate transaction records. Only the trust's name will be recorded as the owner of property, once your offer on a property is accepted. When the country recorder asks someone to sign on behalf of the trust on country records, the "administrative trustee" will scrawl his or her illegible signature on the dotted line.

Likewise, once it is time to buy the insurance policy to cover the structure and personal property inside the house, the administrative trustee can do this on behalf of the trust. Conceal yourself entirely by using a trust to own your home. A trust has no registration requirements anywhere, so be assured that your name will remain a secret to only those who see the trust itself, which ideally should include only the trustees, grantor, the attorney who forms the trust—if one is used—and the notary public who notarizes the signatures on the trust paperwork (the attorney or his associate may notarize the trust).

Trusts are very private indeed and remain the entity of choice for owning a personal residence. Do keep in mind that insurance correspondence, tax bills, and other mailings should go to a mail-drop address—not the residence owned by the trust.

FINANCING

Serious privacy seekers are careful to conceal their names from databases that reveal them as individual owners of property. Lending institutions—which include all mortgage companies, savings and loans, or other companies that agree to carry your note on a piece of real property—will be a weak link indeed to your personal privacy program. In fact, you will need to eliminate these traditional sources of funds entirely for securing financing for the purchase of your personal residence.

The reason you cannot use traditional loans for the financing of property is because lenders on property will use you and your all-important Social Security number to identify the property. Additionally, they will not want to keep your home location private and will, in fact, place the actual home location—with you listed as the owner—on credit bureau reports, while reporting your payment history on a monthly basis during the course of your loan on the property.

Also, since these mortgages are sold on the mortgage market, another lender will most likely become your mortgage holder within a period of time, and the new company will repeat the process of reporting the payment of mortgage payments to the credit bureaus, thus assuring that everyone who sees your credit bureau reports knows exactly where you reside, how much you pay for the privilege of living there, and how timely your payments have been during the life of the mortgage. Privacy-conscious homeowners do not use traditional lenders to finance their residences.

While mortgaging a home with traditional lenders will cause privacy invasions, borrowing money from an individual to buy property outright is an option for you to consider. However, regardless of safety precautions taken, when you borrow money from any source for the purpose of purchasing a home while using your true name, an invasion of personal privacy is possible or even likely.

A more prudent method of borrowing is to utilize an *LLC*, with the collateral being the real estate plus assets held by the LLC. This enables you, as the manager of the LLC and trustee of the trust holding title to the real property, to have no credit checks or personal assets pledged for securing the property. Expect to pay a higher rate—perhaps as much as 200 basis points or more above the best rates offered by traditional mortgage companies—when you borrow from an individual, however, because those who loan money on real estate typically have customers who are "high risk" borrowers, and this is the price you can expect to pay for privacy.

When you borrow money from a private individual, expect to have money for 10 percent to 20 percent of the value of the property as a down payment. Also, the lender will want the property as collateral for the loan, and a provision to "foreclose" on the house will be included in the contract—so don't become delinquent on your house payments.

Depending on market conditions, some sellers of homes will be willing to carry the loans on the property they sell. The real estate being sold will be used to collateralize the loan, and the note holder will exercise the right to take the house back in the event timely payments are not made on the loan. Again, if you purchase a house this way, always make absolutely sure that no private lender accesses your credit bureau report. In the event Mr. Lender does access your credit file, your residence and name will be included on the inquiry, and if you are serious about your home privacy—and you should be—you will need to move in order to preserve your privacy.

Doing business while using an LLC as the borrower, with the company supplying collateral and a down payment as well as guaranteeing the loan, and using the trust-owned real estate as the primary collateral for the lender, assures your personal privacy. For privacy, you may want to use only the company name and an alias during this type of transaction. This is a sure way to avoid having your true credit report accessed by the private lender.

Making sure that you are not linked personally to the home you live in is the most important aspect of your total privacy program. Protect this sacred information at all costs as you make your life private.

Using property or assets you already own or control to fund the purchase of a home is a viable option and offers privacy as well. A margin loan borrowed against securities held can be obtained with a telephone call to your stockbroker. Competitive rates will be given when amounts over $100,000 are borrowed. These loans are based on the broker call rate and vary widely from brokerage company to company. Rates will depend on the stage of the business cycle and the demand for money at the time the loan is made.

Pension funds and life insurance policies also can become borrowing sources for your home if you choose to tap these sources for cash. Borrowing against assets held in company accounts you control or own will enable your use of the funds as you see fit and offers the most private way of borrowing for real estate purposes. Your debt obligations will be to the stockbroker, pension account, or life insurance company and will not be tied to the property itself. So you are able to keep your source of funds for your home purchase completely private when borrowing from these sources.

Borrowing from a company under your management and control—a Nevada Limited Partnership, for example—and then accessing personal credit lines to pay this debt, creates a private source of funds for purchasing real estate. When the financial institution reports your payments of principal and interest on a credit line account, only these records will become credit bureau file records. The original borrowing agreement from the entity under your control will remain in your confidential company files. Make certain that all creative financing is within the guidelines and agreement you have made with the creditor.

UTILITIES

While using a trust for the purpose of owning your home, be certain to obtain all utilities privately. As the account holder of the various utility companies, you offer private investigators, snoops, stalkers, and identity thieves one of the best and easiest sources to make their way into your private life and discover where you reside.

As discussed in the previous chapter, privacy seekers never, ever obtain utilities or any other services for home use in

their true names. For those purposes, you'll want to retain the services of a "professional nominee" to open utility accounts, pay bills, and prevent any paper trail from leading to your true name.

While many who live privately employ the services of nominees as needed for securing home utilities, some excellent communicators have managed to negotiate for services and often bypass using nominees.

Utility company representatives who are flexible often waive privacy-invasive account requirements. Utility accounts have been opened in the name of trusts, alternate names, and company names. Nominal deposits have been made in lieu of providing a credit report.

It is advantageous to have bills sent to a distant mail nominee's address—away from the actual residence—and to use a dedicated telephone number as a contact.

Alternate-name debit cards are also valuable for the anonymous payment of services when accounts are held in an alias.

SELLING YOUR HOME

For privacy purposes, when selling your home, use a broker who is under contract not to reveal any information whatsoever about you or your family—including your true name—to anyone. Only the trust's name should be used when reference is made to the owner of the house. Your administrative trustee can stand in for you in the event you need someone while selling the house. However, this will rarely be necessary, as your reliable, carefully selected real estate broker should be able to do everything without your participation, thus preserving your privacy.

Show the house by appointment. Do not be present when the house is being shown. That's what real estate agents and brokers do best. Do not involve yourself in the process of selling the trust-owned home.

OUTSIDERS AND OUTSIDE SERVICES

Plumbers, carpenters, roofers, carpet cleaners, housekeepers, electricians, and gardeners are just some of the service people who will make their way into your private home life by necessity. Carefully screen these subcontractors prior to forming written contracts with them and have them come by appointment only. Use the trust's name only when reference is made to the ownership of the property.

Use your alias when dealing with all service people relating to home repairs and maintenance. Pay for all services in cash, obtaining receipts in the name of the trust. Using an alias assures your confidentiality in records of payment for services and also preserves your anonymity.

FAMILY AND FRIENDS

For a high level of privacy and home security, do not reveal your home address to anyone except your closest friends and relatives. Many privacy experts recommend that you don't use your home for large re-unions but rather rent a neutral building for this purpose. Children and one's spouse need to be aware of the family privacy goals in order to make your home privacy plan effective, so discuss this and establish policies that serve you best about inviting guests to the house.

Also, your association with neighbors affects your personal privacy, so decide with whom you want to associate as well as what personal information you choose to reveal. Less is best, generally speaking.

As you read this book and decide on your privacy goals, you will become the best judge of how to handle your own home security, and that includes those you welcome into the house.

When it comes to your home and personal privacy, there's not just one right way to do things. Be creative. Adapt the suggestions present-ed here to your own situation. Living privately shouldn't be an overly difficult burden. You can find ways to live privately, yet stay well within your personal "comfort zone."

Perhaps you should have only a select few friends and relatives come to your home, with each family member clearing invitations with you and your spouse to assure you of the identity of each house guest prior to their arrival. Above all, enjoy your home while living a secure and private lifestyle.

HOME SECURITY MEASURES

Travel to and from your home should be practiced with caution to prevent unwanted individuals from dis-covering your resi-dence. Be aware of the cars around you as you

approach your own neighborhood. If you are uncertain about anything or anyone, take a route away from the home until you are confident no one is following you. Driving extra miles, while intentionally moving away from any neighborhood near your home, is worth the extra time and expense when you are unsure about those who surround you when you drive.

Shred all paperwork prior to placing it in the trash. Do not reveal your name or company name on anything sent to the trash bins. Identity thieves will not bother you when they can find no individual links to your trust-owned house. Keep your trust-owned car garaged while not using it. Cover the vehicle identification number (VIN).

Some privacy advocates remove the number designating the house's street address for privacy. Keep certain valuables and important files and documents off site at your storage facility rather than at home.

A "safe room," whether completely hidden from view or designed by plan and made safe with high-security locks—such as the Medeco brand—offers you and your family a high measure of security in the event of an attempted break-in. I have used a walk-in closet equipped with a Medeco lock that can only be unlocked with a Medeco key from the outside. However, from the inside, a simple knob allows the person to unlock the door. Emergency provisions and survival supplies can be stored inside your safe room, which may be your refuge in the event you are terrorized at home.

Frankly, I have mixed feelings about "safe rooms." On one hand, I believe they are valuable as a place where kids can escape when and if they are home alone and someone attempts to break in. On the other hand, children old enough to be left at home alone are capable of defending property and themselves. Teach them how.

Alarms can be valuable, but given the choice, I prefer barred windows, a good fence, and high-quality, secure locks. Also, alarm companies compromise your privacy a great deal, and I do not recommend you use them unless there are special circumstances that make it worth the obvious compromises. For home security, many prefer a well-trained dog combined with a 12-gauge shotgun.

THE AMERICAN DREAM—OR ARE YOU DREAMING?

The ownership of real property is a source of great wealth in America. You too, can profit by owning your home, providing you buy it right and sell it right. Real estate, like other assets, is cyclical, so be aware of this historical fact rather than expecting the purchase of a home at any price to yield high returns on your investment. Be aware that your property can decrease in value as well.

Aside from the profit potential of home ownership, consider the other important parts of the investment equation. What are your needs? A family of five may be able to justify the expense of a 2,500-square-foot home, while a single individual may be best served by placing his capital in liquid assets and renting an apartment.

How many people really consider their time in maintaining a home when they calculate their return on investment? Coordinating home repairs, maintenance, and buying and selling the property can require the time equivalent of a part-time job. Are you paid well for this time spent on your home? Do you factor in the expenses of property taxes? How do you feel about paying the government roughly 1 percent to 3.75 percent of your home's value each year for the privilege of "owning" your home?

What about home maintenance, repairs, structure and property insurance, real estate commissions, and the illiquid property and time associated with selling during a poor market? How about the potential for loss? Many regions are affected by economic downturns more than others, so be cognizant of these facts when chasing the American dream of home ownership.

Financing, depending on the source of funds used, as well as the demand for money when borrowing, will be important considerations when purchasing a home. So far as personal privacy is concerned, you can still make your life private when owning a home—providing you utilize the tactics disclosed in this book. Recognize the fact that I state over and over: privacy is always more expensive than living the "normal" way of life. And this becomes even more evident as you practice privacy while owning your home.

SUMMARY

1. Be aware of the potential dangers of revealing your residence address and establish suitable privacy measures. Avoid using your true name for any service or correspondence associated with your residence, unless legally required to do so.

2. A revocable trust as the owner of the home—with an administrative trustee—enables you to live in your residence anonymously.

3. Non-traditional home financing is necessary for home ownership privacy.

4. Utilities obtained by "professional" nominees prevent any link to your true name in utility company databases.

5. Do not, under any circumstances whatsoever, receive any mail, packages, or special deliveries at home.

6. Sell your home anonymously by using a broker who is bound by contract to keep you anonymous in the transaction.

7. When contracting outside maintenance services and personnel, use the trust's name and an alias; make all payments in cash.

8. Educate family and friends about the necessity for home privacy.

9. Secure locks, a shotgun, and a watchdog are the preferred tools for anonymous home security.

10. Consider the advantages of a safe room in your home.

11. Carefully plan your home security and allocate money for the additional expenses required for home privacy.

NINE

Storage

"When neither their property nor their honor is touched, the majority of men live content."—Niccolo Machiavelli

PRIVATE RECORDS AND VALUABLES

Certain documents, valuables, possessions, and permanent records that you plan to keep long term need to be stored carefully—for accessibility when you need them, as well as for the protection of your private business.

Although you may believe you have taken steps to secure your home, it is prudent to have an off-site storage facility, as well as a safe deposit box, for safe-keeping items you don't want to risk losing through theft, government seizure, fire, or other disasters.

Among items you may want to secure off site, away from your residence or office, are:

▶ Vehicle titles

▶ Original copies of business entity and trust documents

▶ Spare firearms and ammunition

▶ Alternate identification documents

▶ Credit cards

▶ Rare coins and jewelry

▶ Confidential correspondences

‣ Sensitive reference books, tapes, and CDs

‣ An emergency cash fund

‣ Original copies of insurance policies

‣ Tax records

‣ Property deeds

‣ Original copies of rental agreements

‣ Warranties

‣ Bonds

‣ Stock certificates

‣ Gold and silver

‣ Original copies of business agreements

‣ A packed suitcase

‣ Personal diaries and copies of writings

‣ Hard drive copies

‣ Any other personal and business items you deem necessary to store for safety, privacy, and loss prevention.

In the case of records and documents, insurance policies, credit cards, and other materials you need to retrieve on occasion, copies can be stored in a secure filing cabinet so that you have convenient access when necessary. Bank account and credit card account numbers can be blacked out in part, with code numbers added, to prevent anyone from obtaining them in the event of a home or office break-in. The original credit cards should be kept off site.

STORAGE FACILITIES

Making your life private is always more expensive and more inconvenient than living in the style of the masses. Once you accept these facts and commit to living as a privacy seeker, the extra expenses and time spent handling your private business affairs become accepted, necessary costs of doing business. Storing property and private documents away from your home or office offers high-level privacy at a reasonable cost.

Storage facilities—those small spaces available for rent to store your property between moves—offer privacy seekers an option for holding permanent records and property that should be kept away from the home or the office for ultimate security and privacy.

My own experience in dealing with these companies has taught me that bigger is better, and I recommend you consider the large chain companies over the Mom and Pop operations. Furthermore, I advise against utilizing family and friends' homes and garages for holding your personal records and property in order to save the costs of a storage facility company. Nor would I opt for renting a private individual's garage for this purpose, as you will have less quality control over your stored property.

The best storage companies offer access seven days per week to renters, with convenient hours beginning in the early morning until late in the evening. Shop around and use a company in a middle-class neighborhood. Pick a ground-level or second-level space within close proximity to the office, whenever possible. Use a company that employs 24-hour surveillance cameras and has a staff person on the premises at all times.

THE RENTAL APPLICATION

Applications for a space to store business and personal property will not present problems for the privacy seeker. These companies have been known to readily accept alternate identification, providing it is of good quality and you choose to hold it in your alternate name for secrecy.

You may want to use your true name and official identification, while holding the storage space in a company or trust's name. If you elect to hold it in the company name or in the name of a trust, be sure that the records reflect the business name only while keeping your name, individually, off the records

Use your offshore address as a reference if an address is required—or perhaps an out-of-state mail-drop address. Your objective, when renting a space at a storage facility, is to leave no evidence of you as an individual having an account. Renting in either an alternate name or a company name, without your name associated with the account—except as an authorized person to enter it—will prevent your name from coming up on the company record of accounts in the event a private investigator, the police, or government wants to look into your affairs.

For privacy, pay your bills with money orders, and pay them on time.

Generally, only a few days are needed as advance notice to management when you choose to vacate, and fees are paid for rent on a month-to-month basis without a lease commitment.

CODES AND CAMERAS

As you enter the storage facility to access your space, you will be videotaped, and your entrance records will be tabulated by the code you use to enter into the common area, which is time-stamped by the security equipment. Keep this in mind, and when you move sensitive items from the automobile to the rental space—guns, for example—keep them concealed and out of the visual records by wrapping them in a blanket as you transport them from the car to the storage space.

Keep the written code for your secure storage bin in a safe place and eliminate a portion of it by using coding that only you can decipher, for added security and privacy.

Your automobile also will be videotaped as you drive it onto the property and enter the secure gates to the storage bin area. This makes it imperative that you follow the guidelines outlined in the "Travel" section so that your identity cannot be detected through Department of Motor Vehicles automobile records.

POLICE RAIDS

You should realize that these facilities are susceptible to police raids, and you will want to keep this in mind as you relate to management during the application process for a storage rental space, as well as when others, such as movers who assist you, become aware of your storage facility contents.

Preserve the privacy of your sensitive items, which are no one's business, by transporting them yourself while alone, making sure to keep them under wraps from the security cameras. Give movers your alternate name only and inventory your moving contents, making sure that everything is accounted for once the move is complete. Do not discuss specifics of your personal or business life with them, making sure to be vague when asked questions that could compromise your privacy.

When you do have occasion to deal with management, which will usually be limited to the time spent completing the application for service, be sure to act as professionally as possible and keep copies of all contracts and agreements associated with your rental agreement.

Because you are a paying customer, management will want to avoid conflict with you, so do not arouse suspicion by asking unnecessary questions regarding what is or is not allowed to be stored on the premises. Your manner and appearance should make a favorable business impression as you deal with the company representatives.

In the event that you become sought by any government official, police, or private detective, your name should not come up when searches are made of the names holding accounts with the storage company. Proper registration of your rental space in either a separate business entity or trust or an alternate name should keep your true name off all records in the customer database.

Furthermore, when and if automobiles are used as a method of finding those hunted while comparing and matching account holders with automobiles entering the premises, your name will not surface if the car you operate is held in the trust's name only, without any association of your true name with the Department of Motor Vehicles or other state vehicle registration agency documents.

VISITS

Because you want to be discreet about where your property, documents, and other private items are stored, pay attention during travel to and from the storage facility. Private investigators love to follow subjects from work to see where they do their private business and spend their time. Do not allow your secure storage location to be detected by anyone.

Investigators may bribe the company representatives or may even arrange to break into your storage space to obtain the information necessary to discover your asset locations or other personal business information, when the value of their case is increased by such a discovery. Visit your rental space during odd hours, whenever possible, to lessen the chance that your secure site will be found. Weekends and early mornings are a good choice, as Gumshoe will be asleep or at the barbecue as you do your necessary private business.

SAFE DEPOSIT BOXES

A safe deposit box held in the name of a Nevada Limited Partnership offers a secure and private way of storing tangible valuables, including gold, silver, rare coins, jewelry, and precious stones. Confidential documents of companies under your control, as well as registration documents and private, permanent records may also be stored in a safe deposit box.

Remember, you do not own it. The partnership owns it. So even when you are sought or wanted, this is not your property. It belongs to the partnership and cannot be tampered with by those seeking you or your personal property. Even so, be as discreet as possible about all accounts, safe deposit boxes included, which are under your control, because investigators and government agents have been known to do anything possible, including bribe bank employees or break into any facility that contains information which will strengthen their case file.

Those who desire total secrecy when storing valuables in a safe deposit box may contact 24/7 Private Vaults, Las Vegas, Nevada (see Chapter 18). Remember that if no one knows where you store your valuables and confidential documents and information, they have no way of abusing the property. Secrecy is by far your best defense against having your valuable property and information found. So, be prudent and keep your storage locations a secret.

SUMMARY

1. Permanent records, valuables, sensitive equipment, and other items that are extremely private should be stored away from your home or office. A storage facility and a safe deposit box offer secure ways of storing this type of property.

2. Alternate names can be used, as well as trust names and business entity names, for storing property in storage rental facilities.

3. A Nevada Limited Partnership or other entity that holds your investments may be used to hold a safe deposit box. Store tangible valuables and permanent record items in a safe deposit box.

4. Choose a large storage company with several locations whenever possible.

5. Select a good location and properly secure the space with quality padlocks.

6. Storage bins are commonly investigated by police, investigators, and government officials, so be certain that vehicles you drive onto the property do not have any links to your true name. Also, be sure to not have your name, only the business or trust name, on the account.

7. Carefully monitor those around you as you travel to the off-site facility, to avoid revealing the location of your property to anyone.

8. Visit the site during odd hours for the utmost in privacy.

9. Keep safe deposit box locations a secret and register and hold the box in a business entity name, preferably a Nevada Limited Partnership. Or, one who desires total secrecy may hold a safe deposit box without providing a name at all, at 24/7 Private Vaults in Las Vegas, Nevada (see Chapter 18 for detailed contact information).

♦ TEN ♦

Driving Secretly

> *"There are two things no man will admit he cannot do well: drive and make love."*
> —Stirling Moss, Hall of Fame race car driver

STRANGERS IN THE NIGHT

Somewhere between the Colorado border and a point within sixty miles south of Cheyenne, I noticed a car's headlights in my rearview mirror. The car was following too close. Perhaps it was using my full-sized sedan as a shield from the heavy fog and rain, which prevented my vision beyond several feet.

I could see there were two figures in the front seat. License plate? A moot point in this fog and rain. I continued north toward Wyoming's capital city, the site of our annual meeting. Perhaps it is meaningless, I thought. Maybe a couple of kids out to hassle a stranger. Maybe blinded travelers using me as a guide. My imagination? Perhaps.

The fog intensified. I could hardly see at all. April showers, in the form of wet, sleet-like moisture, stuck to the windshield. It was cold. The car was still behind me—still following too close. I was concerned, yet optimistic, and I continued to monitor the car through my rearview mirror.

The lights of Cheyenne finally appeared, the fog lifted slightly, and the rain lessened. It was late, and I was tired. The car remained too close to me. Without question, I was being followed. Police? Plainclothes cops?

The exit sign was near, and I signaled and approached a main street, signaled again and proceeded to the section of town where I was staying. The car continued to follow closely, and I was worried. Adrenaline surged, "butterflies" fluttered, and fearful feelings began. The police station was miles and miles away on the other side of the city. And my cell phone did not work in Wyoming.

Driving down a normally heavily traveled main street, our cars were the only ones out at this late hour in the awful weather, and I was nervous. I proceeded to drive for perhaps three more miles, quickly turned onto a side street, made a U-turn and got back on the same main street as before, this time heading in the opposite direction. The car behind mirrored my every move.

Seeing a business parking lot with street lights nearby, I turned into it without signaling, quickly turned the sedan toward the entrance with high beams glaring, grabbed the large-caliber handgun from the seat, and shifted into survival mode. I was ready.

The driver of the car passed by the parking lot entrance, cut off his lights, and sped into the night. Finally, I breathed. A thousand thoughts raced through my mind. Later, I could not sleep. I will remember this night forever and am glad I was fully prepared.

THE ANONYMOUS DRIVER

After the above true incident occurred, I was not worried about being found by whoever attempted to intimidate me, for reasons still unknown to me today. In order to become "invisible" as a driver for all practical purposes and to be able to thwart the efforts of would-be thugs who may not have your best interest in mind, you must separate your identity from the automobile you drive. This is important, as many who terrorize motor vehicle operators have ways of accessing registered owners of vehicles through DMV databases.

Typically, those attempting to identify the driver of a car will use people as resources who can easily find the "owner" of the vehicle without letting the sought individual know of the investigation. Friends of police and law enforcement agencies, detectives and police, private investigators, and online services may be used to find the registered owner of a car—usually an individual who is also the primary driver.

Therefore, to protect yourself, you should have no personal ties to the car you drive, which is registered in one of the fifty state vehicle registration agencies. The best way to hold ownership of a motor vehicle for privacy purposes is through the use of a trust. The trust may be either "revocable" or "irrevocable," and you may discuss your individual requirements with your attorney prior to deciding which you should use for automobile ownership purposes.

Always choose a name for the trust that has no relationship to you individually. For example, Judy Jones may form a trust to hold title to the car she drives in the name of "The Western States Irrevocable Trust." As trustee, you—the driver of the car—will be in full control of the car legally owned by the trust. So your responsibilities are the same as they would be if the automobile were titled to you personally.

Also, the trust, as owner of the car, will not relieve you of any liability for damages in the event of an accident. Liability insurance, as well as other coverages you deem necessary, should be included on the automobile insurance policy.

The purpose of using a trust to own the car you drive is to prevent anyone who searches the DMV database from identifying you as you drive. A trust has no registration requirements in order to be a legal entity. Therefore, it is a tremendous privacy advantage to use a trust for car ownership instead of a *corporation* or a *limited liability company (LLC)*—two other common entities used for holding title to vehicles.

Also, a trust holding title to the car is more desirable for insurance purposes, because many insurance companies will not insure automobiles owned by a corporation or an LLC. And those that do will sometimes insist on insuring the vehicle as a "business use" vehicle, and the rates will be considerably more expensive.

As the trustee of the trust that owns the car, you will need to be underwritten for insurance just as if you were the sole owner of the vehicle. That is, your driving history and other relevant information will be considered prior to the issuance of an automobile insurance policy. While some companies will resist insuring you if the car is owned by a trust, the number that will write a policy far outnumber those that will insure a business-owned car held in the name of a corporation or an LLC.

So you will have privacy, once you structure the ownership of the car as property of a trust, plus, you will have accessibility to insurance coverage on the vehicle. *Remember: Driving a car owned and properly registered in the name of a trust prevents anyone from obtaining the driver's identity.*

AUTOMOBILE REGISTRATION: PRINCIPLES FOR PRIVACY

First, let me address a common concern regarding separating a person from a car previously registered in his or her own name. Some authors who provide information on human "disappearing" acts preach of the necessity of selling or ditching the car if your name appears anywhere on the ownership history of the vehicle.

I believe this, for the most part, to be overkill, but you may disagree and prefer to drive a completely "clean" car, free of any ties to you through current ownership or historical ownership records. In the event you are trying to conceal your true name while driving and do not want to rid yourself of your current car, now registered in your own name, a sale can be arranged whereby you "sell" the car to the trust formed to hold title to the car.

True, the DMV record history will reflect you as the previous owner, but really, consider the risks and damages of someone figuring out that it was a "dummy sale" arranged by you in the first place. Your risks in such a transaction are minimal, especially when you consider the difficulty anyone will have locating you using the address information given for DMV registration purposes, which I discuss later in this chapter.

In order to accomplish this "dummy sale" of a car from an individual to a trust, one must first present the trust of which he or she is trustee, along with the car title, to the DMV office or other state agency that registers automobiles. A tax must be paid on the "dummy sale" of the car as it changes ownership from an individual to a trust name. New license tags for the car may be purchased once the registration and ownership have changed to the trust.

Let's review what records are now available in the DMV database. First of all, Snoopy would have to know which state DMV database to attempt to access if you register the automobile in a state other than the one in which you reside or spend most of your time. Second, you may choose to register your car in a state other than the one in which your state-issued driver's license is obtained (see Chapter 4, "Government Identification") in order to have maximum driver secrecy.

So considering all of these precautions, in the event a private investigator or identity thief has only your name and a few old mailing addresses (information that is available on most people), what critical information does the investigator have for locating you? Only outdated, useless addresses. Nothing more. He or she will need to "search" databases state-by-state for a car registered in your name and will find nothing when a trust is used to "own" the vehicle. You may elect to buy a new car in the name of a trust, rather than selling the one you own individually to the new trust owner, to prevent any link to you, whatsoever.

Even if you were found in a DMV search, and the address given to obtain a driver's license is a mail-drop address, the investigator or identity thief has nothing (see Chapter 12, "Private Mail"). And since the name of the trust that owns the car is unknown, it will be virtually impossible for anyone to discover your vehicle.

When registering the automobile with the DMV, pay particular attention to what information is given to DMV personnel. In truth, the entire staff there probably will not have seen six trusts among them, so expect "supervisors" to be called to the scene, especially once you politely outline your requirements for registration.

A review of the trust paperwork—particularly those parts that state the trust is entitled to hold property and the part that provides you as trustee the right to do the bidding for the trust—must be shown to the DMV when registering the car. Copies of pertinent pages of the trust may be required by the DMV. This information will be buried on microfiche and will not appear on any registration records.

In some cases—many, in fact—the DMV will attempt to tie your name to the trust. Why? Because Big Bureaucrat always wants to control those who pay his bills. You. Typically, those "supervisors"—ever so loyal to the government's cause of control over citizens through the retention of confidential information, without respect for privacy, yours and mine—will want to include you as "trustee" on the vehicle registration documents.

Do not associate your name with the trust on the vehicle registration. Instead of using your name as "trustee" following the name of the trust, use only the trust's name and address as illustrated below:

XYZ Irrevocable Trust
123 South Private Street
Anytown, Guesswhichstate 00000 U.S.A.

Furthermore, it is not necessary or desirable for your name to appear on any correspondence from the DMV, and it will not, if only the trust's name is used for the registration of the automobile. Personnel at the DMV will not even know the name of the trustee unless you tell them after the car is properly registered.

For those who doubt that even these proven, precautionary measures will prevent their names from surfacing in DMV databases, you may elect to include an administrative trustee in the trust that holds title to the car. This "trustee" can provide to DMV personnel his or her name, the portion of the trust allowing such a trustee to register the car, and the right of the trust to hold property.

It will be necessary to customize a portion of the trust, giving these powers to the administrative trustee.

When done as just described, the administrative trustee fills in for the trustee when the car is registered and titled in the name of the trust. This procedure will only be necessary as each new car is purchased by the trust.

ACTUAL CASE EVENT

Let me relate a true story of my experience with the DMV that pertains to the registration of a car that I previously drove. A mail-drop operator had neglected to forward correspondence to me regarding an insurance premium balance due on another insurance policy, unrelated to the automobile policy on the trust-owned vehicle, but with the same company. The amount had been increased without my knowledge, as I had properly paid the premium for this other policy.

However, a computer-generated bill was sent to the trust's address, and since Ms. Bookkeeper failed to send it to me (sometimes this happens, as people make mistakes), I was unaware of the bill, which was not significant—perhaps $10, as I recall. However, the balance of the bill owed on the policy completely unrelated to the car policy was tied to my name and account with the insurance company, and the failure of paying the balance in full on one premium, for some unknown reason, caused the computer to cancel all policies under my name.

Hence, my automobile insurance policy was, at least in theory, "cancelled" by a computer, and I was unaware of this supposed cancellation but discovered the error while on a "working vacation." Having received a telephone voicemail message from the car insurance company representative, requesting my attention to the receipt of a "refund check," I called back to request an explanation for the check.

Next, I began a two-day ordeal of wading through the customer "no service" department in an effort to resolve the issue. Try as I did by speaking with supervisor after supervisor at this East Coast–based insurance company, I could not convince anyone to listen to my explanation or change their records to reinstate the car insurance policy.

Furthermore, the premium period for which the policy had been paid had not expired, so legally, I was still insured in view of the prepaid premium amount left on the one-year policy period. And I had not cashed their check as they encouraged me to do, to help them make a case for my being insured for only a portion of the policy premium period.

Following my unsuccessful attempt to correct the insurance company error, I decided I no longer wanted to do business with this company, due to their mishandling of my affairs. I promptly wrote a summary letter outlining the entire affair, and mailed it by certified mail to the attention of their chief executive officer.

I began shopping for insurance via the telephone and also called the DMV to inquire about their records pertaining to automobile insurance on the vehicle and whether a cancellation notice from the insurance carrier had been filed. Most states require insurance companies to submit insurance policy status reports of drivers regularly via electronic correspondence so that uninsured drivers are flagged within the system.

Once I reached the DMV personnel, I made a startling discovery. I was very discreet and provided a first name only and used the title of a "clerk" calling on behalf of the trust that owned the vehicle. I said my call was regarding records of insurance coverage at the Department of Motor Vehicles. I asked the DMV supervisor whether their records reflected the cancellation of the trust's automobile insurance policy.

Not only was the supervisor unable to associate any insurance coverage with the car, within the entire registration history, neither did he have any record whatsoever of any "trustee" or other "owner" on the DMV records, other than that of the trust itself.

So essentially, here is what happened: The car was properly titled in the name of the trust only, with no mention of me as trustee on the title or registration. Even though the DMV required me to provide a copy of two pages of the trust, these records were not available—at least not accessible to this supervisor.

Also, I had properly insured the car under my name while disclosing to the insurance company that the car was owned by the trust. The insurance company did issue a policy and most likely reported the coverage to the DMV, but the identifying names of the trust and the driver—yours truly—were not effectively cross-referenced—at least not so that this supervisor knew anything whatsoever about any driver of this car.

Based on this information, it was impossible for anyone who would "run" the license tags through the state database of registered cars to identify me as the driver of the car. A high level of vehicle privacy had been created, with no DMV records containing my true name. Of course, the DMV supervisor wanted to know my name, and I, of course, obliged him by providing a first name only and explained my role as a "clerk" once again. I was asked to provide names of all trustees, and I did not, of course, know who these people were but advised him someone could call him back within five business days with the answers to his questions.

To sum up, when properly registering a vehicle, remember to be insistent on your requirements. Learning the proper people skills required to deal effectively with Big Bureaucrat is essential. Always be polite, dress and speak well, and be candid about your privacy requirements. You have a right to this discreet way of driving a car, so utilize all the tools available and learn to communicate your needs to those who have the power to help you accomplish your automobile privacy goals.

Concerning the car insurance problem previously mentioned, I was later contacted by a manager at the insurance company who offered to reinstate the policy, two months after the error had occurred, of course. I refused, informed him I had found a more service-oriented company to handle my business, and bid him good day.

VEHICLE CHOICES

What type of car should you as a privacy-seeking driver? Will certain types of cars attract attention and perhaps bring unwanted trouble from the highway patrol or the local police? The type of car you drive is your business and a matter of personal choice. The choice of automobile you drive is far less important than how you drive it, and you should drive defensively and adhere to the speed limits and traffic laws. Drive a car that satisfies your comfort, space, and budget requirements, while remembering that a plain, medium-priced car with a common color will create an impression of your being an average person—exactly the image a privacy seeker should desire.

BUYING A CAR PRIVATELY

When buying a car, one can ensure privacy by paying the seller in nontraceable cash—sometimes a cumbersome affair, due to the amount required to buy a car these days, although cash assures no banking records directly related to the car you drive. However, a cashier's check can also be used. Keep in mind that the bank will reference a bank account—yours or one you control—when they issue a cashier's check, as the days are gone when one can buy a cashier's check anonymously.

So when you use a cashier's check, the account held at the bank, whether it is a business account or a trust account (see Chapter 15 and Chapter 17) will be on record as a link to the cashier's check used to purchase the vehicle. But for the ultimate in security and privacy, use cash or money orders as payment for a vehicle.

While buying a car from a private owner is more private, due to fewer people knowing your business, there are benefits to using the services of an automobile dealership. A dealer will have more cars available for sale and will make your shopping much more simple than fishing around through newspapers and on the Internet attempting to find "private owners"—who are often mini-dealers themselves.

As for price, the private individual has less overhead than a dealer, of course, but always check "blue book" or other standard references before you plunk down your cash.

PRIVATE AUTOMOBILE SALES

Selling the old car or trading it in is usually a part of buying a new one. Suffice it to say, discretion should be used when selling a car. Avoid having prospective buyers come to your home or office to see the car. Instead, sell it on consignment with a reputable dealer or company that handles these sales. Also, certain companies—CarMax, for example—buy cars from individuals. Insist on a cashier's check made payable to a company account or trust account, or accept cash for the sale of the car.

When trading for a newer model and purchasing from a dealer, use your illegible signature to sign the car over to the other party on behalf of the trust, the owner of the car. Then remove the tags and mail them to the DMV or other state agency that registered the car, with a letter explaining the car has been sold.

DMV COMMUNICATION

As previously noted, you can effectively communicate anonymously with the government, the DMV, or whatever agency registered the car to avoid unnecessary personal contact. For example, upon selling one automobile and replacing it with the new car, you sign over the title to the new owner, signing on behalf of the trust as the trustee. Then remove and return the tags to the DMV as explained above.

Privacy-conscious people handle this and all correspondences to state government pertaining to the automobile in the manner illustrated on the following page, without ever including their true name on the letter. In the event a telephone call becomes necessary, privacy advocates use a "pretext" first name only and represent themselves as a temporary employee calling on behalf of the trust.

Correspond in writing to DMV offices as follows:

Department of Motor Vehicles
1000 Great Big Lines Street
Mostanycity, Whatever State 00000

"Dear Sir or Madam: Please find the license tags for Vehicle Identification Number 1234567890, registered to The Blue and Red Irrevocable Trust. The car has been sold, and we request any refunds be made payable to:

Standards High, LLC,
777 Private Way,
Myfavoritecity, 5hh 12356, New Zealand.
Sincerely, Trustee."

RENTAL CARS

Driving a rental car provides a high level of travel privacy, because the rental company is the registered owner of the automobile. When you rent an automobile, you are required to provide a copy of your state-issued driver's license to the car rental company. A major credit card will normally be required as a security measure, though not necessarily as a method of payment for the rental.

Use a company debit card issued by MasterCard or Visa for this purpose, as no reporting is done to the credit bureaus on these cards, and your whereabouts will not be known by anyone except the rental company and the bank that holds the business account.

Another more secure option is to use the "prepaid" version of MasterCard or Visa—another form of debit card (see Chapter 15, "Anonymous Banking")—that is available for purchase at check-cashing stores. These cards function as a bank account as one "loads" the card with cash at the check-cashing store. The cardholder can access the account online, does not receive mailed statements, and the issuing bank does not report account activity to the credit bureaus.

A few car rental companies accept cash deposits in lieu of credit cards, however. So you may want to use one of these companies whenever you rent a car. Also, though only a few car rental companies resist accepting debit cards—insisting instead on credit cards only—it is worth checking ahead of time to be certain you indeed can use your debit card—whether in your name, the name of a trust, or a company name.

PRIVATE-PARTY RENTAL CARS

A most secure and private way of traveling by car is through the use of a private-party rental automobile. For example, a person desiring privacy forms a "personal and confidential" agreement to lease or rent a car from an individual in exchange for a rental fee. Generally, the "owner" agrees to keep the car insured and gives the driver discretion on use of the car. Maintenance costs are negotiable.

This method entirely eliminates the need for forming a trust, making any personal appearance whatsoever to any government registration agencies unnecessary, thus relieving the driver of any insurance responsibilities. Although expensive, this is a high level of driving privacy.

CAR REGISTRATION COMPANIES

You know your government has reached the depths of the Third World once companies begin offering "car registration" services. There are companies that offer to do the work necessary to register a car for you. Usually the most valuable service they offer is standing in line for you so that a half day is not wasted at the DMV office.

My experience has been that these companies are not, for the most part, experienced in dealing with anything extraordinary, such as properly registering the vehicle in the name of the trust. Also if you entrust one of these people with the time-consuming task of dealing with your inefficient car registration government agency, realize that they may botch the job entirely by not registering the car in the trust's name only, without mention of the trustee. And once this error is made, it is not easily undone.

Also, it will be necessary for you to provide a copy of at least a portion of the trust to strangers—generally not a good idea. The solution? Do it yourself or perhaps allow an office manager whom you believe is competent to handle this task for you.

DUAL REGISTRATIONS

Sometimes privacy seekers elect to have their car registered in more than one state in order to present themselves as a "local" by having a car that has tags and registration in the state in which they "reside." This remains a personal choice, and in order to most effectively blend in with the local population, it may be a good idea.

However, you may drive a car with license plates that are from any state so long as substantial time is spent in that state. Also, some hold the belief that it is advantageous to appear to be a "non-resident." Law enforcement officials are sometimes more lenient with tourists and business travelers regarding minor traffic violations.

So in fact, it may behoove you to be on an extended work assignment or to be vacationing from the state in which the car is registered. Prepare your explanation in advance of telling your story.

AUTOMOBILE INSURANCE

While all states require drivers to carry liability insurance at set minimal limits, an insurance company representative, quoted in an Insurance Institute study, concluded that in some metropolitan areas, 55 percent of the drivers are uninsured. Typically, drivers who do not want to keep their cars insured due to astronomical insurance costs buy policies, pay only for a minimal amount of time—perhaps one month—provide proof of insurance to the DMV to register their car, and later allow the policy to lapse.

In certain areas of the country, the statistics pertaining to drivers operating motor vehicles without insurance is even more alarming. Sixty-three percent of the drivers stopped in Arizona for violations did not have automobile insurance. Ninety-seven percent of the 63 percent who were driving while uninsured were illegal aliens. (Source: Jim Dallas, radio talk show host. "Wake Up America," KDWN radio, Las Vegas, Nevada, July 28, 2006.)

This means that the responsible drivers have to foot the bill for those who negligently shirk their duty, in order to cover themselves for any potential liability in the event of a catastrophe. As I review my car insurance policy—the premium of which just increased another 20 percent even though I have no claims, no tickets, and no accidents, going back many years—I notice that the largest increase in premium is in guess which category? Why, the uninsured/under-insured section of the policy, of course. You and I, the responsible ones, are paying the insurance company costs for accident claims involving uninsured or under-insured drivers.

The most simple and time-effective way to shop for automobile insurance is by using the telephone. This eliminates the wasted time spent traveling to and from insurance agents' offices, not to mention the privacy-invasive aspects involved in making the deal in person. It should be understood that insurance company representatives for the most part are ignorant about their own products whenever you present them with anything out of the ordinary.

For example, I contacted two representatives of the same insurance company, asked if they would write a policy for me to drive a vehicle registered to a trust, and received a "Yes" from one and a "No" from the other.

Also, expect in your quest to "drive in secrecy" to devote substantial time to researching companies and communicating with insurance personnel. Supervisors will be called to the phone, long hold times will be experienced, but eventually your efforts will be rewarded, and you will be able to buy the policy and meet the legal requirements to operate the automobile.

Some privacy-aware people do not provide a home address for insurance correspondence but instead utilize another address to handle the correspondence related to the insurance policy. This mailing address, where the car is "domiciled"—whether it is now or was for a period of time when you purchased the policy—will serve as your correspondence address (see Chapter 12, "Mail: Creating an Illusion"), and a voicemail telephone number may be used as well, rather than a direct telephone line tied to you.

Preferably, you should use the services of MoneyGram to pay insurance premiums, in order to obtain immediate confirmation that the payment has been properly credited. Also, a faxed confirmation of insurance coverage is valuable and necessary. This can be carried in the glove box of the car to serve as proof of insurance coverage until the policy is received.

Insist that both you and the trust are included as the "insured" on the insurance policy. Typically, the proof of insurance will indicate that you are the insured, while the "Big and Wonderful Irrevocable Trust" is an "additional insured" party—really just a formality, but an acknowledgment that the car is held and legally owned by the trust, rather than you personally.

During the underwriting process, do not provide your Social Security number. Sometimes, underwriters insist on it. Once again, the information you will be required to provide will depend largely upon who is on the other end of the phone, as representatives and supervisors within the same company will "require" different information in order to bind your policy. Keep in mind, however, that the insurance company salesperson can obtain all necessary information about your driving history without your Social Security number, so don't let him convince you that he has to have it to do his job.

A *Comprehensive Loss Underwriting Exchange (CLUE)* report—information available to insurance companies concerning current and prospective drivers—can be obtained with only a full name. So can a "soft inquiry" to certain credit bureaus, but I would not allow an insurance company to access my credit bureau report. In order to prevent this (see Chapter 19, "Credit Bureaus"), I recommend that you "freeze" your credit bureau files.

It will be necessary for you to give the insurance company your driver's license information, and some will insist that you are licensed within the same state in which the car is registered and titled, while the state that issued your license will not matter to others, so long as it is valid. If you are dissatisfied about any requirements that affect your privacy, you can either shop for a policy with a different company, negotiate your differences, or make changes to enhance your privacy after the deal is done.

For example, you can "move" and obtain a license in another state after having given the insurance company representative your driver's license information.

INQUIRING MINDS WANT TO KNOW

As you travel during your normal day and when traveling long distances, keep an eye out for those who may want to know your business, for whatever reason. Remember my opening story at the beginning of this chapter? To this day, I do not know why I was followed. Women, especially, are vulnerable to being stalked and followed home from the workplace or from social events so that stalkers can learn of their place of residence. One tactic to help you avoid unwanted contact from others is to never provide your home address to anyone, excepting a very few family members and trusted friends (see Chapter 6, "The Mobile Lifestyle: Living in Secrecy," Chapter 7, "The Anonymous Resident," and Chapter 8, "Private Home Ownership").

As far as driving is concerned, be aware of those cars close to you as viewed from your rearview mirrors. If you are suspicious of anyone, record license plate numbers for future reference. Alter your routes home from work and other trips, pay close attention to cars in your mirrors when leaving social functions, and do not discuss your home with anyone except those you want to know this information.

AUTOMOBILE DOCUMENTS

As a privacy practitioner, you should keep automobile titles in a safe place, perhaps in a safe deposit box or a secure storage bin away from your home and office. The car registration, proof of insurance, and your driver's license are important pieces of information that you will be asked to produce by law enforcement in the event you are stopped for any violation. These documents may be kept in a safe and secure place inside the vehicle, which should ensure privacy, especially if the car is equipped with an alarm system.

ACCIDENTS HAPPEN

Avoid unnecessary attention from law enforcement by following all the rules of the road. Drive safely, and don't exceed the speed limit. In the event you are given a traffic ticket, whether it be a simple parking violation or for a moving violation, you may choose to pay it immediately, unless the officer is clearly wrong, and you want to contest it. But, in this case, weigh the time and costs of fighting the offense.

If you are involved in a motor vehicle accident, whether you are at fault or not, exchange information with the other driver and report the incident to your insurance carrier and to the DMV, when you are required to do so according to the laws in your state. If bodily injuries occur as a result of an accident, you may become either a plaintiff or a defendant in a civil lawsuit. In the event an accident happens, you will be grateful for the privacy tactics you have in place, as it will be extremely difficult for the other side to investigate you, as happens in normal circumstances when a party is on either side of a personal injury case.

BIG BUREAUCRAT'S EYE IN THE SKY

An acquaintance received a notice to pay a ticket in the amount of $330, which he was unaware of receiving. Imagine that. Automated ticketing equipment. The bill, received at his home address, came with a cover letter, complete with a court date. Also included was documentation of the intersection location where the camera was installed to catch such speeders, a time stamp, the recorded speed, and information advising him that his license plate and photographs of him and his automobile were captured and now on record as evidence of the violation.

So without a defense, he paid his $330 fine—as did an entire room full of people who appeared for similar offenses. Cameras monitoring drivers. Think of the cost of this type of device. No wonder they charge $330!

SUMMARY

1. Properly registering a vehicle in the name of a trust formed specifically for holding title to a vehicle prevents anyone with license plate and registration information from identifying the driver. There are no state registration requirements for trusts. Do not have your true name associated with the car registration on any DMV or title information. For vehicle privacy, one may choose to use a state for car registration that is different than the state where your driver's license was obtained. Privacy advocates never use their true names when corresponding in writing or by telephone with the DMV concerning the trust-owned car, unless a specific law requires this.

2. Privacy seekers use a discreet mailing address to receive vehicle-related mailings, as well as a voicemail telephone number for their contact information.

3. Properly insure yourself, and include the trust as an "additional insured" on the automobile insurance policy.

4. Buy and sell automobiles using cash and money orders, for high-level vehicle privacy. Dealers and private parties may be used for purchasing and selling cars.

5. Carefully monitor vehicles around you as you drive to prevent being followed to your workplace or home, and be careful who knows where you work and live.

6. Keep the automobile title off site and the vehicle registration, proof of insurance, and your driver's license locked in the car. In the event of an automobile accident or receipt of a ticket, follow all the laws associated with your reporting requirements and payment of fines.

ELEVEN

The Private Passenger

"Let us not look back in anger, or forward with fear, but around in awareness."—James Thurber

FLYING THE FRIENDLY SKIES

Smoke filled the room. People lay on the floor huddled in corners, some sleeping, others eating, all captured—at least temporarily— and unable to contend with the armed guards preventing them from continuing their journeys, whether to Grandma's house for a visit or to a distant city for an important business meeting.

Where did this happen? In Russia in 1995, as I presented my U.S. passport, along with the required "invitation visa," which they claimed to be a fraud so that another one could be sold to me, thus causing me an unpleasant wait of five hours and a fee of $350 for the privilege of entering that country.

The same scenario repeats itself throughout airports in the U.S. today as passengers are halted by Big Bureaucrat's travel security forces and kept at bay until employees—often minimum-wage-paid and broken-English-speaking—allow them to continue their journey.

Other examples of such unnecessary, blatant, abuse include:

1. In December 2003, U.S. security officials detained a British Airways Boeing 747 on arrival at Reagan National Airport near Washington, D.C. and spent several hours searching it. The plane's 247 passengers and seventeen crew members were allowed to leave the airliner three hours later.

2. Bob Rajcoomar, a naturalized citizen and former U.S. Army major from Lake Worth, Florida, was detained and held in a filthy cell for about three hours. Following his release, he was given no reason for his detention.

3. Passengers aboard an airplane traveling from Denver to Philadelphia in February 2005 were detained when a woman who fell ill during the flight was believed to be carrying a contagious disease. Later, it was reported that the woman had developed a simple rash. The delay lasted one and one-half hours.

Despite resistance from privacy advocates, the U.S. government plans to develop a computerized system to probe the backgrounds of all passengers boarding flights in the United States. Under this system, passengers will be given scores with a numerical rank and color codes that quantify their perceived threat to the airplane.

Today, flying on an airplane is the most privacy-invasive form of travel. You will be required to show a government-issued form of identification prior to being allowed to board an airplane and, if your name matches anyone on the "no-fly" list, expect to be delayed or disallowed to fly at all until you have been cleared by the government's Transportation Security Administration (TSA).

Or, you may be hauled away in handcuffs. Security personnel will undoubtedly question you at length whenever anything out of the ordinary occurs as you attempt to board an airplane on U.S. soil. When you make a reservation to fly on an airplane, your name is entered into the airline's database and "bounced" off a list of criteria supplied by the U.S. government to the airlines for use in their database. Your name, address, and other information is screened and may cause your name to be flagged and make you subject to questioning or detention prior to boarding an airline.

Or, you may appear on the TSA "no-fly" list or the Homeland Security watch list. Or, you may be profiled by the Computer Assisted Passenger Pre-Screening System (CAPPS) and either be detained or kept from flying until you are cleared. Of course, if you are on the TSA or FBI wanted lists, forget about it—you won't be flying anyway, except perhaps to a federal prison.

Also, you can expect to make it into a number of secondary government databases—among the names the airlines will not reveal, if in fact they even know these names—if your name is flagged, once it goes through the screening process within the airline's database following your ticket purchase or reservation.

Some individuals have bypassed the databases containing lists of those flying or scheduled to fly by presenting a name very similar to their own with perhaps a first letter replaced with an incorrect one, in order to prevent their true name from being discovered as a passenger scheduled to fly. Then, as the airline ticket is purchased, right at the last minute, the mistake is pointed out to the airline ticket agent, who verifies you by checking your *official identification*.

TRAINS

Trains have tightened their security drastically over the past several years in an attempt to ward off and discover those undesirable passengers who might wish to harm property and the folks aboard.

A government-issued identification document—a U.S. passport, driver's license or state I.D. card—is required as you board the train. Conductors also may verify your identification at any time during the trip, according to one Amtrak representative. Trains have become an expensive way to travel as fuel costs and travel costs in general have increased. They no longer offer travelers a viable alternative to plane travel, either from a cost standpoint or for privacy. However, travel by train can be a fun experience as you can comfortably travel, see the beautiful countryside, and sleep for a couple of nights in the cabins available to rent as a part of your travel ticket. The cost, however, may be several times the cost for traveling the same distance by airplane.

SHIPS

Ships, whether cruise ships or freightliners, offer no better privacy than commercial airplanes or trains. They are a fun means of travel, however, and feature many luxuries. Cruise ships resemble a floating city, complete with recreation facilities, restaurants, movie theaters, casinos, and shops. This means of travel also affords a great way to meet new friends.

BUS TRAVEL

Buses are the privacy-minded traveler's dream! Commercial bus companies will sell you a ticket and take you anywhere within the forty-eight contiguous states of the continental U.S. without any identification requirements whatsoever.

Perhaps this leniency, so far as I.D. is concerned, has something to do with the fact that buses are not subsidized by the government when they manage their business poorly, unlike both the airline industry and Amtrak, which have both been bailed out in the past and disallowed to fail.

Buses, while not as speedy or as comfortable as trains or planes, provide a form of completely anonymous travel if you desire it. Just buy your ticket, using any name or company name you choose, present it to the driver when you board, and you will not be included in any databases or required to prove who you are. For those individuals who want to travel privately, for whatever reason, without the possibility of being traced, bus travel is the best option available as far as public transportation is concerned.

While it is the slowest form of public transportation, schedules are usually reasonably accurate, and you will arrive at your travel destination on time, in most cases. If it is necessary to leave one location without a trace and a car is not available or not the best idea, a commercial bus trip will give you the complete privacy you need. Consider using a bus as a means of travel if circumstances require moving to another location with security and privacy.

TRAVEL BY TAXI AND SHUTTLE

For short trips, when your car is not available, while away on business, when you are vacationing in a distant city, or for airport trips, a taxi or shuttle bus provides an efficient and private—albeit expensive—way to travel.

Be sure not to disclose your true name or room number or address when you call for either a taxi or a shuttle. Also, meet the driver at a neutral location—either another hotel or at an address other than your actual residence. As you are being transported home, from the airport, for example, make sure you do not reveal your home address, but rather have a designated spot for your drop-off arranged—a commercial office building or other location which is relatively close to where you actually live. Pay for services in cash.

SUBWAYS AND METROS

Subways and metro rail systems and their passengers are under scrutiny by law enforcement and government agencies in major cities throughout the United States—including Atlanta, Baltimore, Boston, Chicago, Cleveland, Newark, New York, Portland, St. Louis, San Diego, San Francisco, Seattle, and Washington, D.C.

Law enforcement is everywhere on the subways. Expect very little privacy as you travel on a subway. Government and police routinely check the identification of subway passengers. This is an undesirable way to travel if you value your privacy.

CITY BUSES

Bus travel within a city will not present any unusual concerns for those who want to travel without being identified. Travel passes usually can be purchased without providing any identification, unless you need to prove eligibility for an age- or handicap-related discount. If you don't mind the waits between buses, this is a cost-effective way to move about a major city.

Bus service varies greatly from city to city, so be aware that frequency, routes, and general slowness of buses can affect your schedule. Bus travel in the city may serve a purpose on those occasions when the trip is short and it is convenient for you to take a bus.

DELIVERY CARS AND SHARING RIDES

Look in the newspapers or search online, and you will discover advertisements offering you the chance to deliver a car from one major city to the next, free of charge, or perhaps offering you payment for your driving services. Both automobile dealers and private individuals advertise for these services. This can be an effective way to go from one city to another.

However, you may be closely monitored by the company or person who is going to retain you for the service. In the best-case scenario, expect to show your driver's license and complete a form requesting personal information prior to taking the car. Dealerships and others who need to make sure the car is accounted for may want your Social Security number, will surely record your name and driver's license into their own database of drivers, and will sometimes request a credit report. If you choose to deliver a private-party automobile, you can negotiate the personal information requirements or look for an advertiser who requires you to reveal less.

Some car-delivery services also require that drivers be bonded. This typically involves the purchase of a short-term policy from a bonding company as security to guarantee that the driver will perform on his commitment and will not abscond with the vehicle.

Overall, the choice is not such a bad idea for private travel, particularly when you are able to keep your name out of huge databases and if you are able to supply only minimal information to transport the car and yourself to a desired city.

Individuals advertise for others to accompany them cross-country for companionship and to share expenses. This is an option for those who require complete privacy when traveling. Check out all of the people with whom you will be traveling by running their names through the people-search databases—which reveal public records and criminal histories—prior to agreeing to make the trip. This screening will lessen your odds of being associated with undesirable people as you travel. The last person you want to be on the road with is a person with a criminal record or one who has a history of DWI or other driving-related offenses.

HIGH-LEVEL PRIVACY TRAVEL RECOMMENDATIONS

If you are being hunted by someone who is serious about finding you and has adequate funds to spend for your investigation and apprehension, you will want to employ unusually high security and privacy tactics to make certain you are not discovered by the investigator, stalker, or other enemy who is searching for your whereabouts.

Keep in mind that being hunted is never pleasant, is quite stressful, and your success in avoiding those who are looking for you will be highly dependent on your attention to details in every aspect of your life. Travel is no exception. Driving an automobile is high-risk travel for a person who is wanted and whose name has made its way into law enforcement databases, even though that person may be innocent of any crime.

Even though you may take the steps to ensure that the automobile you are driving is not traced back to your true name, you can be stopped while driving—and then the gig will be up. Examples of those who make their way into law enforcement's databases and are hunted are the numerous, innocent, mistakenly designated "deadbeat dads" being hunted.

If found, they wind up being detained, arrested, and taken to jail—sometimes due to mistakes made by incompetent child support enforcement agency personnel who fail to properly credit Dads' payments, thereby throwing an honorable, law-abiding father into arrears. This negligence by the state creates a criminal charge and a search for Daddy by the county sheriff's department, investigators, and other local and government law enforcement officials after a period of time.

Other times, one is falsely accused of any number of crimes, is totally innocent, and believes his/her only recourse is to escape and avoid the problem. Sometimes one is hunted by an enemy, and police refuse to offer them protection. This is yet another example of why you may choose to handle the problem by relying on the privacy advantage of secure, high-level private travel.

In the event you decide your situation warrants a very high level of privacy, be sure to avoid conventional travel means. Driving an automobile, flying on an airplane, and taking a train are not good choices. Also, you are at risk of being charged with a crime if you use a false identification to board a plane, train, or ship or use a fake driver's license in the event you are stopped while driving a car.

It is a better option to avoid the problem altogether by traveling in such a discreet way as to not risk the chance of being discovered in the first place. Hitchhiking used to be a relatively safe way to travel within the U.S. many years ago. Today, I would recommend this mode of travel only if your choices are limited and you believe you are capable of withstanding any type of confrontation you may face as you seek transportation from strangers.

Think it over and seriously consider it as a means of travel only if you have weighed the potential risks and dangers of traveling with someone who is a complete stranger. Traveling with another person who does not know you does offer you complete traveling secrecy.

Advertising for a ride to or from a major city through various newspapers or through Internet advertising will yield responses, particularly when you offer to share the travel expenses with the one providing the car. Here is another opportunity to use another's automobile and their privilege to drive as tools for you to travel discreetly.

Bus travel remains at the top of the list for those who want to go long distances without a trace of their name becoming a part of travel databases. Privacy seekers purchase the ticket in any name they want. You can vanish and go as you please without being tracked or bothered, no matter what your motivation for such travel discretion. And bus travel is the cheapest way to travel, particularly when you purchase a package ticket that gives you unlimited travel within a specified period of time.

Those who are wanted or hunted for whatever reason, or who do not want to make their way into a DMV office to renew their license or I.D. card, for whatever reason, are advised to use "high-level privacy travel recommendations" methods of travel to assure themselves of not being discovered while moving from city to city.

BORDER CROSSINGS

Crossing the U.S. border into Canada currently requires a U.S. passport. Mexico has the same legal requirements for crossing their border. It does not matter how one travels, the requirements remain the same. Travel by bus is the same as traveling by car.

Customs officials are authorized to check your documents as you enter a foreign country. And they will detain you for as long as necessary to satisfy themselves of your documents' authenticity. So don't use phony passports, driver's licenses, or birth certificates. Ever.

If you are wanted and hunted in the United States, I can positively assure your detention when you attempt to cross borders. FBI wanted lists, TSA no-fly lists, *FinCEN* wanted lists and watch lists (see Chapter 27), and numerous criminal database lists potentially contain your name, so be warned and expect to be detained, jailed, and held until whatever agency with jurisdiction over your case comes to take you away.

Crossing the border legally if you are wanted will assure your capture in this data-sharing information age. Of course, human error can occur—which could prevent the system from working as law enforcement and government intends it to work, to prevent anyone from escaping once their name is entered into one of the many databases designed to track and halt the movement of individuals as they cross international borders. And these errors do occur more often than one would think, thanks to the high number of incompetent government workers today. But don't count on it if you happen to be on anybody's wanted list.

For those in the fugitive category or those who are wanted, even for questioning, choices for avoiding contact with government or law enforcement officials are limited to illegally crossing the border on foot, much as the estimated 5,000 to 10,000 illegal aliens do each and every day as they come into the United States without proper legal documents.

In some cases, driving across either the Canadian or Mexican border is doable, if country roads are used, though this is high risk. You will probably not be on either country's international crime watch list unless convicted of a very serious crime or unless you have skipped out on bail and are being hunted by bail bondsmen. Then, expect to be in everybody's criminal database. If the charges are relatively new, your name may not yet be on any other country's criminal watch list.

The rule for border crossings is that unless you are clean, without warrants, expect questions and detention by border guards, followed up by armed officials who will keep you as long as they choose or until you make bail, if you are charged with a crime. In some cases, even civil case litigants' names are flagged at the border, providing those involved in the litigation have the right connections to alert customs officials to be on the lookout for such defendants.

Especially vulnerable to being detained while attempting to cross country borders is the child-support-paying American father whose account may be delinquent but may not have reached the criminal matter stage. Child support enforcement departments in all states closely track all dads ordered to pay court-ordered child support. Because it is a government agency, the child support enforcement division can have names of those who are delinquent (or those accused of being in arrears) placed on customs officials' watch lists. So, if you owe or are accused of owing back child support, expect to be disallowed to leave the country.

TICKET PURCHASES

Even though many airlines claim to retain your purchasing information—including your name, credit card number, address, and other personal data—for only one year, I doubt this to be the case.

Ever wonder how those advertisements make their may into your mailbox? You can buy your tickets with cash—forget about your frequent flyer mileage benefits, coupons, and the many other goods and service benefits for which you may be eligible. Just pay cash. For less scrutiny, buy round-trip tickets; one-way tickets are automatically flagged, and you will surely be questioned when you buy one. Likewise, I recommend paying for tickets in cash when you elect to travel by bus, train, or ship as well. Leave no paper trail, or, if you leave one, make it difficult to follow.

INTERNATIONAL TRIPS

When you take international flights, expect even more privacy-invasive tactics used by your government to thwart any illegal activity, of course. You will have the DEA, ATF, Homeland Security, FinCEN, and U.S. Customs, to name a few, among those who are watching for anyone to break the laws, so be careful.

You will be asked to sign a form declaring under penalty of perjury that you have not taken more than $10,000 out of the country—up from $5,000 some years ago. So don't take more than this amount out of the country, or if you do need to, tell the government that you are carrying an amount in excess of the $10,000.

Sometimes travelers take inconvenient routes to arrive at a final destination in order to avoid having their flights and passports reflect direct routes to banking havens such as Switzerland, Grand Cayman Island, and other countries known to house Americans' money. Canada has been used as a country for Americans to fly from when such a guise is needed.

I think that, for the most part, you will be best served by paying attention to the tax laws and other applicable regulations and concerning yourself with the safety issues of flying today while attempting to fly as discreetly as possible—not for the purpose of breaking any laws, but to preserve your personal and business privacy.

SUMMARY

1. Of all forms of public transportation in the U.S., air travel is the least private, with passengers' names being closely scrutinized by government and entire flights and individuals detained without cause while making plane trips.

2. Trains and ships also require passengers to prove identification by showing government-issued identification. Neither is as cost effective for commercial travel as are airplanes.

3. Commercial buses allow travelers to purchase tickets and complete their journeys without showing identification. Bus travel is the most private way to travel in the U.S.

4. Local travel can be accomplished in complete privacy when taxis, shuttle buses, and city buses are used. Subway travelers are often asked to produce identification, and their luggage and belongings may be subjected to searches.

5. Sharing automobile transportation with others going to the same city offers privacy-minded people the opportunity to travel secretly. Research those with whom you plan to travel prior to making the trip.

6. Delivering automobiles for commercial companies or private parties is an inexpensive travel option. The personal information required will vary depending on the company or individual.

7. High-level private travel is best accomplished by riding a bus, hitchhiking, or sharing a car with another person through a prearranged travel agreement.

8. Border crossings offer authorities the chance to detain those whose names are in several different criminal or other databases.

9. Ticket purchases should be made with cash or a money order.

10. Expect even closer scrutiny when traveling abroad and when returning to the U.S. from a foreign country.

♦ TWELVE ♦

Mail: Creating an Illusion

"Never interrupt your enemy when he is making a mistake."
—Napoleon Bonaparte

INVISIBLE OCCUPANT

The addresses were old. Years had passed since mail had been received there. Two remained on the file records of the three credit bureaus—one, a storefront shared by an adult store and "Mickey's Mail" in an East Coast city; the other, the residence of a retirement-age widow who formerly provided bookkeeping services to small businesses in Michigan.

Investigators' stops at these locations yielded only distant memories of initial meetings or telephone conversations and no meaningful stored records or forwarding addresses, except an address in Panama for Mickey's and a recollection from Widow Bookkeeper that the customer was moving to Vietnam for contract work. Consumer statements on the credit bureau reports referenced the correct address as being half a world away.

Where to start? How much would this cost just to pick up the trail on such a subject? This is the information Alex Corbin purposely created

131

for the benefit of those who sought him, as he received mail and had it forwarded and *remailed* multiple times to prevent anyone from keeping up with his whereabouts—as he made himself invisible.

When being hunted by enemies, it's a tremendous advantage to live "beneath the radar," so to speak, with your actual physical location unknown to those who record and store your personal information in their privacy-invading, life-controlling databases. Keeping personal and business mail totally private will enable the privacy seeker to build a solid foundation for the ultimate in anonymous living.

Having reviewed his three credit reports for the third time in a year, Alex, our fictitious character, noticed that credit inquiries from the district attorney's office were continuing. Investigators had tapped into his credit file monthly for the prior six months in an attempt to locate him by discovering his physical address.

Let's see what they found. Under the address section, his long-abandoned mail-drop addresses were still on the report. Letters sent to these addresses would be returned to the sender, and a direct physical contact at these locales would yield nothing except a storefront address and a residence Alex had not visited in years, if ever at all.

Sometimes, privacy seekers establish mail drops entirely by telephone, fax, and mail, while never actually meeting the person handling the account. Since U.S. credit bureaus will not record foreign addresses as the primary address for an American citizen, Alex had included his "actual address" with the credit bureaus under the consumer's statement in each credit bureau report. This statement noted his actual mailing address, and his "official address," which was a New Zealand office where the manager received and held his personal mail and forwarded it to him per e-mail instruction.

So, Mr. Investigator's efforts were essentially halted once he learned that his subject "resided" in a foreign county—halfway around the globe, no less. And to add insult to injury, the envelopes received by his sister agency—the child support and collection office in Texas—contained Alex's monthly payments with postmarks from different states and countries each month.

These payments were remailed from Hong Kong, London, Sydney, Salzburg, Paris, New York, Vancouver, Los Angeles—take your pick—on any given month as part of his plan to thwart the efforts of the government by creating a physical-location illusion. These tactics helped assure that his actual location would be nearly impossible to discover, even if they increased their investigator force and budget in their

SALZBURG, AUSTRIA

attempt to locate him and serve him with a summons.

Alex expected that the statute of limitations on the civil lawsuit of which he was the defendant would expire long before the government and private investigators found him. And it did.

YOUR MAIL: QUICK LINK TO YOU

Your mailing address is one of the most valuable resources an investigator, identity thief, stalker, or other predator utilizes to locate you. So important is your address that serious privacy advocates never, ever receive anything addressed to them—whether mail or a package or special delivery—at their real home address.

If you want true, high-level personal security, you must make the adjustments necessary to separate yourself from yourself—that is, from your perceived "actual" physical location—the address contained in various databases, necessarily supplied by you for goods and services in order to live in present-day America. If you desire a secure lifestyle, you must create an address that the world will believe is yours, but in fact will be only the location where your mail is received. This "location illusion" must be established and used in order that you are never bothered at home for any reason, whatsoever.

MAIL DROPS: PATHWAYS TO PRIVACY

A mail drop is an address used by a person or a business for the purpose of receiving mail only and does not serve as an actual address for living or doing business. Mail drops come in various forms and types, and they are necessary for the person who desires privacy and freedom in America today, in order to eliminate the possibility of having unwanted government intruders and others enter one's home or business.

The best and most secure form of mail drop is provided by independent business people, not *commercial mail-receiving agencies (CMRAs),* which are actually quasi-government post offices. These commercial businesses require the completion of U.S. Postal Service (USPS) Form #1583A, photocopies of state-issued identification, highly personal secondary identification documents, and the approval of the USPS in order to rent a mailbox to you or your business for the purpose of receiving and handling your mail.

Generally, serious privacy advocates avoid them. There are possible exceptions, however. Occasionally, you will discover a Mom-and-Pop operation that recognizes the privacy-invasive requirements of the USPS and will allow customers to maintain their privacy, but the best idea is to utilize private, independent business people for the purposes of handling your mail.

Having used mail drops for a number of years, I have discovered bookkeepers, CPAs, and secretarial service companies to be the most amenable to handling business and personal mail. It is best to seek out these types of businesses, because due to the nature of their job descriptions, they are most capable of handling the duties of receiving and forwarding mail for customers.

Often, I have cold-called owners of these businesses to inquire about their services. I find the proprietors typically to be grateful for the opportunity of making extra revenue in exchange for providing a mailing address. Generally, they are receptive to providing other services as necessary, including, but not limited to, sending and receiving faxes, mail forwarding to any address in the world, remailing letters as needed, and other routine office services when the need should arise.

I suggest a written agreement be formed, with fees set at or near the rate of the competition—the commercial mail-receiving agencies and the U.S. Postal Service.

MULTIPLE MAIL DROPS

Privacy advocates receive ALL of their mail at mail-drop addresses. A serious privacy seeker might elect to receive life and health insurance premium notices addressed to him or her personally at "Anne's Bookkeeping" in Bismarck, North Dakota, for example. Car registration correspondence might be addressed to the irrevocable trust holding title to a car in Sheridan, Wyoming. If licensed to drive in Arizona, this driver can have an address in that state as well (see Chapter 4, "Government Identification").

Bank, brokerage, and business-name correspondences could come to a small town in Idaho or to an offshore address in Scotland. Secretary of state correspondences—and business correspondences to business entities—could come to an address in Reno, Nevada. And those requiring privacy often receive Internal Revenue Service and Social Security Administration correspondences offshore—a mail-drop in the Isle of Man, for example.

Those living under the radar have also alerted the U.S. credit bureaus of their official offshore address, while providing a consumer statement and completed forms, with proper documentation of the same—and include an "official" address in the consumer statement of each report for TransUnion, Equifax, and Experian. By doing this, all who access these credit bureau files will know that the subject of the files resides offshore, and he or she will establish a higher level of personal security.

Those who are really ambitious can keep anyone from accessing their credit reports, as they establish a "home address" in a state that allows them to "freeze" their credit files. This will prevent anyone except current creditors from viewing any privacy-seeker's credit bureau files unless they choose to unlock the freeze on them (see Chapter 19, "Credit Bureaus").

Another address in Seattle, Washington, could be used to receive sensitive and highly confidential mail under both a non-registered company name and an "alternate name." These are examples, of course. Structure your own mail to be received in any way you choose. Establish a temporary arrangement with a company to receive forwarded mail for a few weeks only, if traveling, but keep it all confidential and remain anonymous.

If you're careful, you can remain beneath the Big Bureaucrat computer and radar system and will never need to be concerned about having unwanted people show up at your door or ever know how to locate you. A good high-level security measure is to establish multiple mail drops.

OFFSHORE MAIL

"Living" offshore or creating a "location illusion" of living offshore has a tremendous advantage. For instance, by establishing an address in another country, you can, depending on the circumstances, "remove yourself" from the jurisdiction of the United States and keep the hunters at bay and make it more expensive for anyone to pursue you and identify your location. This is important if you are sought for any reason—false or just, civil, criminal, or personal—by the government or any private individual or company.

Of course, if you actually are a fugitive, foreign countries in which you are believed to be residing can be contacted and asked to help ferret you out, but even in such a case, the costs become astronomical, and you must be wanted for a serious offense in order for foreign governments to participate in the hunt.

However, remember that nearly anyone can be found if enough time, effort, personnel, and money are expended to locate them. The key is to make it so difficult and costly and time-consuming that your case is placed on the back burner awaiting more money or relegated to the "dead file" and allowed to get cold as you go about your business while taking necessary, prudent precautions for living a safe, secure, private lifestyle.

For privacy matters—in fact, for most alleged civil and criminal matters—an offshore mail drop will be sufficient for high-level personal and business privacy. And if desired, you can establish multiple foreign mail drops as well, or perhaps a single one as a backup in the event an ambitious government or private investigator decides to take a trip to attempt to pay you a visit.

Carefully isolate yourself by corresponding with your mail-drop operator in Sweden or wherever he is located by utilizing secure, encrypted e-mail or a pay telephone or a remailed letter for correspondence, and pay your bills by mailing cash or money orders from remailed locations. Use whatever security measures you believe are necessary and congruent with the amount of acceptable risk for your given situation.

On occasion, the USPS will cooperate with various government snoop agencies and either photograph your mail or open it, photocopy it, and reseal it to gain information about their "suspect." In the event you are ever a target of the Internal Revenue Service, any state tax revenue department, any state child support payment enforcement agency, any federal or state law enforcement agency, or any other state or federal agency or private company that has convinced the post office to cooperate with their investigation, mail that is addressed to you personally may become a part of the files of your enemies.

Therefore, you not only want to receive mail under alternate names and company names but also at offshore addresses, so that the interception of your personal and business correspondences becomes difficult to impossible.

For example, Joe Jones' child support payments, while current, have not been properly credited by a child support payment clerk—whether intentionally or unintentionally, it does not matter. Therefore, a state investigator is assigned the task of seizing Mr. Jones' bank and brokerage accounts for the payments believed to be owed. However, Joe Jones has his personal bank account statements held in the name of "The Big Blue Invisible Trust," without his name as trustee on the statement, and mailed to his mail drop in Sydney, Australia.

His brokerage account statements, held in the name of "Western States Private Woman Limited Partnership" are also mailed to Sydney, as he receives business mail there and has it forwarded from Sydney by way of Vancouver to his non-registered company name of "Maggie's Homewares" in Salt Lake City, Utah, where he picks it up at his leisure.

So without a known name associated with Joe Jones' asset sources—his bank and brokerage accounts—where does the investigator look, and how does he intercept this mail, since there are no U.S. source addresses that receive these bank and brokerage statements?

And because our resourceful Mr. Jones has carefully utilized the "administrative trustee" concept (see Chapter 17, "Private Investments") to conceal his manager status with the Nevada Limited Partnership—the entity that owns his stock brokerage account—he cannot be found by name as an officer or manager of any company in any state, even if all fifty states' secretary of state company records are individually searched for his name—a tedious, costly, and time-consuming task.

Furthermore, the investigator finds that Mr. Jones resides in South Africa, as per the three credit bureau reports that indicate this in their completed consumer statements, which read: "My correct address is: 1234 South Cape Avenue, Pretoria, South Africa." Only long-abandoned mailing addresses in Florida, Georgia, and Colorado remain as ties to Mr. Jones in the United States.

So the investigator is left with little information for locating Mr. Jones. Mr. Jones has effectively prevented his asset locations from being known by keeping his personal and business mail private. However, despite following these precautions, your author has received mail from offshore, with U.S. Customs stamps on it, indicating they have opened the mail for their satisfaction prior to allowing it to be received in the U.S.

In order to minimize government snoops from reading your mail, having it forwarded from a Canadian address into the United States will minimize this invasion of your business and personal privacy. You still can expect your government to steal your privacy on occasion, so be cognizant of their capabilities and be as discreet as possible when receiving mail, both in and outside of the United States.

REMAILING SERVICES

The purpose of remailing letters, payments, or anything, for that matter, is to make the receiver of the correspondence believe the sender is located in another area, whether that be another city, state, or country. Remailing services are abundant and may be found on the Internet via a search.

Typically, $1.00 to $5.00 is charged for the remailing of one to five letters from U.S. or foreign cities. The sender encloses letters to be remailed from the "ruse" location in a larger envelope and advises the remailer to mail those letters he wishes to have postmarked far away from his home in San Francisco, for example.

The recipient receives the postmarked payment or letter from London and believes his mail was sent from that city. Want the Bank for Commerce in Panama to take your account application for a loan seriously? Have your cover letter and application remailed by a remailer in that country. Being investigated during an ugly divorce and child custody and support case? Create a ruse and make it expensive and time-consuming for the other side and, most important, prevent them from properly serving a summons for a U.S. civil case, by remailing letters, alimony payments, birthday cards, and Christmas gifts from faraway New York, Hong Kong, California, or Sweden.

Investigators will never know where you are and will exhaust themselves chasing your last-known location by fumbling through old files, making useless telephone calls, and investigating previous address information and people to attempt to find a tie to the place where the last child support payment or letter was postmarked.

All to no avail, of course, because for the cost of a few dollars you have prevented your enemies from knowing your real location and have given them time-consuming and expensive false leads to follow. Remailing services are excellent resources for privacy. Use them for security and peace of mind as the need arises.

BUSINESS MAIL

As previously mentioned, business mail received in company names only, at offshore locations, offers the best security for keeping government and others out of your business. Keeping business correspondences, especially sensitive ones, separate from your true name will prevent you as a privacy seeker from having any known association with an employer, agency, or company under your management and control.

Practitioners, attorneys, doctors, and others who necessarily deal with the public may want their office mail sent to another location from their practice or business site location, or they risk the same intrusion as anyone knowing their physical locations. Office location and physical presence of the business person or professional can be limited to only those seen by appointment. For personal privacy, do not receive either business guests or business mail at home under any circumstances.

PICKING UP MAIL

For high security, utilizing several remailings from various mail drops is the best idea, with the final packages containing either company mail or personal mail from different locations being sent to a convenient mail drop that is accessible to you. An understanding bookkeeper receptive to your unannounced walk-ins without an appointment is best, or you may want her to send it to yet another mail drop—perhaps a Mom-and-Pop shop—for your pick up. One with 24-hour access is great, but not entirely necessary.

Always park your car some distance away so it will not be identified with you, should your bookkeeper sell you out and have Mr. P.I. at the ready were you to be hunted for any alleged offense. For an added measure of security, open an account with Ms. Bookkeeper or the like under an alternate name, while using a fictitious business name—one not registered anywhere, of course—for the purpose of breaking the trail to you individually, once the mail finally comes home to roost.

This strategic plan of combining several remailings of your packages of mail, with the final stop being to a person or company not associated with those names in the packages, will give you a very high level of mail security.

SUMMARY

1. Home addresses and business addresses should not be used for receiving mail. Instead, create a mail drop—an address with a company or individual for the purpose of receiving mail only—in order to shield actual home and business locations.

2. Do not receive any correspondences where you live. For the highest level of privacy, receive business mail at a mail-drop address serviced by a nominee you have chosen.

3. Use mail-drop addresses for the receipt of all mailings, while creating an address distant from your actual location. Your address is the closest link to your actual physical location, so for privacy purposes, create multiple addresses, both offshore and in the U.S.A.

4. Serious privacy advocates do not use postal boxes or commercial mail-receiving agencies that insist on privacy-invasive information in order to provide mail services. They use bookkeepers and secretarial service providers—or individual mail nominees—distant from their actual location.

5. Business mail should be received separate from personal mail.

6. Personal mail and business mail can be received offshore and remailed to a convenient U.S.A. location under a non-registered, fictitious business name or alternate name.

7. Pick up mail discreetly and unannounced under an alternate name or company name.

♦ THIRTEEN ♦

Telephone Communication

"Electric communication will never be a substitute for the face of someone who with their Soul encourages another person to be brave and true." —Charles Dickens

GOVERNMENT MONITORS CITIZENS

Worried about your personal and business telephone calls being unlawfully intercepted by identity thieves possessing unblocked scanners? Does it concern you that your cell phone and unlisted land-line telephones may not be as private as you think and that crooks desiring to know your most important, secure information could be monitoring some of your conversations?

These are valid concerns for all of us as we communicate by telephone, and the list of potential thieves about whom you should be concerned includes your own government. President George Bush authorized the unlawful tapping of American citizens' telephones without obtaining court orders to do so, according to the December 19, 2005, edition of the *Australian*. The story has been widely reported by major worldwide sources—including many in the United States—as well.

Bush defended the eavesdropping program as "critical to saving American lives." In one of his

weekly radio addresses, the President stated that "its purpose is to detect and prevent terrorist attacks against the United States, our friends, and allies."

According to an article published in the *East Valley Tribune* (Arizona) on May 13, 2006, Qwest Communications refused to provide the government access to telephone records of its fifteen million customers. However, AT&T, Verizon Communications, and Bell South all released customers' phone records to government agents soon after September 11, 2001.

LAND-LINE TELEPHONES

The land-line telephone in your home is the least secure telecommunications tool you own. It is not only wishful thinking to believe you can depend on it for timely communication, based on the number of call backs it takes to reach someone today, it is risky from a privacy standpoint to have one in your home in the first place. I am not saying you need to throw it out—at least not until you have a better and safer alternative—but consider the risks of having your telephone number traced to your residence.

Think you can block caller I.D., screen all your calls with an answering machine on your land-line phone, and depend on your telephone company to honor your privacy by not revealing your "unlisted" number to anyone? You're not only gambling, but you're also taking a risk when you have a way to be called back on a land-line telephone at home.

With a little work, Gordo, the resourceful convicted credit card felon who is looking for a new score and a new identity from which to launch it, can soon be at your door peddling insurance or offering home-improvement items or carpet cleaning, for example, with the underlying intention of finding out more about you. That's the way professional identity thieves and other "fraudsters" work. In fact, the professional criminals—the ones who are successful—plan a caper for several years prior to striking. How do you suppose felons spend their waking hours in prison?

So start your privacy plan by considering how to make your telephone communication system as secure as possible. You may choose not to have a land-line telephone at your residence, because anyone who is called—with the assistance of *69 or other telephone company codes and perhaps some help from an understanding operator—can take the necessary steps to find your home number.

And you do not want the wrong people knowing your home number, because it can be used to locate your actual street address. And therein lies part of the potential risk of having a land-line telephone in your home. Throughout the course of making everyday calls from the home phone, someone at your home will leave the number to be called back. Then a name will be associated with your "unlisted" telephone number. The party or business who has collected it may record it, and your home number and name may find their way into any number of databases. Before you know it, your name and number will be included in a national database that can be accessed by anyone who knows either your name or the phone number of your "private" home phone.

Reverse reference searches are capable of revealing your name and phone number when either is known. Once the number is known, it can easily be traced, with the cooperation of a telephone company employee or a friendly phone company operator. The investigator or crook researching you will then have a clear path to your door.

If any of these subtle methods of finding your home address fail, Gordo and his gang can retain the services of a private investigator who has telephone tracing equipment, or collect on a favor due at the phone company, and then you will be found. Count on it. Strongly consider discontinuing the use of land-line telephones at home when your personal security and privacy are high priorities.

PAY TELEPHONES

Public pay phones are becoming less common today, and even these are traceable back to your calling location. However, they represent the most private means of communicating by telephone, so find one located in a quiet area, take your list of names and numbers to it a couple of times per week, and make those sensitive calls without risking having your home or office location revealed to the person or business whom you are calling.

Privacy has to be a priority in order to inconvenience yourself and pay the added expenses related to secure telephone communication. Traveling to a pay telephone, tolerating the noise at the less-desirable locations, and paying the high costs required to use a pay phone may cause some hesitation about taking all the necessary precautions for telephone privacy. However, the discipline required to do it right pays huge dividends in the form of knowing with certainty that there is no link between the telephone from which you are speaking and your home address, thus giving you absolute assurance that you and your family cannot be unknowingly traced through telephone communication.

Pay phones have certain restrictions as well. Most of them cannot receive incoming calls, which can be a handicap to effective and timely communication. However, this can be used to your advantage as well. If Mr. Blumberg is out to lunch, simply leave instructions with the operator to relay the message to him or do it yourself on his voicemail. Then send him written confirmation of your message, try ringing him later, or do it by written communication entirely and be done with the task, instead of playing phone tag—a waste of your valuable time.

Also be aware of the possibility of government agents and police monitoring certain public pay telephones. They can listen in on any citizen's calls they choose without court order or cause and without criminal suspicion or activity. And if justification is ever required, although it won't be, government agents can use any number of Patriot Act provisions or homeland security reasons for listening to your routine telephone calls while attempting to gather as much personal information about you as possible during the course of the call. So with these real possibilities in mind, be careful about what you say, whom you call, and how long you stay on the phone.

TELEPHONE CALLING CARDS

Prepaid telephone calling cards are popular today and eliminate the need for a long-distance service carrier if you do have a land-line telephone, in your office, for example. These cards are available at all major grocery and drugstore chain stores at reasonable prices. Using a telephone calling card can provide an element of privacy as you make local and long-distance calls from your office telephone or a phone in a hotel room, for example.

However, I have discovered inconsistencies in the information revealed when caller I.D. is used by whomever you are calling with a calling card, so be careful. You should "test" each new calling card you purchase by calling someone with caller I.D. and asking them about what is shown on their monitor as far as the number and location you are dialing from is concerned.

Also, never buy additional minutes on the same card by charging it to a credit card—instead, purchase a new card, with cash, of course. Destroy used-up phone cards to eliminate any records of your previous telephone calls made with the card. When local calls are made, instead of dialing direct, key in the entire phone number, including the area code. This causes the service number for the calling card company to be displayed, rather than the phone you are calling from.

Calling cards should be used as you make calls from pay phones as well and will prevent the number of the pay phone from being shown on caller I.D. The phone call can still be traced back to the phone location, even when the number is not shown on caller I.D. Be sure to test each new phone card so that you are aware of your risk when making telephone calls.

Another technique you can use when making calls from a hotel is to use a name different than that used to register at the hotel. For example, when you use your alternate name of "Perry Doolittle" to register at a hotel and have a need for a temporary office worker, use the name of "Tom Schmidt" to inquire as to the costs and availability of office workers for your business stay in Atlanta. This way, if Suzie Clay, the resourceful recruiter who works on commission and is just shy of her sales quota, decides to find you by using caller I.D. to trace you back to your hotel, there will be no such registrant on hotel records.

VOICEMAIL

The most effective means of insulating yourself from unwanted telephone callers—while providing no clue whatsoever about your actual physical location—is to use a standalone voicemail service.

For the highest level of security and privacy, do not use a telephone company. Instead, shop around for a company that rents phone numbers to individuals and companies. Choose one that is highly flexible and will allow you to do the entire process over the telephone without ever producing any identification or in any other way link you to the service.

For $10 to $15 per month, without a service contract, you can have voicemail listed in whatever name you choose, complete with the same voicemail features offered by the telephone companies. Companies differ as to their policies on offering services, so look for one that suits your privacy needs.

I have opened service accounts with these companies for years in several names for added security and am aware that this is easily done, although you will have to make some calls to find the right service. For added security, you may elect to use two different numbers, perhaps in different states, to conceal your actual physical location from those with whom you make telephone contact.

Serious privacy seekers often have a West Coast telephone number and another on the East Coast, to give the impression of being far away from their true home base, which may in fact be in the Midwest.

These simple telecommunication privacy tactics are often highly effective, particularly when several numbers are used when making contact with the same company or individual, because the other business or individual will assume you are a frequent traveler who is difficult to reach and will never know that your only contact is a voicemail phone number. These services are limited to receiving your calls and messages only, so recognize that your only reason for buying the service is to establish a telephone contact for you or your business.

For the ultimate in security, do not use your actual voice on the message center feature of the voicemail service, but instead rely on the pre-recorded voice provided. This way, no one can tie you to the phone through voice recognition technology or establish your identity by hearing your recorded message.

Also, the telephone message system will allow you to screen those callers you want to call back and those calls that go into the delete file, so your hassles with unwanted solicitors will be minimal and will not waste your time.

A standalone voicemail in another name with an independent company usually won't make it into the common databases that are available for reverse searches to locate individuals and telephone numbers, so your voicemail provides an exceptional privacy advantage. Also, just in case someone did record your name in such a database, this is no problem, because your true identification will not be known anyway, since the number was secured in your alternate name.

So far as billing is concerned, the company issuing the voicemail telephone number will want a billing address, although they will not use it for billing, in most cases, but will record it in their customer records database.

A reader writes that he uses the services of a California company that rents voicemail numbers in several states, and he prepays the service three months in advance. His billing address for the phone number is a private school in Panama City, Panama, and he has no idea whether the company bothers to send the bills, since he has no association with the address.

Based on this fellow's extensive experience with privacy, and my own, there are many companies who will provide this simple service of giving you a source of telephone contact—the only purpose of a voice-mail service—while preserving your anonymity. As always, when dealing with confidential service providers such as the company providing your voicemail, call them infrequently, and call them from a pay phone whenever phone contact is necessary.

ANSWERING SERVICES

Live answering services place a layer of privacy between you and those trying to reach you by telephone. Credibility is also added to your business when you have a person available to field your calls during business hours. For reasonable fees, you can obtain a 24-hour answering service and return calls as you choose, or, for additional fees, receive forwarded calls from the number you rent from the company providing the service.

These services not only offer convenience but privacy as well, because calls are made to another business telephone number, which provides a buffer between your phone and your callers. For high-level privacy and to eliminate your phone number from being captured—at least by ordinary means—consider having your calls forwarded from your independent answering service to your cell phone.

The main advantage of utilizing an answering service, however, is to have a person available to take your calls at all times. The privacy features associated with using a third party to take your calls is an added benefit of the service. When you seek the highest level privacy features, so far as telephone answering services are concerned, retain an offshore secretarial service or pay your offshore mail-drop nominee additional fees to take your calls.

Phone numbers that are out of the country and are your primary telephone contact number will strengthen your telecommunication security system by creating a belief that your physical location is offshore. However, be aware that calls placed to and from offshore numbers are the most likely of all telephone communications to be monitored by government, so exercise extra precautions when using them.

ANSWERING MACHINES

Answering machines were once used to screen calls and provided a way to avoid unwanted calls and callers. Because they are tied to a land-line telephone, the location of the machine taking your messages can easily be traced back to its physical location—usually your home or office. These devices have been replaced for the most part by voicemail, and those serious about telecommunications privacy do not use them.

PAGERS

Although pagers have been replaced by cell telephone features that alert you when someone is attempting to reach you, a small telephone pager is not expensive and may be useful. Unlike a cell telephone, pagers cannot be tracked. Pagers will give you immediate notification of calls while your location remains unknown even to those with the most sophisticated scanners.

A cell phone can be kept turned off and carried on your person and used whenever calls are received through pager messages, for a high level of telephone security. Or a pay phone can be used to return the most confidential calls, if you believe using a cell phone poses a security risk.

YOUR TELEPHONE NUMBER

As previously mentioned, your telephone number is an extremely important and reliable link to the real you. Investigators and identity thieves rely heavily on telephone numbers to stalk and locate their prey. So the number you provide to the world should be the standalone voicemail phone number you secure in your alternate name from an independent company that rents communication services.

Your best choice for a billing address for this service will be in a faraway land where English is not the first language. When you handle your telephone contact information number in this fashion, you will save yourself a great deal of trouble in the event someone wants to locate you—whether you are aware of being hunted or not—as your trail will lead to a dead-end locale in the world of cyberspace. The company renting phone numbers will have no ties to your true name.

Also, chances are good that the source where your number originated—the independent company which provided the phone number to you—will be difficult to identify as well. However, if the source of your rented number is discovered, you are not going to be bothered, because your account is held in your pseudo name and, as far as the billing address in Argentina is concerned—forget about it.

For further protection, voicemail numbers, so far as I know, are hardly ever included in telemarketing databases. Why? Because they will never reach anyone by calling voicemail, plus, the company renting these numbers gets them from another source, and these numbers turn over every year or two—so the validity and inclusion of these on a marketer's phone list is unlikely.

Also, the alternate name you provide when you obtain the phone number would be the name associated with the number, even if it were in a collected list of phone numbers, so the true you would never be discovered in any case.

Sometimes it becomes necessary for you to give out a phone number as you do official business—to your attorney, for example—and then your true name and the voicemail number become linked. When it is necessary to provide your true name and telephone number to businesses, government, or individuals, a standalone voicemail number provides the best telecommunications privacy. Those who need to reach you will still have a means of contact.

Most of the companies with which you do business will request your telephone number as a reference on your account or other records. For those requesting a phone number for you or any trust or company you manage, a voicemail number will be sufficient and will not compromise your privacy.

CELL TELEPHONES

Telephones are never really secure, as all telephone conversations can be monitored by unblocked scanners, and the words of each party may be deciphered. With this potential privacy hazard in mind, I recommend you treat all conversations as if they were being monitored and carefully avoid providing sensitive information when speaking on any telephone.

Cell telephones have become nearly a necessity for business people the past few years. In order to communicate effectively with those with whom you must stay in touch, carefully evaluate what privacy features are important to you.

First, realize that the traditional way of obtaining a cell telephone is not for privacy seekers. In fact, mainstream telephone companies offer all sorts of incentive programs if only you sign a two-year service contract and provide a detailed list of your most confidential information for their files. They will want your home address, Social Security number, a credit card number, a copy of your driver's license, and authorization to pull your credit report.

All of this for the privilege of allowing you to buy a cell phone and pay phone bills every month. Privacy advocates never, ever provide their Social Security number, true name, home address, credit cards in their true name, or any other banking information to a cell telephone company. And they do not under any circumstances allow a cell phone company to view their credit reports.

In fact, never provide any information to any telephone company about the real you. Because if your true name makes its way into any database associated with your real home address, your Social Security number, and other confidential and personal information, you become a prime target for identity theft and any number of other crimes, not to mention the many, many databases that will store your name and information and will in turn supply this information to numerous telemarketers. These, in turn, will call you and attempt to sell you services and goods as well as share their information about you with other companies who will do the same.

Privacy and freedom require initiative and creativity on the part of the individual seeking it, so be aware of what it takes to gain near-total privacy as you create a means of being available to only a select few through the use of cell phone communication.

Due to the huge demand for services from people who have no credit in America—mainly the illegal-alien Mexicans who cross the southern borders each day—certain cell telephone companies have relaxed their policies for providing cell phone service in the past few years. More competitive "prepaid" cell phone services have made their way into the marketplace. These plans, without contract obligations, are the most attractive to the true privacy seeker.

Today, TracFone and Net 10 offer preloaded phone cards for purchase. Neither company requires any name registration for cell phone users. Choose a phone that offers services you need and requires no contract. Buy it and register it in your alternate name, or in no name at all. Prepaid cell telephones may be loaded with minutes by paying cash at stores, charging the cost of minutes to an anonymous debit card, or by purchasing prepaid cell phone calling cards with cash and loading the minutes yourself. Companies offering prepaid phones and minutes offer different payment options.

In any case, your priority is to have no link between the real you and your cell telephone registration. A billing address will also be requested, though there is no reason for the company to verify it, so use your judgment as to what you give them. One effective method, which I do not necessarily recommend but am aware of being used without difficulty, is for a lower-forty-eight resident to provide a billing address that leads to a tiny Alaskan town. No doubt promotional materials and other advertisements make their way to that faraway place, at least part of the time, but the cell phone user has no knowledge of it, and his important mailing address will not become known to the phone company.

An offshore address, which will be equally effective for telephone privacy, may be used. Cell telephones, you remember, are only traceable when turned on, so keep yours off when you are not using it unless you're expecting an important call. Also, for added security, two telephones with numbers from different geographic regions are effective. Consider this if you are really worried about being located.

The obvious advantage of using a cell phone for most of your calls, except the really sensitive ones for which you should use a pay telephone, is the convenience, of course, as well as the difficulty others will have finding your actual location. When cell phones are on, they send out a continuous signal identifying the nearest cell tower, hence your location can be determined, at least nearly so, depending on the quality and sophistication level of the equipment being used to locate the signal.

TRACING CELL TELEPHONES

Only law enforcement personnel, crooks, and government agencies will own unblocked scanners capable of identifying and locating a cell telephone. Because your cell phone number and location at the time you make or receive calls is detectable, it is imperative that this number—as well as the name to which it is associated—has no links whatsoever to you.

Making sensitive calls while in a moving vehicle will prevent scanners from finding your true location, due to your movement. Because of your ability to move when a cell phone is being used, as well as the fact that it cannot be traced when it is turned off, a cell phone is not likely to create a risk of you being located if you use it sensibly.

In the event you find yourself being stalked or followed or otherwise come under suspicion, changing the phone service and number will prevent tracing the phone to you. Whenever given the choice, privacy experts use a pay phone instead of a cell phone, however, and avoid communicating sensitive information by phone, including their true name and other personal data.

Business calls requiring one's true name and confidential information pose risks, so recognize these risks and strive to minimize making this information available to anyone who may be monitoring your phone calls.

HIGH-LEVEL PRIVACY TELEPHONE TACTICS

It is best to avoid using your true name, especially your last name, whenever possible during telephone calls, for privacy and to prevent anyone scanning your conversations from learning your true identity.

All toll-free numbers, which are quite popular among businesses and government agencies, automatically retrieve the phone number from which you are calling. This is done through Automatic Number Identification (ANI)—an 800 number feature to identify their customers, of course. When you call on a cell telephone, the cell phone number will be revealed. A pay phone is your best choice for calling toll-free numbers.

You can make it difficult for those wishing to locate you by subscribing to Voicenet, a service available to those who want to provide an impression of being in a different city than the one in which they are actually located. If you are in Dallas, for example, you can be called at a Delaware number and still receive the call in Dallas. This company can be reached by calling 1-800-385-5710, or you can see their website at www.voicenet.com.

When you want your calls blocked from caller I.D., press *67, which provides per-call blocking on outgoing calls from land-line telephones. You must remember to use the code on every call you make, however. Radio Shack also sells a blocker that prevents your phone number from being seen by those using caller I.D.

For emergency calls, use your cell telephone, if possible, to ring 911, to avoid having a valid address traced to the location from which the call is made. Of course, your cell telephone will reveal its actual number, but the address will not cause you a problem, even if someone wants to use it to find you. The name associated with the cell phone is your alternate name, or no name, so you'll be spared providing any information, should they want to make a file on you, as they typically will when emergency calls are made.

If you are still worried, even when these precautionary steps are taken to protect yourself from privacy-intrusive government agents, police, and the like, you could change your number and start anew with the same company or another company. In fact, for the ultimate in privacy and security, you may change numbers every year or three anyway, thereby breaking any accumulated links to you and your number.

FAXES

Sending or receiving faxes normally poses the same risks for revealing your location as do land-line telephone services. Call-forwarding services can be used to prevent the tracing of your fax location, but be careful with these services, as they sometimes fail, either through human error or by equipment malfunctions.

Overseas fax numbers provide the best location cover, and a number of companies will provide these for you for the asking in conjunction with other office services or as standalone services available upon your request. Shop for these services via the Internet, and you will locate several which will accommodate you and your office requirements.

Voicemail and a personalized answering service, combined with a fax service in another country, are viable choices for the business person or entrepreneur who travels frequently, or for the stateside man or lady who wishes to be shielded from the outside world under the guise of a phone and fax number from abroad.

Fax services can be purchased for about $10 a month that allow you to send and receive faxes via computer. Also, you may choose a distant area code from your home base if you want to create a location illusion. When you consider this means of communication, remember that certain identifying information is used by those with the wherewithal to afford it—mainly government—which can record your computer's I.P. address. So if this is a concern, utilize a proxy server and other software to shield your computer from those who might see through the fax number you present from computer-generated faxes as you pretend to globe trot around the world.

The most confidence is gained by utilizing the services of third parties to send and receive whatever faxes become necessary, providing these are not too frequent. Office managers and secretarial services, particularly those operated by proprietors, are usually willing to provide fax services as a part of their normal office routine service. Your mail nominee is a good resource for faxing confidentially, particularly when you utilize offshore nominees to receive and forward your mail. They in turn can re-fax, or scan and e-mail the document to you at your secure location so that timely receipt of the information is possible without sacrificing your privacy.

TELEPHONE MANNERS

How do you answer your telephone? Never use your first or last name as an opening greeting, even for a voicemail, or you risk losing the telephone anonymity this chapter is all about. Answering the phone with a simple "Hello" will work fine, as you then wait for callers to state their business, giving you the option of continuing with the conversation or quickly terminating the call.

Developing a good telephone voice through practice will go a long way in your phone privacy as well as provide you with the ability to effectively communicate by phone. Clear diction is best achieved through emulating those who speak well, so listen to the professional radio talk show announcers and others.

Those with whom you speak on the telephone will gain an almost immediate respect for you and make it a breeze for you to terminate unproductive calls if you speak with a pleasant, clear voice. Likewise, important calls will be more efficient if you stay on point and know when it's time to end the telephone call.

IS YOUR PHONE TAPPED?

Gone are the days when debugging equipment used by a detective could locate devices used to listen in on your most sacred telephone conversations. Today, scanners from a distance can intercept and decipher your phone conversations. If you are being stalked or hunted, you will want to avoid phones, except for pay phones, and make calls on a very limited basis from cell phones, while changing your cell phones often. Throw-away prepaid cell phones are another option to avoid having a monitored phone conversation traced back to a phone linked to you and in your possession.

Follow the golden rule of all communication: "Think what you say before you say what you think." Your phone probably isn't tapped—certainly not in the traditional sense of containing a small bug-like device as seen in detective movies. But be aware that telephones are indeed tapped—and often—these days, although this is done from a central location and through the use of a computer that is able to monitor your calls without anyone entering your office or residence to plant a "bug" in your telephone.

Avoid discussing anything that could incriminate you for any reason whatsoever while on the telephone, but at the same time, do not overly restrict your supposed freedom to speak freely. Establish a balance, follow all the laws of the land, and have your most serious chats in person or thorough the use of codes and prearranged substitutions. For added protection, shred prepaid phone cards once they have been used.

PHONE BILLS

The most notable paper trail left on your telephone communication history is the billing associated to your name and telephone number. A prepaid cell telephone will not generate phone bills and, when listed under your alternate name, the real you will not be tied to the phone calls made and received on the phone.

You have no doubt watched enough detective shows to know that phone bills and records provide investigators with valuable investigative resources if they have a reason to gather information about you or your business. So take steps to ensure that no records exist of your telephone calls.

When you establish all telephones and related telephone services in an alternate name with no link to you, a purely fictitious, non-existent person will take the proverbial fall for you if one is taken. So avoid the traps most amateurs fall into, and never allow another person—not a friend, relative, or even a nominee—to establish a telephone account and phone number for your benefit. Because if those records come under scrutiny, your friend, relative, or nominee may very well point criminals, investigators, the police, the IRS, or whoever is looking for you, in your direction very quickly.

Establish all phone services yourself in alternate names and use faraway billing addresses, if any are required, which have no association with your true name. Pay all prepaid cell telephone bills with cash at the phone store or with your alternate name debit card. Other phone bills, voicemail service bills, pager bills, and the like should be paid with money orders. Use a different signature on money orders than the one you use as your true name signature.

Net 10 and TracFone are two companies that sell cell telephone cards with up to 1,500 minutes on a card. These cards may be purchased for cash and loaded onto the phone manually. Neither of these companies require identification information.

SUMMARY

1. Government poses the biggest threat for privacy-invasive monitoring of your private and business telephone calls and other forms of communication.

2. Land-line telephones are not private and are easily traced. Reverse-reference checks compromise your name and telephone number, so do not hold any telephone numbers, voicemail telephone numbers, pager numbers, or answering service numbers in your true name. Use alternate names and company names for privacy.

3. Pay telephones allow you to use a third-party telephone with no ties to a traceable name, business, or home location. Pay phones may be monitored.

4. Telephone calling cards should be purchased with cash and replaced when the minutes have expired. Test each new phone card for caller I.D. security features.

5. Voicemail telephone numbers should be purchased from independent communication companies.

6. Answering services can forward calls to a cell telephone as necessary.

7. Answering machines are traceable to the telephone location.

8. Pagers offer a cost-effective, secure message-receiving service.

9. All telephone numbers should be held in alternate names or company names.

10. Prepaid cell telephones, purchased in an alternate name or in no name, provide the most secure means of anonymous telephone service. Turn the phone off when not in use.

11. Caller I.D. blocking devices and telephone number diversion services allow privacy during telephone communication.

12. Fax numbers may be "call-forwarded" for privacy. Computer fax services may be useful for security and privacy. Third-party faxes offer the most secure and anonymous fax services. Use offshore nominees for sensitive faxes.

13. Treat all telephone calls as if they are monitored.

14. Pay all telephone bills and other communication bills with cash, money orders, or with alternate name debit cards.

◆ FOURTEEN ◆

Computer and Internet Privacy

"Computers can figure out all kinds of problems, except the things in the world that just don't add up."—John Magary

COMPUTER PURCHASES

Purchasing a computer for home or office use should be handled much as other equipment purchases—as discreetly as possible. Remember that every computer—laptop or desktop personal computer (PC)—has its own identifiers, including a serial number as well as a unique fingerprint—the internal IP address.

Even though there is a variety of protective security measures you can take to conceal most, if not all, of your information and activities while using a computer, it still behooves you to purchase your computer with cash and register it in an anonymous name. Likewise, with software purchases. Don't use your true name when buying computer products in stores or online.

It becomes even more important to remain anonymous while using a computer to correspond via e-mail and perform research on the World Wide Web than in other facets of one's business and personal life, because many times, the user will have no idea who or what company they are dealing with while online. Hence, the need for complete anonymity.

COMPUTER CHOICES

Today, a variety of fine brand-name computers is available that will serve the casual user and professional alike. Desktop PCs are the least mobile and are vulnerable to having an installation of a keylogger program, while laptops are completely mobile—a valuable security feature itself.

A laptop can be carried and kept with you whenever you leave the home or office, much like a briefcase, enabling you to keep your data with you or close to you at all times. Laptop computers, due to technical advances of the last few years, can serve as your primary computer, which increases security and control over the unit due to the increased mobility capabilities of these smaller, portable machines.

BACKUP DATA

You can keep the computer external hard drive, backup storage hardware device, or CD-Rom disks containing your important data files, in an off-site location for security purposes. Keeping important data at a storage facility or safe deposit box will prevent the possibility of being wiped out completely in the event of theft, a system crash, virus, or other catastrophe. Separating the backup data from the computer in use is advised.

Continuous online backup of data is available through a company called Data Deposit Box for a charge of one cent per megabyte. Data Deposit Box makes instant online backups whenever your files change. Their website is at www.datadepositbox.com.

Removable hard drives enable the user to store and manage data on magnetic disks. The huge storage capacity, as well as mobility, make these devices ideal for large files.

INTERNET SERVICE

At the heart of your computer privacy plan is the company supplying you with access to the Internet—your Internet Service Provider (ISP). Today, it is almost essential to use high-speed Internet service, and these services come in a variety of forms. High-speed wireless providers, DSL providers, T-1 line service companies, and cable companies compete for the high-speed Internet market. Even companies providing "accelerators"—which are add-on features for dial-up telephone connections—claim they are in the high-speed Internet service provider category. Though dial-up Internet connection speeds simply cannot compete with those offered by high-speed providers, some dial-up ISPs do offer "accelerators" that offer a significant measure of improvement.

A number of companies offer Internet service via satellite—a convenience, although an expensive one, for those located in remote areas.

In all cases, your computer security begins when you buy services giving you a connection to the Internet. So, positively do not register your service in your own name or use any address that is traceable to you. Instead, utilize the paid services of a nominee to subscribe on your behalf and hold the account in his or her name. Refer to Chapter 24, "Nominees," and apply these principles to obtain anonymous Internet service.

Certain people requiring privacy have purchased high-speed Internet services using alternate names, used distant mail-drop addresses for billing, and paid for the services with alternate-name debit cards or money orders. This type of discretion in purchasing and maintaining service has eliminated the need for a nominee.

REGISTRATIONS AND SUPPLIES

Companies that sell computer products—both hardware and software—want to track their customers, as do grocery stores, cell phone companies, and many others. Provide bogus information about yourself to avoid unnecessary contact with telemarketers and other solicitors, privacy-invasive mailings, telephone calls, and spam in your e-mail box.

In order to make convenient software and computer-related purchases online anonymously, you will need a Visa or MasterCard debit card issued in an alternate name or in no name, such as is possible while using a PrivaCash Visa or MasterCard. Their website is located at *www.privacash.com*. This anonymous, worthwhile tool enables you to keep your true name out of the hands of the companies that sell these products, as well as hackers or others who make it their business to intercept personal and confidential identity information from online customers.

Debit cards with the capability of complete online account maintenance are the best for making online purchases. The use of true-name credit cards compromises customer purchases in spite of using security software to block account names and account numbers. Hackers may still retrieve this sensitive information, and the information will still be contained on the user's hard drive.

BASIC PROTECTION

Windows Operating Systems have firewalls that help protect your computer. A firewall is supposed to block computer viruses and worms from infecting your computer. Also, the firewall asks for your permission to block or unblock some connection requests. A firewall will not eliminate computer viruses or worms that have already infected your computer, nor will it stop you from opening an e-mail that contains dangerous attachments. And a firewall will not block spam from your e-mail inbox.

One available security/anti-virus protection program that offers comprehensive protection is *Norton Internet Security* by Symantec. The twelve-month subscription to the program can be purchased at *www.Symantecstore.com* for about $78.00. Included in the program are a variety of basic privacy and protection services.

It automatically downloads new protection updates and protects one's personal information on the Internet. The subscriber is notified about Internet threats, and the computer equipped with this software blocks Internet worms at the point of entry. E-mail and instant messages are scanned for viruses, and a spam blocker can be activated and programmed to block specific users and key words contained in the e-mail text or subject heading.

Viruses, worms, and Trojan horses can be removed with this program—even when they're already in the system. The user's computer is hidden from hackers, and inappropriate or distracting websites are blocked. On-line intrusions are blocked and "phishing" e-mails are filtered out. Virus infections in compressed file archives are detected in real time. Spyware and adware are detected and pop-ups are blocked. This program provides the user with control over all incoming and outgoing Internet traffic and is compatible with Win XP Home/Pro, and Win 2000 Pro.

Lavasoft offers Ad-Aware SE, a free version of Code Sequence Identification (CSI) technology, which provides a user's computer with protection from known content as well as advanced protection against many unknown variants. The program is designed to be compatible with Windows 98, 98SE, Win ME, Win NT 4, Win 2000, and Win XP Home/Professional. Lavasoft products can be found at www.lavasoft.com.

ZoneAlarm provides basic protection from hackers. Their easy-to-use firewall blocks hackers and other unknown threats while preventing them from intruding into a system and automatically makes a computer invisible to all on the Internet. Their website is located at *www.zonealarm.com*.

The Anonymizer, a security/anonymous surfing software package, provides subscribers with a good deal of anti-spyware protection as well as digital shredding capabilities. Their real IP address can be hidden and another substituted, enabling the surfer's computer to remain invisible. Certain financial institutions which allow online account access have software that detects the Anonymizer program, limiting the account once bogus or previously troublesome I.P. addresses associated with the Anonymizer are detected. The Anonymizer website is located at *www.anonymizer.com.*

CYBERSPACE TRAVEL

Millions of people travel the Internet to search for readily available information. With a virtual library at the user's fingertips, surfers can pull up articles, books, and websites and make contacts worldwide within minutes. Unfortunately, cyberspace has its share of snoopers—in government and con-man form—so protecting one's anonymity must be a priority in order to reduce the risk of losing identity, money, and information to theft.

Recognize that your computer is a potential open book without the proper security software. While Windows Operating Systems come equipped with basic firewall protection, you need to go far beyond the basics to protect yourself from intrusive threats. As with all privacy endeavors, preparation and knowledge offer the best avenues for success. Recognize the challenges that will be faced and keep up to date—the price is indeed high in the event your computer is successfully attacked.

HACKERS

How do hackers get into your computer? Through a variety of ways, depending on their skill level, the type of information available to them, and the type of hacking equipment they have at their disposal.

1. **Casing** is the acquisition of targets and information gathering. Also called footprinting, it involves profiling your Internet presence and security while you believe you are surfing safely. The hacker is planning an attack through Casing. Several items that may be used for targeting by a hacker include: Domain name, IP addresses, Network Blocks, TCP and UDP services, System architecture, Access Control lists, Intrusion Detection systems, Workgroup names, Routing tables, and Networking Protocols.

2. The most common hacker activity is known as **Port Scanning**. The hacker's goal is to determine the user's operating system and specific applications currently being used. A computer is vulnerable following a port scan because the hacker learns which

applications are capable of being invaded, as well as the security level of the operating system itself.

3. **A PING Sweep** is used to obtain a list of all devices. A hacker may order the ping program to sort IP addresses at a domain. Individual machines, network printers, and device information may be obtained through a ping sweep.

4. A computer or network may be actively spied on by a **Sniffer** who scans available resources.

5. **IP Scanning** is done with a Traceroute tool used to intercept hops in the packet flow. Passwords and other unencrypted information can be stolen, and all traffic to an entire domain name can be redirected to another website.

6. A hacker may **Register Grab** by remotely connecting to an application via telnet. Once the Enter key on the keyboard is pressed a few times, platform-specific information comes back.

IP ADDRESSES

IP means "Internet Protocol." IP addresses are similar to phone numbers in that a caller on the telephone must know which number to dial in order to reach someone at another telephone. When a computer connected to the Internet needs to send files or other information to another computer, the IP address must be known. IP addresses are shown in numbers of four groups separated by decimal points. Examples are: 10.43.985.4 and 187.165.76.331.

Every computer on the Internet has a unique IP address. The address can change when the computer is connected behind a firewall within a network, when dialing into an Internet Service Provider, and when connected to a broadband service using dynamic IP addressing. An Internal IP address is a non-routable IP address. It is a unique identifier that is specific to a single computer.

SPOOFING

E-mail "spoofing" occurs when an e-mail message appears to have come from one source but was actually sent from another. This caper is pulled by tricksters and identity thieves in an attempt to con the targeted person into revealing confidential information that will enable them to access secret data—financial accounts, for example.

COMPUTER THEFT

Regular system backups—with those backups stored either in a safe deposit box or at the off-site secure storage facility—allow you to recover data in the event your computer is lost or stolen. Providing no one is looking for you, and providing you have no clues leading to your actual home address, the chances of your computer being stolen are reduced drastically.

Laptops are convenient to carry with you whenever you leave home or the office. It takes only a minute or two to unplug, disconnect, and pack up a full-sized laptop computer. In the event a computer is stolen or lost, the data on it may fall into the wrong hands, and the owner will want to make the calls necessary to change whatever confidential information is stored in certain files. Banking, brokerage, credit card information, and passwords will be vulnerable, so recognize the danger of having this information used to access your money.

However, even if a theft does occur, verbal passwords on the accounts may prevent the thief from stealing money owned by you or under your control. Other information—your photographs, letters, e-mail and anything else you want to keep a secret—can be accessed by others if you lose your computer for whatever reason, so guard your computer to prevent your private information from becoming known by someone else.

E-MAIL ACCOUNTS

Nearly everyone who uses a computer corresponds by e-mail, due to its instant communication capability and the conveniences of e-mail and cost savings over postal mailing or telephoning. E-mail accounts vary greatly in their security capabilities, although someone with the skill and the right programs can decipher even the most complex codes, passwords, and encryptions.

Ensure against future potential problems by constructing e-mail letters and messages so that no personal information is revealed. Avoid writing something that could come back to haunt you if your computer is ever stolen, lost, or seized. For e-mail account security—although even the best are not really totally secure—you may want to visit the following sites and consider opening an e-mail account with one of these companies: www.hushmail.com, www.s-mail.com, and www.mail2web.com.

Regardless of the type of e-mail security features available on your particular account, you should avoid opening unknown e-mail attachments. Be certain that you know the source of each attachment. Otherwise, you may expose your computer to a virus that even the best anti-virus software can't stop or cure.

Using encryption and e-mail remailers adds some security to your e-mail communication. But even if you use remailers, you can sometimes be traced, and encrypted letters can be made readable once they are discovered by the right people with the right programs to decipher the encrypted communication.

PASSWORDS

A password should be constructed with the intention of making it as difficult as possible to crack for anyone who attempts to log into your secure information. Use passwords with mixed alphanumeric characters that are easy for you to remember. The use of short words combined with numbers or symbols is effective. For example: pigs-8sky and roof:tarbaby0.

PHISHING

Phishing is the practice of sending e-mail to a user while falsely claiming to be a business soliciting legitimate products or services, when in reality, a scam to obtain private information from the target is the objective. This technique is often successfully used to steal crucial identity documents and information about one's property and money.

During 2003, many users became victims of a phishing scam when e-mails were received by an eBay imposter claiming that the users' accounts were about to be suspended unless their credit card accounts with the real eBay were updated. This "phisher" spammed many eBay account holders and defrauded many who took the "fishing" bait.

PROXY SERVERS

Web proxy servers are specialized HTTP servers. Proxy servers are used to allow internal clients the ability to access the Internet from behind a firewall. Security is given to those behind the firewall. Proxy servers are generally implemented on a per-access basis. A proxy server allows calls to FTP servers. A complete proxy server allows communication between all Web protocols, with the most important ones being HTTP, FTP, Gopher, and WAIS.

OFFSHORE PROXY SERVERS

Using an offshore proxy server in a privacy-friendly country is akin to using an offshore bank—in the 1970s. While using an offshore proxy server, your Internet activities are protected, because most threats to your Internet and computer privacy are local and come from employers, business competitors, local governments, identity thieves, investigators, and nosey neighbors. Breaking through the privacy barrier provided by a proxy server in Eastern Europe may not be possible.

SECURE BROWSERS

Mozilla's *Firefox 1.5* contains an intuitive interface that blocks viruses, spyware, and pop-up ads and also delivers web pages at a high rate of speed. Firefox enhances user security while you are on the web. All personal data can be deleted with a Clear Private Data tool with only a single click. Personal data such as browsing history, cookies, web forms, and passwords can be removed.

Notrax is a secure web browser that leaves no trace of Internet activity on the user's PC. It erases session files, cookies, and cache while using secure deletion methods while browsing and when exiting browsing sessions. Cache is stored and erased in memory and is encrypted.

ANONYMOUS INTERNET SURFING

Programs that will allow the privacy advocate to hide sensitive and private files from prying eyes are available. Browser favorites, history, cookies, and image cache are completely hidden through the use of software designed to make the Internet experience a private affair. Two companies that provide applications for this purpose are at *www.anonymizer.com* and *www.privacy.com*.

KEYLOGGERS

If you use a computer at home or work, your activities may be monitored by those who want to spy on you. A spouse, a significant other, an employee, a person who is under government surveillance, or an identity theft target may be watched through the use of a keylogger program. Programs are sold for these spy-like purposes, and you could have your entire computer use history tracked without being aware of it.

Keyloggers are software applications that monitor a user's keystrokes and then send the information back to an investigator, sophisticated identity thief, stalker, or other party attempting to gain crucial information about a target. This can happen from your e-mail correspondences or your server on the web. The software "logs" can then be used to find key information, such as online brokerage or banking information, complete with your passwords and account names.

Hardware keyloggers are devices placed between the keyboard and the computer. These can only be installed by someone who has physical access to the target's computer. Anonymous living will, for the most part, eliminate the capability of one becoming a serious target of a keylogger.

Software that uses a hooking device uses Windows function SetWindowsHookEx( ) to monitor keystrokes. Any application that calls SetWindowsHooksEx( ) will be able to steal passwords. Notable keyloggers include the *Blazing Tools Perfect Keylogger, Spector, Invisible Keylogger Stealth,* and *Key Snatch.* Keyloggers can be used on both individual and networked PCs.

ANTI-KEYLOGGING SOFTWARE

Preventive keylogger software can be purchased from a number of companies. Signature-based keylogger programs are applications that typically identify a keylogger through files or DLLs that are installed plus the registry entries made. Hook-based anti-keyloggers are more effective than signature-based anti-keyloggers.

REMOVING KEYLOGGERS

According to *SpywareRemovers Review,* the top spyware/adware/malware remover programs found at their respective websites are as follows:

XoftSpy	www.paretologic.com,
NoAdware	www.noadware.com,
Spyware Nuker	www.spywarenuker.com
Pal Spyware Remover	www.palsol.com

PC Magazine contributing editor John Dvorak has recommended *SpyCop* for looking for secret keystroke-logging software. *SpyCop* software is located at *www.spycop.com*. *SpyCop* reportedly stops the potential for password theft, keeps e-mails private, and instantly kills message and chat spyware. It stops surfing monitors and keyloggers and prevents online credit card theft. Banking information is protected.

SpyCop prevents the unauthorized transfer of data and stops spyware that can help identity thieves steal your identity. *SpyCop* detects over 400 surveillance spyware products. *SpyCop* will alert the user when spyware is being used to record chat conversations and e-mail messages. It will find the intruder and allow the user to disable the spyware. *SpyCop* effectively destroys keylogger programs and protects the system against intrusions.

TROJAN HORSES

A Trojan horse is a harmful application that is masked by appearing to be a good program. Trojan horses are spread by hiding them inside a normal distribution of software programs. Trojan horses are also spread through e-mail. The attacker will send the target an e-mail with an attachment called something designed to appeal to the receiver such as "beautiful women.exe."

If the attachment is opened, the Trojan horse can infect the receiver's system—unless it is detected in time by security software and either removed or quarantined. Chat systems such as AIM, MSN, or Yahoo Messenger are also used to spread a Trojan horse.

A Trojan horse virus is a virus spread by a user who executes it. For instance, a Trojan horse virus might require a user to open an attached file to an e-mail message. In order to protect yourself from being infected by a Trojan horse, do not run programs sent by e-mail or chat systems. One company that markets software for the removal of the Trojan horse may be found at *www.tech-faq.com*.

CARNIVORE

"Carnivore" is a computer used by the FBI that is equipped with software able to scan Internet traffic at a high rate of speed. It attaches to an ISP and is used legitimately by way of search warrants on particular subjects or illegitimately to watch everyone using a given ISP.

A privacy site, *www.Privacy.org*, recommends consumers ask their

ISP the following questions concerning Carnivore: (direct quotes of recommended questions are taken from this website).

1. *Has the FBI ever asked to install Carnivore (or EtherPeek, or any similar system)?*

2. *Has Carnivore (or a similar system) ever been installed in their facilities?*

3. *Is Carnivore (or a similar system) now installed on their facilities?*

4. *If yes to 1. or 2., what was the ISP's response? Did the ISP offer to obtain the information under court order so that Carnivore would not be necessary? Did the ISP retain counsel to fight such a broad search in the courts, and appeal it to the highest level?*

5. *If yes to 2. and 3., what steps did the ISP take to assure that the privacy of its users would be protected? Did the ISP gain access to Carnivore's source code to verify FBI claims? Did the ISP check the information FBI obtained from the Carnivore machine, either remotely or through physical collection of recordable media?*

6. *If yes to 2. or 3., is the ISP aware of any other capabilities FBI might have installed?*

7. *If FBI or any government agency gains or attempts to gain access to all user traffic information on the ISP, will the ISP inform its users? Under what circumstances will the ISP inform its users of unwarranted monitoring by investigators?*

These questions may serve as a screening mechanism for privacy-conscious individuals and businesses to use when they shop for an Internet Service Provider.

DELETING FILES AND FOLDERS

Anyone using a computer over time can accumulate files that could either cause simple embarrassment or result in the user being questioned by authorities who obtain information via the Internet, from e-mail correspondences, or other world wide web sources.

For privacy-seekers, the complete deletion of sensitive files from the hard drive is the desired objective. While this may be impossible to do without the right software—and in fact some say it is impossible anyway—there are companies that sell software for this very purpose. One such company can be found at *www.stompsoft.com*. This company sells a product purported to permanently delete files without the possibility of recovery. The software—*Digital File Shredder*—shreds, obliterates and renders unrecoverable any file or folder you designate to be deleted from the hard drive.

File Shredder Pro will shred information contained in the recycle bin, as well as e-mail contents, individual files and folders, and Internet/Windows "tracks" (such as find history, run history, clipboard, common dialog history, temp files, recent documents, *index.dat* files, cookies, IE and AOL cache, IE and AOL history, auto complete files, and Microsoft Office recently opened documents). Additionally, a system cleaner is sold to eliminate all traces of Internet activity

DELETING HARD DRIVES

Every bit of information ever entered on a computer hard drive potentially can be recovered. Whether one accumulates sensitive data that will compromise personal privacy, or business-related information, steps can be taken to destroy or wipe a hard drive clean. And since data recovery can destroy lives and data recovery companies are on the rise, an understanding of how to prevent this recovery is essential for computer privacy.

Forensic software programs, including *enCase* and *F.R.E.D.*, allow data recovery of all information ever downloaded onto a computer. Police, investigators, government agencies, bosses, spouses, and identity thieves buy these programs and scour computers to attempt to bring old data—believed to be deleted—back to life.

One program that claims it can destroy all data once and for all without the danger and risk of having anything recovered ever is *Sneakyclean,* located at *www.sneakyclean.com.* Another program, *WipeDrive,* is marketed by Whitecanyon software, which sells software to prevent identity theft and other privacy and security programs. Their website is at *www.WhiteCanyon.com*

If you believe that these programs will fail to wipe the slate clean on all past computer activity from an old computer that is to be donated, for example, you may remove the hard drive and saw it into pieces or use a welding torch to cut it into pieces and place the separate pieces into several trash bins. Now your "shredded" hard drive cannot cause any future problems.

USING THIRD-PARTY COMPUTERS

Public computers found at Internet cafés, libraries, copy stores, and airports are cheaper than buying your own computer and offer privacy and security—when you use these third-party computers correctly. In order to avoid sharing your personal and financial information with potential identity thieves and others, some basic rules should be followed when using public computers.

Your login information should not be saved. Log out of websites by pressing logout on the given site rather than by closing the browser itself. This will help guard against other users accessing your information. Disable automatic login features that let you save your passwords. Never leave a computer you use in a public place logged on. Your unattended computer will allow someone else to view your sensitive information.

When it becomes necessary for you to leave—even for a brief period of time—log out of all programs and close all windows. Once you have completed your work on a public computer, erase all of your activity. In order to eliminate temporary Internet files and your history, find the appropriate features inside the browser.

Public computers will probably have common browsers on their machines such as Internet Explorer. You can delete your activity under Internet Options while using this browser. Also, under the General tab, you can delete files and cookies. Under History, click to delete the history of files visited.

Beware of snoops looking over your shoulder while you are using a public computer. Position yourself in a spot that enables your computer to have minimal exposure to people who may want to steal your sensitive information and passwords—even if this means waiting for a computer with an ideal location within the library, café, airport, or copy store.

Try to avoid entering your most sensitive information when using a public computer. Sometimes identity thieves and other crooks install software on a public computer that will record every keystroke and then email all of the captured information back to the installer's remote computer or server.

Positive aspects of using a third-party computer include a useless IP address and Internal IP address for identifying you as the user of a certain computer—providing you have not given your true name to those renting the machine to you. Libraries may require the computer user to provide a library card to use their public computers. Certain cafés in Europe may demand a user's I.D. card prior to using their computers.

So make decisions that allow you to maintain your privacy if you take advantage of the convenience of public computers.

COMPUTER SERVICE AND REPAIRS

For many computer users, services and repairs from computer service personnel are a regular part of office maintenance. Of course, there are security and privacy advantages to performing the maintenance and repairs yourself, providing you have the necessary skills, time, and expertise.

If it becomes necessary to use an outside service company, follow the privacy guidelines stressed throughout this book—utilize companies and individuals who have been prescreened and meet them for the repairs at a neutral site or at their shop and await the repairs being completed during the same workday whenever possible. Also, keep your true name and home or office address out of their customer databases. Pay cash for services and repairs.

PRIVATE DOMAIN REGISTRATION

Anyone can access "Whois" and determine who is the registered owner of a given domain name—unless the registrant pays extra for "private registration." Private registration of domain names is important so that no one will be able to identify you through domain names you own for a specified period of time. It is possible to leave no trace of your true name and location through privacy tactics used to register domain names. You should own domain names completely anonymously in order to avoid unnecessary intrusions from anyone—all government agencies and identity thieves included—as well as private investigators who may be investigating a particular person or business behind a domain name.

Private registration of domain names is available from companies that provide "private" registration services for an extra fee. Without this service, the "owner" may be subjected to unnecessary inquiries and spam, as the information on record should be accurate—at least at the time the domain name is purchased.

But the shield provided to protect the identity of "private" registrants of domain names can be easily penetrated by government agencies, with little resistance from the company claiming to provide anonymous domain registration. (This is the reason for the Nevada LLC and trust manager—even though these are privately registered, when government uncovers them, nothing will be revealed except a trust manager with a foreign mail drop.)

Avoid using nominees to hold these domain names. Instead, utilize the same principles outlined for holding other companies under an owner's control. A Nevada LLC as the actual owner, with an irrevocable trust as the "manager" and an offshore address, is a good structural choice for holding domain names.

An alternate name can be the contact person and become the "representative" for the company whenever telephone or email contact is necessary. These privacy measures become even more necessary during the current zeitgeist, as government readies itself to continue its illegal spy activities targeting citizens' computer activities and telephone correspondences.

Website owners with domain names under their control may become the subject of such investigations, so it is important to leave no traces to your true name and location when you purchase and register domains. Always pay for domain names with money orders. Some companies accept only credit cards for payment, so to cover your tracks entirely, find a company that accepts money orders.

SUMMARY

1. Computers purchased with cash and registered anonymously will not compromise the user's privacy. Laptops offer higher security and are easily transported.

2. Store backup data off site or with a third-party data storage company.

3. For confidentiality, nominees can purchase Internet service.

4. An alternate name and an anonymous debit card for online purchases of supplies and equipment will prevent links to one's personal and confidential information.

5. Anti-virus programs and security software can conceal a computer's real I.P. address while on the Internet and eliminate access to surfing activity and records.

6. Hackers steal identities, money, and information and threaten personal security.

7. Computer theft is a common occurrence. Guard your computer and keep up-to-date backup data. Removable hard drives may add to data security.

8. Take care to avoid revealing highly sensitive business and personal information through e-mail correspondences. Encryption and passwords will add to security.

9. Phishing via e-mail is an identity theft threat that warrants special attention.

10. Proxy servers offer anonymity. Offshore proxy servers add security and the advantage of an offshore jurisdiction.

11. Internet privacy can be enhanced through the choice of browsers; privacy software programs can make the user anonymous during web surfing.

12. Keylogger software monitors the target computer keystrokes. Anti-keylogger software removes keylogger programs.

13.	A Trojan horse is commonly spread through e-mail and chat systems.

14.	Carnivore—the F.B.I. computer—threatens the privacy of all who use computers.

15.	The best defense against intrusions is anonymity in all computer-related tasks.

16.	Deleting files, folders, and hard drives completely can be accomplished through the use of the appropriate software or by physically destroying hard drives.

17.	Third-party computers eliminate a trail to the user's I.P. address and registration information but may have keylogger software installed on them.

18.	Screen computer service personnel; pay cash for products and services.

19.	You can register domains anonymously using a Nevada LLC and a trust manager with a "manager" contact address located off shore.

FIFTEEN

Anonymous Banking

"It is well that the people of the nation do not understand our banking and monetary system, for if they did, I believe there would be a revolution before tomorrow morning."—Henry Ford

WHERE'S THE MONEY?

As you take the necessary steps to make your life private, consider making your personal money become "invisible," with no obvious links to you. This secrecy in your normal banking routine will shield your funds from the prying eyes of identity thieves, investigators, would-be wage garnishment agencies, and others who want to know the source and location of your money.

For those who live in the U.S., high-level banking secrecy is best accomplished by using an American bank. Access to your funds and timely clearance of checks and other negotiable instruments is assured,

while a high level of privacy is also achieved, providing that you carefully take the proper steps to open a bank account and maintain confidential banking practices for maximum privacy.

Due to the importance of keeping your personal money a secret, you should devote as much time as necessary to establishing and maintaining a high level of banking security. Once you follow the routine outlined in this chapter, no one except the bank with whom you do business will know where you house your money. True banking secrecy—with you in full control—is doable in the U.S. Learn to do it right, and you'll benefit from anonymous banking.

TRUST ACCOUNT

The most private and cost-effective way for a U.S. citizen to handle his or her personal finances is by opening a non–interest-bearing checking account in the name of a trust in a United States Bank.

First, a trust must be created with a name that has no similarity to your true name. You may employ an attorney to create a trust, or buy a blank generic trust form at a legal forms store—or at some office supply stores—then fill in the blanks for the name, address, *grantor,* trustee, and other essential particulars and have the document properly notarized. Then you'll have a legal document that is a separate entity capable of holding a bank account and other property for the benefit of others.

Generally, a revocable trust is used for banking purposes, because it can be changed as necessary by revisions that you, the trustee, see fit to make. Consult your attorney for changes if the need arises. One important advantage of using a trust to hold personal money is the privacy associated with the entity itself. A trust does not have any registration requirements anywhere—unlike an LLC, limited partnership, or corporation.

Also, these business entities are designed to separate you from personal money and other assets. A bank account held by a corporation, LLC, or family limited partnership cannot be used for depositing your personal checks, for example. A trust can be used for the deposit of checks to the trustee(s) individually, as well as to deposit and clear checks made payable to the trust itself.

Thus, a trust titled as The Midwestern Beechwood Trust, of which Joe Able Jones and Kathy Bertha Klinkensmith-Jones are trustees, may be used for the deposit of checks made payable to The Midwestern

Beechwood Trust, Joe Able Jones, or Kathy Bertha Klinkensmith-Jones. In this illustration—a purely fictional one—additional flexibility is possible regarding acceptance of checks, because the bank will surely accept checks made payable to one trustee, Kathy Bertha Klinkensmith-Jones, in either her married name alone, married name with the hyphenated maiden name, or maiden name alone.

Additionally, both trustees could, without a doubt, simply have checks made payable to any combination of their initials only, followed by their last names, which adds even more privacy for the person or persons behind the trust account. However, for the utmost in privacy, the trustees will be best served to use the trust's name as the payee name when receiving payment by check, as no one except the bank where the trust account is held will be aware of the identity of the trustees and *signers* on the trust account.

Once you have formed a trust for the purpose of holding a checking account, you as trustee have total control over decisions regarding how the account is handled, all the while preserving your anonymity, even when and if you sign a check drawn on the account. While the bank in which the trust account is held will have your name as "trustee" and "signer" on the account records, the trust will be on record as the "owner" and account holder of the checking account.

Please remember that you as trustee are not the owner, only the

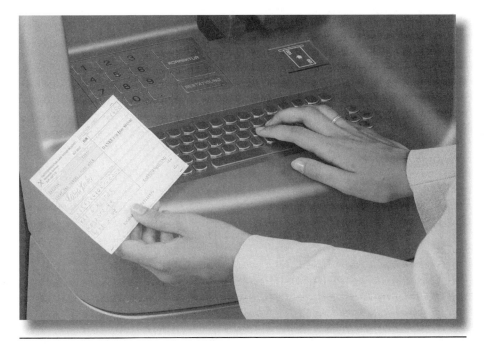

signer, of the account. A non–interest-bearing account is recommend-ed, because the purpose of the account is to store money short term as well as to clear checks, whether these are made payable to the trust's name or to the trustee(s).

A trust, the most private of all legal entities, when used for the pur-pose of holding a checking account, will entirely eliminate the need for any trustee and signer to have a checking account in his or her name. However, any trustee and signer can make withdrawals in person or from an automatic teller machine (ATM) as he or she deems necessary, deposit checks made payable to any trustee or to the trust, utilize the Automatic Clearing House (ACH), receive and send money via a bank wire transfer, write checks on the account, use the account for the pur-pose of purchasing cashier's checks, or use any other banking service offered by the banking institution.

The one exception that may be unavailable to trust accounts is on-line banking, which in my experience requires privacy-invasive person-al information about the trustee. And since our primary goal of using a *trust checking account* is for the privacy associated with this account, I do not recommend that trustee(s) provide unnecessary personal in-formation to the bank just for the privilege of being able to access the account online.

In order to open a bank account in the name of a trust, it is necessary to obtain a tax identification number from the Internal Revenue Service. A Form SS4 must be completed and sent to the IRS for a number to be assigned to the trust. Some very particular trustees have been known to add an "administrative trustee" to the trust for the sole purpose of delegating to this person the respon-sibility of obtaining the trust's employment identification number (EIN).

Whoever completes Form SS4 will be required to provide evi-dence in writing of his or her eligibility for obtaining the EIN on be-half of the trust. Any trustee should have the power to do this and must sign the form under the penalty of perjury, swearing to have this power under provisions of the trust. Make sure that whoever requests the EIN is authorized to do it according to the provisions of the trust.

A company tax identification number or Social Security number must be provided by the person signing the Form SS4, thus provid-ing the IRS a paper trail linked to the trust's tax identification number. Although privacy is sacrificed by providing the IRS with an identifying number of the trustee who completed the Form SS4 for the trust, this is not meaningful. The bank account will not generate a 1099 form, since no interest is paid on a non–interest-bearing checking account. Essentially, the IRS will never know or care about the trust's checking account.

And when an administrative trustee obtains the tax I.D. number for the trust under their Social Security number or a company EIN with which they are associated, the trustee(s) may become entirely disassociated with the IRS tracking system—depending on whether the administrative trustee knows the trustee(s) by name.

CHEXSYSTEMS: BANKING'S BIG BROTHER

Banks employ *ChexSystems* and similar services to access historical bank records under a huge database. The key identifying information is the Social Security number. This ferrets out the bad boys and girls who skipped out while owing any bank money for checks written on accounts with insufficient funds, the check-kiting crowd, and just plain old "bad check" writing and other common and uncommon forms of fraud that cost banks money.

Depending on the level of seriousness of the problem, those whose names cause the computer to "ding" once their Social Security number is entered may be banned from being customers of the bank for five years or longer. I have been told, however, that the records never actually leave the ChexSystems database.

How to handle the ChexSystems inquiry? Sometimes an empathetic banker who has agreed to respect your privacy by using only the tax identification number of the trust (and not your Social Security number) on the trust bank account will enter your name and Social Security number into the ChexSystems database and, once you prove yourself free of problems in the banking world, the banker will purge it from the banking records. Thus it is used only temporarily, perhaps for a minute or two, and is not kept in the bank's records.

Another idea is to provide business and banking references to the bank manager in addition to using your people skills to convince the banker of your integrity.

My first choice is to have no information required whatsoever concerning past banking relationships. Sometimes regional banks and small community banks, particularly in medium-sized cities and small towns in western states, are receptive to customers who appear to be business-minded new "residents" who have recently relocated. Favorable impressions made on bankers can lead to leniency for the prospective new customer, providing that he or she convinces the banker that a productive future banking relationship will be the result of the account about to be opened.

When dealing with the ChexSystems issue, in the event it comes up, be prepared to present your best case to convince the banker of your worthiness as a new banking customer. Dress well, appear well groomed, speak with clear diction, and deal with the bank manager only. Your tone and position should be firm but not overbearing.

Realize, too, that providing too much information to a bank compromises your privacy, and you may be best served by negotiating the amount of information requested by the bank. Dealing with bank managers is paramount, because they often can override certain policies when presented with a rationale to do so by a fluent, on-point discussion from a convincing business person.

So feel free to make whatever privacy requests you see fit, including waiving ChexSystems, prior to agreeing to open an account.

Of course, you should not do business with a banker or a bank unless you are satisfied that your personal privacy requirements are met to your satisfaction. There are many banks in the United States, so find one that will handle the trust account with your privacy in mind, thus minimizing your chances of having any account security breaches or unnecessary risks of theft of the trust's money.

Until recently, when they changed their policies, an organization known as Americans for Lawful Financial Independence and Information (ALFII) promised that members could open an association bank account for personal or business purposes, and that neither a Social Security number nor *employer identification number (EIN)* would be required to open the account (see Chapter 17, "Private Investments," for more details).

BANKING SIGNATURE

The trustee's privacy is assured when a unique, unidentifiable signature is used for banking purposes. Anyone who happens to see the signature associated with the trust account will have no idea of the identity of the trust's signatories, when an illegible scrawl is placed on a check drawn on the trust account. And this is exactly what you want for privacy purposes.

Practice producing a consistent, illegible signature that cannot be associated with your true name, and use this "mark" when your signature is required. Your signature must be consistent, because the bank will store it and access it from the signature card when certain types of banking services are performed. Cash withdrawals will require your signature, which will be checked and verified against your original signature card being used as a signature reference.

Account signer signatures are checked prior to bank wires being sent, when withdrawing cash, and when checks are presented for payment, although banks often fail to scrutinize signatures closely. Identity thieves and other criminals will often attempt to copy the signatures of those whose identity and money they intend to steal, so make yours absolutely impossible for them to associate with your name

TRUST ACCOUNT REQUIREMENTS

Make twelve different telephone calls to bankers asking what information is required to open a non–interest-bearing checking account in the name of a trust and expect to talk to no more than one person who is able to answer your questions. The other eleven may place you on hold, ask supervisors what is necessary, and talk to you through the other person as you inquire about what is actually needed by the trustee to open an account in the trust's name. The level of ignorance about trusts and business entities is so high among American bankers that you may find yourself educating a bank assistant manager on the meaning and powers of a trust as a holder of assets.

My advice is to remain patient and humble as you field elementary questions about the trust and the trust documents. It is to your advantage to tell the banker what you as a trustee require, that is, a non–interest-bearing checking account to hold funds and clear checks made payable to the trust and/or any trustees and signers on the account.

Also, because privacy is your primary goal, explain your privacy objectives to the banker. You will best utilize your time by screening potential banks via telephone to determine how amenable their managers are to assisting you in your quest for banking privacy through a trust account. You'll generally find bankers in medium-sized cities and small towns most congenial and easiest to do business with.

Regional banks, money-center banks, or small community banks can serve you equally well, however, providing they are willing to meet your banking services and privacy requirements. Banks generally want to see and photocopy portions of the trust. The title page, signature page (which indicates the trustee's names and notarized signatures), and that portion stating the trust has the capability of owning property, including bank accounts, will be required. Do not provide copies of anything else.

The bank has no business knowing all of the particulars of your private affairs, so use your discretion and provide only what is absolutely necessary to open the trust account. The bank will require the trust's tax identification number for their banking records, and most banks also will ask for your Social Security number as a part of identifying you as a signer on the trust account.

When you question the bank about why your Social Security number is necessary, remember that the trust's tax identification number meets the only IRS requirement banks must verify for trust accounts. The banker will typically tell you that due to the Patriot Act, they are required to have it in their records. The Patriot Act requires banks to "know their customers" and does not specifically require the trustee or signer's Social Security number.

It is best not to argue the point, however, as being right and winning a debate on the banker's turf accomplishes very little. Your time is better spent finding a bank and banker who will do it your way, and while your risk of having your personal SSN on the account is debatable, some people have avoided giving it by explaining their privacy requirements to the bank and screening potential banks who will open the trust account using only the tax identification number of the trust with identity documents only of the trustee.

I have opened business accounts and trust accounts without ever providing my SSN to the banker. This was done after 9/11/01 and implementation of the Patriot Act. So, don't let anyone tell you it cannot be done. If your SSN is on the bank records, with other trustee information on the trust bank account, you as a signer risk being discovered in the event assets are searched under the trustee's name. This is relevant, because a trust, while a very private entity, will not serve to protect you as trustee from any personal debts or other liabilities.

Asset searches vary a great deal as to their sophistication and thoroughness. The risk of a trustee being discovered while a search is performed under his name and while being associated with the anonymous trust's name as a signer on the account will depend on how the account records are stored by the bank—as well as the criteria used and information available to those doing the asset search. With this in mind, take special precautions with this account by keeping the balance low and not providing your SSN to the bank, whenever possible to do so. Certain privacy advocates do not reveal their mother's true maiden name to banks.

In addition to these precautions, see to it that the bank titles the account in the name of the trust only, without you as trustee being on the bank account, title records, or statements that are mailed each month. Insist on having the statements mailed as follows:

Midwestern Beechwood Trust
123 South Privateandfree Street
Anytown, Moststates 77777, U.S.A.

Banks sometimes include the name(s) of the trustee(s) on the statement as well as on the title of the account. Insist that trustee(s) are not included on either and speak to a high-level bank manager to accomplish this important privacy security measure. A story regarding a previous identity theft—or identity theft attempt—will add a great deal of weight to your case for having everything on record at the bank in the trust's name only, without mention of any trustee.

TRUSTEE REQUIREMENTS AND BANKING SECURITY

Use your U.S. passport as your primary identification document when opening an account in the name of the trust. An additional secondary identity document, such as an insurance card, is generally all that is required for your identification. However, in certain cases, a driver's license from the state where the bank is located will be required, so you may need to make adjustments or look for a different bank. Banks often require a local mailing address at the time the account is opened, although they will often send the statements anywhere in the world once the account has been opened for a period of time.

Use a local nominee to receive the mail for the trust. Later, you can have bank statements mailed to your offshore address—that of a new nominee, who will forward the mail back to you as per your request. Receiving statements for the trust account out of the country, preferably in a western European country, will reduce the chances of having government snoops perform a *"mail cover" operation*—a covert affair in which your business and/or personal mail is officially investigated without your knowledge.

Likewise, private investigators, identity thieves, and other criminals will have more difficulty stealing your mail when it goes straight from the bank to your offshore address. However, customs agents sometimes open and inspect mail coming into the country, so you can expect this to happen. To reduce the chances of U.S. Customs knowing your business by way of opening your mail, use two mail drops—one from Europe, followed by a Canadian mail-forwarding service, which you instruct to send mail on to your American mail-drop address.

Receive the trust bank statements from your mail forwarding nominee under an alternate name or a non-registered company name in order to remain anonymous to any government snoops or potential identity thieves who may be attempting to trace you and your money. Mail received in the U.S. from Canada is the least likely of all countries to be opened by U.S. Customs.

U.S. banks, unlike foreign banks, are usually unwilling to hold bank statements for long periods of time, so you will need a reliable nominee to receive the statements. When the statements contain only the trust's name, address, account number, and banking activity, without mention of the trustee's name, identity thieves have no resources from which to draw.

Without a signer's name, the potential thief will be left with only the bank as a source of your true identity. The bank will not provide this to non-customers, so the would-be identity thief or other snoop or crook will move on to another person without such a high level of banking privacy.

HIGH-LEVEL PRIVACY RECOMMENDATIONS

Request that the bank hold and not return the few cancelled checks that are written on the account. For additional account security, instruct the bank to place a pass code on the account that must be recited whenever any signer calls regarding the account.

This will eliminate identity thieves from tampering with your money and account, even if they should discover your mother's maiden name, your SSN, the trust's tax identification number, trust's name, address, and any other information that might persuade the clerk at the banking center boiler room to release information that could result in theft. With the pass code word in place, your account will remain under your full control.

Do not give anyone your code name or other personal and confidential banking information. In fact, I do not recommend that you share any information about your business with anyone who does not have a need to know it. Shred and discard the checks the bank gives you following the opening of the trust account. Order new checks beginning with a high number from a mail-order house or use a computer program with check paper to print your own.

Do not have any name or address printed on the front of the check. The bank's name, the trust account number, and routing number—as well as sequential check numbers—are all that should be on your checks, for maximum personal security.

This is all the information required for the checks to clear through the Federal Reserve Bank system. A check with only the bank name, account number, and routing number will increase your privacy a great deal, because crooks often trace the account holder, even trust account holders, through names and addresses—so include neither on your checks.

Banks will not authorize their supplier to print the checks this way, so you will have to take care of these important tasks yourself. When you receive checks, money orders, cashier's checks, insurance drafts, or any negotiable instrument for deposit into the trust account, do not endorse it with your signature, because it is possible that someone could then copy your signature and find a way to discover your identity.

Instead of endorsing checks, order a rubber stamp that states "For Deposit Only," along with the bank name and the account number. This rubber stamp, too, will require a special order from a mail-order house that supplies checks and banking supplies. Some office supply stores will also produce rubber stamps as per your special order.

TRUST ACCOUNT DEBIT CARD

A trust account MasterCard or Visa debit card can be a good addition to your privacy arsenal, providing you are able to convince the bank to produce it with only the trust's name on it. Typically, the bank will print the trustee's name only on the card or, in some cases, the trust's name with the trustee's name beneath it. When questioned about it, bankers will usually not have a good explanation as to why they issue the cards this way, but I have found that when the right managers are confronted, they will see to it that the card is printed as per your request.

Sometimes this takes some doing, but it is worth your while to have it done so that your name does not appear on the card. When the trust's name is all that is printed, you have an *anonymous debit card* that is valuable for securing hotel rooms and making anonymous purchases, with only the bank knowing who is behind the trust account debit card.

Also, a debit card issued by either MasterCard or Visa provides the same purchasing conveniences and versatility as a normal credit card, minus the credit bureau reporting, which enhances your privacy and lessens your chances of having personal information stolen. Use a code to access your account through the ATM machine that is uncommon and known only to you—do not share it with anyone.

DUAL TRUST ACCOUNT PRINCIPLE

For banking secrecy, establish two separate trust accounts with different banks. Use one bank for normal deposits of payroll checks, insurance drafts, government checks, or any other payment received and payable to you or the trust. Also write checks, withdraw cash for cashier's checks, and send and receive wires and utilize the ACH features on this account.

This account becomes the "public" trust account, as any one of those businesses, agencies, or individuals who have issued checks to the trust or trustees can discover your account number and bank when they retrieve the check which they have issued to you, providing you have deposited said check to the *public trust account.*

As soon as funds clear in the public trust account, withdraw the cash, keeping only a minimal balance in the account. Then convert this cash from the public trust account into money orders, stamp them "For Deposit Only," and deposit them into the second trust account, designated as the "private" trust account.

Do not write checks, use the ACH feature, send or receive wires, or purchase any cashier's checks with this account—as an account source of funds and reference account. Keep this account private by depositing only cash and money orders into the account. Make cash withdrawals only from this account, making it the ultimate *private trust account.* This system allows you to have a high level of security with two separate trust accounts being used for maximum privacy.

The public account becomes your "full use" account, while the private account becomes your "restricted use" account. By combining the two accounts, you as trustee gain full use of the trust as a privacy feature by being able to fully use the public account while maintaining secrecy through limited, restricted use of the private account. Maximum privacy is achieved through this system of banking. For an additional layer of banking secrecy, use two separate trusts for these two bank accounts.

TRUST ACCOUNT LIMITATIONS

The purpose of using a trust account for banking is to shield yourself from those who want to know your financial business. By establishing a separate entity in a name unrelated to your true name, as well as having a separate trust tax identification number, you are able to privatize your banking activities, providing the additional privacy tactics are followed as described.

Keep in mind that there is no way to keep a collection agency, a court, or a government agency from seizing this account if the account is discovered, and you, as trustee, are personally liable for a debt. A trust does not protect you from any personal liability, debts, or judgments. So realize that the purpose of this type of bank account is the privacy associated with clearing trust and personal checks and the ability to store personal money in the trust's name.

CHECK-CASHING STORES

Many people successfully handle their personal finances without using a bank. Pseudo-banking businesses—those check-cashing stores you see on every corner, particularly in the Southwestern United States where the demand is great—have become a tremendous growth industry, due to the estimated 5,000 to 10,000 illegal-alien Mexicans who cross into the United States each day and need a way to cash their earnings collected from employers who break laws by hiring them.

You, too, however, can increase your privacy by using these businesses to clear checks if you require the highest level of financial privacy available and don't mind the outrageous fees they charge for routine check cashing services. Fees range from approximately 2.9 percent on payroll checks to 5 percent on personal checks and money orders, to astronomical rates of 15 percent of the check amount on insurance drafts. Multiply these fees at annual percentage rates, and you will see why this is a growth industry.

Check-cashing companies provide these services to customers who are either on the lam, illegally working in the country, have previously had banking problems and are unable to open accounts with banks, or require very high level financial privacy and do not want to risk clearing checks through a bank or having a bank account of any kind.

CHECK-CASHING STORE EXPERIENCES

As previously mentioned, I receive mail under alternate names and company names. On one particular occasion, having ordered merchandise by mail under an alternate name, I had to request a refund from the business that sold me the item. A telephone call to the company resulted in a promise to refund the money following the return of the item to their factory.

At that time, I did not give any thought to the name the refund check would be made payable to, but the only name the merchant had in reference to my order was my alternate name, so within a couple of weeks, a check for the returned item was received with my alternate name as the payee.

After receiving the check, I decided to present it for payment at a local check-cashing store, and I recall that the amount was under $50, so I did not anticipate any problem, as it was rightfully my money regardless of whether the payee section was in my alternte name or my true name. Of course, there was no government record of my alternate name identification, so it could not be verified through any database.

However, the check was verifiable and determined to be genuine by the check-cashing store, with sufficient funds available in the account from which it was drawn, which was in another state. I was asked to endorse the check and then received my money, minus the check cashing fees, of course.

On a second occasion, I received a refund check from a state government agency for a car registration, and as the automobile I drive is titled in the name of a trust only, without mention of myself as trustee, the check was made payable to the trust. Now, this particular trust—one of the irrevocable variety—was created for the sole purpose of owning the car in order to provide a high level of security as I drive.

This check, an amount under $100, could not be deposited in any account under my control, and the trust holding title to the car held no bank accounts, had no tax identification number, and I had no desire to obtain either, yet wanted the money due me. Several calls were made to banks where I am the signer on various business and trust accounts as well as to a stock brokerage firm with which I had a long-term business relationship.

I explained the circumstances and offered to produce the trust documents, in original form, complete with notarized signatures. But this simple service of cashing the check payable to the trust of which I was trustee was refused by all institutions, in spite of my business relationships with them. Banks and other financial institutions will often accept checks without all the I's dotted and T's crossed but will not clear a check made payable to a complete stranger or strange entity—as was the case with this trust check.

So in spite of having a long relationship as a trustee and signer on accounts with banks as well as being the signer on business accounts, I was unable to cash this check with any bank or financial institution.

I called several check-cashing stores, and one manager advised me that he expected they could cash the check. My U.S. passport was presented as well as the original trust, and I advised the supervisor that I would not authorize them to make a copy of either for their files. Viewing the passport with a matching name on the trust naming me as trustee was sufficient for their purposes.

So following this brief period of proving my identity, plus the completion of a very short form with my name, offshore address, and two unverifiable references as well as a contact phone number which was also not linked to me, I was out the door, minus my 4 percent in fees, of course.

These experiences taught me the value of these businesses for those requiring extremely high level security as far as their finances are concerned. You could operate completely anonymously—either while using an alternate name, or while using a trust without a tax identification number yet using your true identification—in the event you receive payment for goods or services under the name of a trust of which you are the trustee.

In either case, the only remaining available records of the transactions would be the endorsement signature on the check and your name and address in the check-cashing store's file. This limited information does not pose privacy problems if your address in their files is from another country, if there is no photo identification in their records, and if they have no phone number tied to your true name.

I was advised by the manager of the check-cashing store that I could now cash any check made payable to any trust or business entity once I provided the proper paper documents indicating my power to sign on behalf of the given trust or business. No tax identification number or Social Security number is required if you choose to operate the way I have described in the above actual case.

In the event you are exempt from paying taxes in the U.S.A., authorization to do the signing on behalf of a trust or business entity—as documented in the paperwork of the entity itself—is all that is required to clear checks made payable to this same entity. This allows you essentially to operate entirely beneath the normal highly scrutinized system of banking and employment records kept on individuals in the U.S.

So in the event you ever need the highest possible level of financial privacy, you now know what is possible through the use of the many check-cashing stores, that will give you high-level anonymity for your finances—in exchange for huge fees, of course. Check-cashing stores offer those who wish to minimize their chances of becoming victims of identity theft an extremely private means of converting checks into cash. If you use these stores, you reduce the risk of having your assets stolen, since no information is available on your money anywhere.

ALTERNATE-NAME BUSINESS ENTITY CONCEPT

While on the subject of very high-level financial privacy, a method exists whereby you can utilize the protection of a business to conceal your identity as well as protect your money. While this is not a recommendation, I am aware that this method has been successfully used by individuals who required an extremely high level of privacy.

Let's consider the case of a woman I will call Betty Muñoz. Betty Muñoz was hit with a double dose of bad luck during the course of two years when her ex-husband engaged in a stalking campaign that included the bugging of her telephones at home and at work, as well as unannounced visits to her home. The man, a convicted felon, reportedly abused her on multiple occasions. All of this was done in spite of a court-issued restraining order.

After a period of time, Betty, believing that her life was in danger, packed her suitcases and left the state in search of freedom from her tormentor. Soon she encountered another problem, one familiar to many Americans today, as it is the fastest-growing crime in the U.S.A. While trying to do her routine personal banking, Betty discovered she had become a victim of identity theft. Although the culprit—an illegal alien Mexican woman who assumed Betty's Spanish surname successfully for over a year—was apprehended, our victim was left penniless, deep in debt, and without her once-spotless credit report.

Having had her personal bank account stolen and her credit cards used without her authorization by the identity thief, Betty sought out a solution while the problems were being sorted out by law enforcement, the bank and credit card companies, the three major credit bureaus, the Social Security Administration, the Department of Motor Vehicles, and others.

Left with only the cash in her pocket, she formed an LLC under the name of Susan Flowers, LLC, obtained a tax identification number for the business, and obtained good-quality alternate identification in the name of Susan Flowers. She used a commercial bank to open a non–interest-bearing checking account under Susan Flowers, LLC. The banker was privy to viewing the proper company documents—which included the *articles of organization* and the LLC's tax identification number.

Her true identification documents—those of Betty Muñoz—were used, of course, for the bank's identification requirements of the signer on the business account. Once this was completed, our previously abused identity theft victim began reshaping her life in complete financial privacy. Being a medical technician, Betty (a.k.a. Susan Flowers) began working on a per diem basis for a local medical registry.

Our resourceful lady had previously met with the director of personnel at the registry and explained her privacy requirements, presented herself as a manager of the aforementioned LLC, and offered the services of the company—her medical technician skills, in fact—in exchange for the usual and customary rates paid to registry medical technicians.

Now there happened to be a shortage of qualified medical technicians in the area, and since our enterprising LLC manager was in demand, she was advised to provide the LLC's tax identification number and begin work as per the job referrals provided by the employment coordinator of the medical registry. Soon, she began circulating to whatever hospital required her services—or rather the LLC's services—and checks began coming to her mail drop in the name of Susan Flowers, LLC.

And since no employer's new-hire records or any employment-related database contained her true name, only the LLC's, she escaped any possible discovery through her employment and was, at last, free of her abusive ex-hubby or anyone else attempting to learn her location by way of her employer.

The LLC bank account was used to clear checks received and made payable to Susan Flowers, LLC, from the medical registry. ATM machines were used for cash withdrawals as Betty began paying her bills through the use of money orders and cash, by necessity, due to the ruinous effects of the identity theft crime. High-level privacy was also achieved by paying her bills with cash and money orders only.

Because she needed to recoup her losses suffered through her identity theft ordeal, Betty began working a second job as a medical caregiver to elderly patients whose relatives hired her under her alias, Susan Flowers. She found these jobs herself without the assistance of the medical registry—the main source of her income.

For privacy reasons, Betty Muñoz had assumed the name of "Susan Flowers" for everything except the most official portions of her business life. Her checks for the second job were made payable to "Susan Flowers"—her alternate name—and were accepted by her bank without so much as a raised eyebrow, into the business account of Susan Flowers, LLC.

This illustration—an actual case history with name changes to protect the victim—provides a case study of what is possible when one has a need for a very high level of financial privacy and personal security. While it is not a recommendation, and the author does not condone this type of activity, it affords high-level privacy.

NOMINEES AND BANKING

Privacy authors have advised the use of nominees for banking purposes, or the use of another individual to hold your money and have the signing power on bank accounts in order to conceal the actual "owner's" identity. While I believe nominees have an important role in your quest to make your life private, I do not believe a nominee should be used for banking purposes. Remember, whoever is the signer on the account either owns or controls the money in that account. Privacy-conscious people can avoid any potential disaster by properly setting up a checking account in the name of a trust as described in this chapter for the purpose of holding personal funds. Or choose to use any of the other privacy options in this chapter to accomplish anonymous banking in the U.S.

PEOPLE SKILLS AND BANKING

As you strive to make your life private and escape the horrible, time-consuming, expensive, growing, crime of identity theft in America, realize that your success will depend on your ability to deal with those who set policies and restrictions on your banking activities.

I asked three different bankers at the same large money-center bank about the requirements for opening a trust checking account. Each gave me different answers concerning requirements of the trustee's Social Security number being necessary on bank records. During a small sample study, I asked ten bankers with mid-level management responsibilities key questions about the United States banking system. All ten believed the Federal Reserve Bank was a part of the Federal Government.

It should concern you as a banking customer that the bankers you are dealing with do not know that the Federal Reserve Bank is a private corporation. The Federal Reserve Bank is no more a government agency than is Federal Express. With this in mind, you must make adjustments as to your expectations about bankers and their knowledge of their business. Do not expect those in charge of making the decisions about the trust account to have a thorough knowledge of the language of business.

It is to your advantage to act as patient and humble as possible, while remaining firm about your privacy requirements. Treating everyone as your equal is always the best policy as you recognize the limitations of those in the American banking industry. Successful banking for the privacy seeker involves the utilization of effective communication as well as the patience to wait until you find the right bank manager for your particular requirements.

Excellent people skills and your ability to effectively communicate will, in my experience, far outweigh the bank's manuals and the policies of corporate officers. Most business deals are negotiable, and your banking is no different. Take your time, select your bank and banker carefully, and clearly tell those with whom you are dealing about your specific requirements.

SUMMARY

1. Anonymous banking assures protection from identity theft. Americans are best served by using a U.S. bank for timely clearance of checks and bank drafts.

2. For high-level banking privacy, use a trust for holding a non–interest-bearing checking account. The trust name should not be similar to your true name.

3. Trusts, the most private entities, have no statutory registration requirements .

4. Trustees are assured anonymity when a trust account is opened and maintained properly, and such an account has all the versatility associated with a personal checking account. For maximum privacy, only the trust's tax ID number should be on the bank account records. Trustees and signers should avoid providing their Social Security numbers to banks.

5. The use of ChexSystems is negotiable; avoid having your name run through this database. Bank managers have discretion concerning use of ChexSystems.

6. Use an illegible signature when you sign banking documents and checks.

7. Interview potential bank managers by phone for trust account requirements.

8. Work with upper-level bank managers to accomplish banking privacy. Account statements and the account title should contain only the name and address of the trust, not the trustee, to avoid association with the trustee and trust bank account.

9. Use your U.S. passport as your primary identity document for banking purposes.

10. Bank statements should be sent to your offshore address for maximum privacy.

11. Discard bank-supplied checks. Order or make your own without any name or address on the trust account checks for high-level banking privacy. Use a rubber endorsement stamp with only the bank's name and the trust account number.

12. Obtain a debit card with only the trust's name and make deposits by mail and withdrawals in cash at automatic teller machines for privacy. Keep the card in a secure location.

13. The dual trust account principle provides the advantage of a full-use trust account and the security of high-level banking secrecy.

14. Trust bank accounts are for privacy and do not serve to protect the trustee from any liability or to act as an asset protection entity.

15. Check-cashing stores provide an extremely high level of financial privacy.

16. The alternate name/business entity concept has been successfully used by those requiring privacy in their employment and banking activities.

17. Nominees who open bank accounts on the privacy seeker's behalf have legal control of the bank account. Maintain control over your money rather than trusting your funds to a nominee.

18. Effective people skills enable the individual to obtain the best services during the process of banking and managing personal finances. Recognize the limitations of bankers and obtain all the knowledge necessary for effective, private management of money under your control.

♦ SIXTEEN ♦

Private Bill Payments

"A man is rich in proportion to the number of things he can afford to let alone."—Henry David Thoreau

CASH

Using cash for paying routine bills reduces the paper trail on your purchases—a positive step in your lifestyle plan to keep identity thieves and others from gaining access to your confidential information. Cash is seemingly a totally discreet way of settling your bills. Right?

Did you buy groceries today? How about three days ago? Most of the readers of this book purchased items in a grocery store within the last week, and since we all want the most for our money, many of us used a store discount card. These are those coded cards you dislike carrying around that, when you forget the card, can be activated when you key in a phone number—or if you have it with you, used for discounts by swiping the card's magnetic strip through the machine at the counter, just as you do a credit or debit card while in the store.

Items on sale at that time are read, and you reduce your bill by small amounts when your purchases include certain items on the bargain list. Cash customers and credit card purchasers alike may use the store discount cards, and both are subject to having their personal information made available to others. So go ahead and use the card, but never tell the store who you really are, and don't provide your true address or phone number.

When you use these cards, be sure to use an alternate name and any address you choose, since they never require a real one, plus a voice-mail or a phone number that has no connection to you. If you provide your real identity data, the stores will surely sell your name, address, phone number, and buyer profile to any number of marketing companies, which will in turn sell it to someone else, and on and on and on.

And one day, some marketing firm's latest new hire could show up at your door. Who might this be? Even Bubba, the 300-pound recent parolee from the state pen, needs to work. Think he doesn't know the ropes and how to get what he needs? Be careful, even as you pay cash for everyday expenses. Take your privacy seriously. All the time. Be discreet, and never provide your true name unless it is for the right reasons. I recommend that you use cash for most everyday purchases.

Accessing the trust account, which you control for your personal finances through the use of an automatic teller machine (ATM), is the most private way to do your banking. If you really want a high level of privacy, use the drive-through ATMs. Be aware that you are on camera any time you are near a bank these days, so if you want to avoid being identified by the cameras as you drive through, place a dark piece of plastic over each license plate temporarily as you use the ATM from the vehicle. And, you can wear a wig, sunglasses, or even a mask as you access funds from the ATM if you are concerned, for whatever reason, about being spied on as you access your money.

Of course, if you follow the detailed privacy recommendations in the "Travel" section of this book (see Chapters 10 and 11), your car will be registered in the name of a trust, and the license plates and registration will reveal nothing about you.

The time stamp and records of the ATM withdrawals at some banks may be able to be traced back to the account accessed when you use the cash machine. For the ultimate privacy and to avoid the highest level of security employed by some banks on ATM customers, use an independent ATM machine at convenience stores and other business establishments. These are owned by non-bankers and, of course, charge fees, but will not be as privacy-invasive as banks. They also will be more reluctant to do the research to satisfy an investigator's requests than the government agency-controlled banks. And contrary to what some believe, these independently owned machines are as secure as those of banks.

Certain bills may be paid in cash via the mail as well as in person. Bills that are due in faraway countries can be paid by using large denomination currency, and you may send payment via DHL or Federal Express—services that allow tracking delivery online.

These companies will ask for your name but won't check your identification, so give them a company name or an alternate name. For paying small debts, simply wrap the cash in tin foil or stationery and mail it certified or as a normally stamped letter.

Recognize that there's risk in doing this, however; you may want to send payment for larger bills in several letters to reduce the risk of loss. However, cash is the only payment method that is non-traceable, so when your privacy is a priority, use it to settle your bills.

MONEY ORDERS

For many years, I have used money orders for paying those bills for which it is not practical to pay cash. Money orders are private, negotiable instruments, much like the older version of cashier's checks, which were almost as good as cash. Today, money orders can be purchased, for the most part, in total privacy and are readily available at numerous businesses.

On occasion, I have been asked for my name when buying money orders and, of course, when and if this happens to you, provide an alternate name. Also, sometimes limits are placed on the amounts you can convert from cash to money orders at stores, all in the name of protecting the country from money laundering, terrorism, and other societal dangers, of course.

When this happens, just smile and waltz down the street to another business for the remainder of the money orders needed. Paying bills with money orders provides you with a payment stub, which serves as a record of the money order sent for payment. With this payment stub and the cash register receipt as a record of the money order purchase, you can issue a stop payment on the money order or obtain reimbursement for it, in the event it is lost in the mail or elsewhere.

Try to avoid losing money orders, though, as the reimbursement of lost money orders costs $12 and may take several weeks. You can purchase money orders from any number of sources, including small convenience stores, check-cashing stores, pawn shops, and commercial mail-receiving agencies. Note that mail centers may place restrictions on the amount you can purchase and will require your name in some cases.

When you need a privacy layer as to your location, sensitive bills paid by money order may be remailed. Send a note with the bill inside a larger envelope, along with a note attached to your offshore mail-drop nominee, instructing him or her to stamp and mail the bill from that location. Any number of remailing services can be found via an Internet search, and you can have bills sent from inside the U.S.A. or from abroad.

So when you do want to make your location unknown to anyone who receives any of your bill payments, create a high-level privacy layer by remailing your bill payments. Type the "payee" information and account number and your name or company name if these are absolutely required, as you pay bills with money orders. Or you may include this information on a separate sheet of paper inside the envelope.

Avoid using your true name unless necessary. Leave the address section blank, and use your illegible signature (as previously discussed in Chapter 15, "Anonymous Banking") for signing the money orders. Or use a different signature altogether when you wish to have no link between your normal banking signature and the one used to pay a sensitive bill.

Keep in mind that since money orders can be traced to the store where they were purchased, as well as to the payee who accepts it as payment for goods or services, some privacy is sacrificed when using them. Although an investigator could discover your general location on the date the money order was purchased, I learned this is quite difficult and unlikely following phone conversations with supervisors at both Western Union and Travelers Express—two companies that sell money orders.

If you believe this endangers your privacy, you can stock up on money orders in the amounts needed to pay bills in the amounts of each bill when you are visiting a location a great distance from your actual address, to prevent even the most in-depth and serious investigators from learning your true location.

As mentioned throughout this book, privacy always costs more than the usual way of living, and of course, buying money orders is yet another added expense you will need to pay to make your life private. Money orders vary in cost, depending on where they are purchased. I have spent $2 for a money order on the Las Vegas strip and have been given free money orders in Utah, Arizona, and Wyoming. Generally they cost from $.50 to $1.50. The maximum amount of a single money order is usually $1,000.

The purchase of money orders is even more confidential at some convenience stores in Arizona, where there are machines that spit out

Western Union money orders after you deposit cash into them. This is an ideal way of purchasing money orders privately. Cameras are installed inside the machines, so like ATMs that dispense cash, these money order machines film you as you use them. So if you are camera shy, wear a disguise to eliminate being tracked.

Money orders are the safest and most private way of paying bills, and unless you are in the real fugitive category, you need not worry about using them as a secure method of paying your bills.

While many check-cashing stores and other businesses produce their own brand-name money orders, experienced privacy advocates often prefer the large, established companies. Western Union and Travelers Express are easiest to deal with, should you need to make a claim for a lost or stolen money order.

MONEYGRAM

In order to receive immediate credit on an important bill due while paying it anonymously at a distance, utilize MoneyGram—an equivalent of a wire-transfer bill-paying service. You will find MoneyGram available for your use at some check-cashing stores and other retail stores, including Wal-Mart. I use this service when I need assurance that a bill payment is credited immediately—an automobile insurance premium, for example.

There are fees associated with the service, of course, but your account is immediately credited, and a receipt is received once the wire has been completed. In order to make a MoneyGram transaction, you need to have the account information for the bill you are paying. You also must complete a form prior to sending the payment, though there is no reason to supply personal identification information to MoneyGram—the company sending the payment on your behalf.

WESTERN UNION

Western Union and other companies offer money transfers in the form of wire transfers, which may be sent to any person anywhere in the world. Western Union offices, located nearly everywhere, offer good—although expensive—service. Western Union offers a convenient way to have cash available upon your arrival at any destination in the world.

The person receiving the Western Union wire transfer will have to provide identification prior to receiving cash. Sometimes the sender also is required to supply verifiable identification.

CASHIER'S CHECKS

Once upon a time, it was a simple process to visit a bank, purchase a cashier's check—a monetary instrument that once was a cash equivalent—and walk out with complete anonymity. Sadly, those days have been gone for some time, and banks now require that you have an account at that institution in order to purchase a cashier's check.

Cashier's checks, formerly given the same treatment as currency, have gone to that favorite of banking favorites, the "three-day hold heaven." Some banks even try to hold cashier's checks longer than three business days when they think they can get away with it.

On occasion, I have been given immediate credit on a cashier's check, but only with a bank manager vouching for me and the account into which it was deposited. Whenever I ask bank managers why a cashier's check would need to have a three-day hold placed on it, I am always told, "too much fraud." I accept the hold because of the few choices available to negotiate the check.

I never believe them, however, because my experience tells me that a check can be verified almost immediately. In fact, when receiving a personal or business check, you as the payee can call the institution where the checking account is held and receive verification of funds being available for honoring the check amount. Bankers can argue the point and say that another negotiable instrument on the same account could be presented ahead of the one being verified and drain the account, thus making it "bounce," but this is not possible if the demand electronically for the check in question is made ahead of the hypothetical large one with potential to deplete the account.

Remember the cases in the previous chapter where the check-cashing stores provided immediate cash to me when checks from distant banks were presented for payment? Those were actual happenings. These pseudo-banks, the check-cashing stores, have essentially the same equipment for verifying checks as do the banks, but are more inclined to offer good service—for exceptionally high fees, of course.

When you obtain a cashier's check from the trust account of which you are the signer, or another business account, keep in mind that the check is traceable back to the account from which it is drawn and to you as the signer on the account. When you utilize the dual trust account principle described in Chapter 15, "Anonymous Banking," access funds from the public account, thus preserving the total secrecy of the private account.

Use generic words such as "trustee" or "manager" for the remitter portion of the cashier's check, rather than using your name, the trust name, or the company name. Cashier's checks require less time to clear than personal checks. And you can request that a portion of the reference number on the cashier's check be deleted to preserve the privacy of the bank account from which the funds were drawn.

AUTOMATIC CLEARING HOUSE (ACH)

Automatic Clearing House (ACH) is an electronic check equivalent. Banks will offer this feature on a checking account as a bill payment option for your convenience, of course. The disadvantage of using ACH with your trust checking account is that the bank and others whom you pay through this method will know your business. That is, when you agree to pay your insurance policy premiums and link the bank account to your insurance company, your bank will know your insurance carrier, and your insurance carrier will know your bank. It's not that they won't get along well, since they are first cousins, but I recommend you not introduce them through your checking account.

Paying routine bills via ACH is not a good choice for privacy seekers. Limit your use of ACH to the task of transferring money to or from your public trust account by utilizing the dual trust account principle as discussed in Chapter 15. ACH is nearly as convenient as bank wires, and transactions can be accomplished by making a phone call and providing a password to your banker or stockbroker.

WIRE TRANSFERS

Wire transfers are the most time-efficient and practical way of making deposits for immediate credit into a bank account and are treated as cash deposits without the obvious cumbersome problem of lugging loads of currency into a bank lobby. As you use the dual trust account principle for privacy, utilize the public account for sending and receiving bank wires, while keeping the private account free of any paper trails or traceable, privacy-invasive transaction records.

This is an important consideration and worth the storage requirements and time required to maintain two accounts, because records of transferring money via wire are kept for long periods of time. I have been told that records of bank wires are kept for both the sending and receiving banks for seven years or longer.

Wire transfers are an efficient and quick way of gaining immediate credit from one account to another—from a brokerage account under your control, for example, into the public trust account of which you are the trustee and signer. Cash withdrawals can then be made from the public trust account, converted into money orders, and deposited into the secure private trust account.

This system increases your privacy and the security of storing personal money—and reduces your risk of having your serious personal money, which is kept in the private trust account, from being discovered by anyone who may attempt to steal your identity and your money. Always remember to keep the balances low in the public trust account—perhaps under $100—because due to the activity on the account, it will be the most vulnerable to discovery.

The private trust account, on the other hand, will have records only of cash and money order transactions, without reference to where they originated, and will remain secure and private.

PERSONAL CHECKS

While personal checks are the least private way to pay your bills, you can reduce the risk of having your personal money discovered, with limited use of personal checks, by obtaining checks without the trust's name or address on them, and by using an illegible banking signature. Leave the reference section on the check blank or include only a portion of the account number of the bill you are paying, and do not include your name on the check.

BANKS AND GOVERNMENT REPORTING

The federal government likes to monitor citizens' banking activities under the guise of fighting the wars on drugs, terrorism, money laundering, and other illegal activities, so they have the capability of viewing all transactions over $3,000 and require banks to file forms and report certain transactions. By doing this, bureaucratic snoops are able to review those making the transactions.

Government wants to control citizens' banking and to track money sources, hence all the bank regulations and banking requirements for opening accounts—all to maintain U.S.-style freedom, of course. Don't try to escape the $10,000 reporting requirement by withdrawing $9,900 from your account, because Big Bureaucrat is watching and at the ready to charge you with a crime for using your money.

This is a crime, known as *"structuring,"* under a law they sneaked in to flag those who intentionally attempt to bypass the reporting requirements for transactions of $10,000 or more. It's advisable to do everything according to government banking laws, while being aware of what has happened to your freedom to handle your own money in the United States.

CREDIT CARDS

Credit cards such as Visa, MasterCard, Discover, American Express, and others that agree to front you the credit for goods and services when you make timely payments on the principal amount of the "loan" have become the most widely used of all methods of paying bills in America. Be aware of the potential dangers you and your money face as you pay your bills by credit card.

When you pay for dinner at a restaurant, for example, using a credit card under your true name, you are sharing your personal and confidential information with far too many potential identity thieves who want to steal your ability to borrow money. I recommend you stop paying routine bills in public places with credit cards issued under your true name.

For the utmost in privacy, use credit cards to pay large bills to companies that agree to not retain your name and credit card information in their databases. This is a tricky situation, so make sure you speak with a high-level manager—a hospital administrator, for example—before paying the balance of your bill with your MasterCard.

Do not rule out the use of credit cards for paying your large bills, because, providing that you are careful and time your credit line use so that you use the bank's money just as the current billing cycle has closed, your float time—that period when you use other people's money without interest charges—can be as long as seven weeks. So if you do it right, using credit cards for paying large bills with interest-free money while keeping your account information discreet makes good sense.

Occasionally, you'll find that those who agree to delete your credit card account information after being paid breach their promise and retain it in their system. When you make this discovery (accomplished by a follow-up phone call to the business thirty days after the payment has been made), you have an easy remedy to be sure you are not defrauded in the future by someone with access to your credit card account number.

Simply telephone the bank that issued the card, explain that the account has been abused by a business, that you risk being defrauded, and that likewise, they risk a monetary loss. They'll quickly void out the old account number and send you a new credit card with a different number. The credit card issuing bank will do this at your request without hesitation, because while you are not liable for fraudulent charges made to your account, they are. So they'll issue you a new account number to reduce their potential for a loss due to fraud.

DEBIT CARDS

Debit cards are issued by banks through their agreement with MasterCard, Visa, and others, and are linked to money on deposit in bank accounts. You may obtain a debit card with your trust account, although, as previously stated, the card should contain only the trust's account name for the ultimate in personal privacy. This allows you to use the card just as you would any credit card, while remaining anonymous as you do it.

Also, debit cards, since they are just a convenient way of accessing your own money rather than borrowing it from a bank, have no reporting requirements to any credit bureau, so no outsiders will be aware of where your funds are being spent. It is most important that the trust's name only, not your name, is on the debit card, so that when a charge is made on the account, your true name will remain a mystery to those accepting the debit card as payment.

Just as you are able to have your trust account bank statement contain only the name and address of the trust, without mention of you or others as trustees and signers, you can arrange to have a debit card issued in the trust's name only. Communicate with a bank manager, a regional manager, or the CEO if you need to, in order to obtain this high-level privacy feature on the trust account. This assures you of anonymity as you pay bills with debit cards.

A bank debit card issued in the trust account name only is, however, the second-best choice for privacy while making debit card purchases.

An even more private way of paying for purchases—one that virtually assures no one can discover your true identity—is to use a prepaid debit card obtained in an alternate name.

ALTERNATE-NAME DEBIT CARDS

A "prepaid" debit card—known also as a "stored value card"—with the MasterCard or Visa logo on it, when issued to you under an alternate name, is the most private way to make credit card purchases. Companies that allow you to obtain such a card in any name you choose come and go, as do their requirements for opening such an account.

Government periodically interferes with those providing these types of accounts, hence the continuous changes for opening accounts by these businesses. You will need to keep abreast of what is happening in the "prepaid" and "stored value" debit card industry in order to find one that will best serve your needs. Check-cashing stores and the Internet are your best resources for finding these accounts, as well as foreign banks, which may accommodate your privacy needs with an anonymous debit card. Brokers for these anonymous debit cards periodically surface on the Internet, although you should be careful when obtaining such services.

The reason these accounts are so valuable is because you, as the account holder, have full control of the account, while using only non-traceable cash to make deposits and withdrawals through the use of stores, for depositing funds, and automatic teller machines, for making withdrawals.

Your confidentiality and privacy are assured, because the paper trail stops at the point of sale. The transactions are reported to no one except the bank that issued the card, so no one will be able to associate the alternate-name debit card to your true name, and only you have access to the account records via the Internet. This is truly a high level of privacy and assures that you will not be traced as you pay bills privately through the use of a debit card in an alternate name.

Certain companies issue debit cards without any name on them. PrivaCash and others do this through their "stored value" accounts, and these accounts have maximum limits of less than $5,000 in most cases.

SUMMARY

1. While cash remains king for bill-paying privacy, carefully protect your true identity and confidential data and home address by supplying limited information to vendors. Be especially aware of the potential dangers of store discount cards.

2. Use your alternate name to guard against having privacy-invasive marketing companies discover your personal information.

3. Automatic Teller Machines provide convenient access to personal money held in the trust account. For the ultimate in privacy, use independent, free-standing ATMs.

4. Money orders offer the payer the advantage of high-level privacy with the loss-recovery features of bank checks. For added security, consider remailing bills that are paid by money order.

5. MoneyGram is a bank wire bill-payment equivalent.

6. Western Union may be used to pay bills worldwide or to send and receive cash to businesses or individuals.

7. Cashier's checks are available to bank customers only. Trust accounts provide the most privacy for personal bank accounts, which are referenced when cashier's checks are used as bill-paying instruments.

8. Automatic Clearing House is an electronic check equivalent provided by banks to account holders. Privacy is sacrificed when ACH is used for paying bills.

9. Wire transfers are the most time-efficient for gaining credit on funds or for paying bills.

10. Personal checks should have no account name, address, or telephone number for the ultimate in security.

11. Use trust account checks for the convenience of paying large bills.

12. The dual trust account principle enables the account holder to maintain one private account while taking advantage of the full use of a less-private public account.

13. Banks report transactions over $10,000 to watchdog government agencies. Do not structure transactions, or you risk being prosecuted for depositing and withdrawing your own money.

14. Credit cards enable you to pay bills using other people's money. Make sure the party receiving the payment guarantees your privacy by deleting your account number from their records once the bill is paid.

15. Debit cards tied to the trust account are secure for routine purchases, providing only the trust's name is on the card.

16. Alternate-name prepaid or stored value debit cards provide total privacy and are the best choice for private bill paying when cash use is inconvenient.

♦ SEVENTEEN ♦

Private Investments

*"Where large sums of money are concerned,
it is advisable to trust nobody"*
—Agatha Christie

ASSET MANAGEMENT

Private investments, as discussed in this chapter, will include liquid investments—meaning all paper assets, including cash, certificates of deposit, money market funds and other cash equivalents, treasury bills, notes and bonds, corporate debt instruments, stocks,

mutual funds, and any other paper investments readily bought and sold through an auction market and easily converted into currency.

The individual investor who desires financial privacy from government, gold diggers, identity thieves, and others will be best served by using legal entities to hold investments. When a business entity is properly formed and registered with privacy in mind, it can shield the privacy-conscious investor from any connection to his investments. It is important for the investor to adopt the philosophy of "owning nothing" while "controlling everything."

In order to do this legally, one will necessarily manage investments through legal entities, properly registered with the secretary of state of the state where the entity is registered, so that the company formed for the purpose of holding the investments is the actual and true legal owner, while the individual controls and manages the property. When investments are handled in an entirely legal way by the transference of an individual's property to a properly selected separate legal entity— a registered company—both privacy and freedom from asset seizure through any future personal liability may be accomplished.

Unless you keep all companies that hold investments properly registered with the secretary of state that require registration in order to be legal entities, the company can be determined to be null and void.

Privacy-conscious investors should consult with a competent attorney for advice on the best entity choices for holding investments. In addition, the company must be maintained properly, with internal paper work and records consistent with the state's compliance requirements. Seek counsel and tax advice as necessary when you have compliance questions.

The examples outlined in this chapter are for discussion purposes only. They have been effectively used and were recommended by an attorney who specializes in asset protection and who has provided advice on privacy. The reader will be best served by obtaining legal counsel and tax advice specific to his or her particular case. Please consider the examples as outlined herein, while always consulting your competent professional prior to structuring your assets for privacy and asset protection.

PRIVACY AND PROTECTION

The following case rulings should convince you of the need to separate yourself from your investments in order to prevent anyone from obtaining information about your property. When investments are properly held in separate legal entities, you control everything, while owning nothing, and you become judgment proof.

1. A passenger injured in a taxi can sue the taxi company's insurance agency for failing to have uninsured motorist coverage (Arizona Court of Appeals). The plaintiff was ruled to be a "third-party beneficiary" of the contract between the agency and the company. The court cited similar rulings from Illinois, Massachusetts, New Jersey, and Tennessee, as well as contrary rulings from Louisiana and New York.
   —Source: Friedman Ranzenhofer, P.C., March, 2005.

2. A high school student from Memphis, Michigan sued his school principal, the superintendent, and all seven school board members because he received an "A" instead of an "A+" in one of his classes.
   —Source: AP/CNN, February 6, 2003.

3. A New York man sued four fast-food chains seeking unspecified damages, claiming the restaurants were to blame for his obesity, diabetes, high blood pressure, and high cholesterol. The man had been eating fast food for decades, thinking it was good for him, despite the fact that the restaurants had posted nutritional information on their food.
   —Source: *The Daily Recorder*, July 30, 2004.

4. A store that sold a gun to a drunken man, who then shot and killed his girlfriend with that gun, is liable for $11.5 million for negligent entrustment. Selling a gun to an intoxicated person presents a foreseeable risk of harm. The gun buyer had consumed a fifth of whisky and a case of beer during the day. Although the store clerk indicated that the buyer did not appear intoxicated, he had to help him fill out the federal firearms form because his handwriting was illegible (Florida Supreme Court).
   —Source: Friedman Ranzenhofer, P. C., March, 2005.

So, dear reader, it is not just doctors and lawyers and such who are sued, but insurance sales people, educators and administrators, school board members, store keepers, and restaurant owners. Remember that if you are named as a defendant in a civil lawsuit, whether it has merit or not, the complaint must be answered, providing you as the defendant are properly served, of course—and the case must be defended. So, in the event you are named in a lawsuit, you do not want to own assets but rather control assets, by being the manager of property that is held by entities other than you.

NEVADA FOR PRIVACY

Johnson and Kleven, LLC, offers some convincing reasons why Nevada is the state of choice for doing business and retaining privacy in one's business affairs. These reasons are listed below.

WHY FORM A BUSINESS IN NEVADA?

- ▶ No State Corporate Income Tax
- ▶ No State Taxes on Corporate Shares
- ▶ No State Franchise Tax
- ▶ No Personal Income Tax
- ▶ No Internal Revenue Service (IRS) Information Sharing Agreement
- ▶ Relatively low Annual fees
- ▶ Minimal Reporting and Disclosure Requirements
- ▶ Stockholders are not Public Record
- ▶ Only one person is needed to create and maintain a legal corporation or LLC.
- ▶ Directors need not be stockholders
- ▶ Officers and directors of a Nevada Corporation or LLC can be protected from personal liability for unlawful acts of the Corporation or LLC.
- ▶ Nevada Corporations may purchase, hold, sell, or transfer shares of their own stock
- ▶ Nevada Corporations may issue stock for capital, services, personal property, or real estate, including leases and options.
- ▶ The directors may determine the value of any of these transactions, and their decision is final.

Source: Johnson & Kleven, LLC., 50 S. Jones Blvd., Suite 204, Las Vegas, Nevada 89107, March, 2005

NEVADA FAMILY LIMITED PARTNERSHIP

Of all business entity choices for holding liquid investments, none offer the privacy and asset protection of a properly formed and registered Nevada Family Limited Partnership. For the purposes of this chapter, a Nevada Family Limited Partnership and a Nevada Limited Partnership are used interchangeably.

The *family limited partnership* is a limited partnership formed to own family property. Most family limited partnerships appoint the parents as *general partners* with each having a 1 percent interest, while the children share the remaining interest as *limited partners.*

General partners have full control over the operational decisions of the limited partnership, so the parents own a small interest in the business, but still control it—an ideal plan for managing investments while protecting the assets of the partnership. Using this form of partnership structure, the parents' exposure to loss of property is limited to 2 percent of the total partnership, as only general partners are exposed to the debts and liabilities of the partnership.

NEVADA LIMITED LIABILITY COMPANY (LLC)
AS GENERAL PARTNER

For maximum privacy, form a Nevada LLC as the general partner of the limited partnership. The parents will split ownership in the LLC at 50 percent each. A single individual may also own the LLC entirely, while using it to become the general partner of a Nevada Limited Partnership.

Thus, a single person may fully control a limited partnership, while having complete decision-making power over it through the ownership of the general partner, LLC. Thus, his or her personal liability is limited to the 1 percent ownership of the General Partner LLC. The remaining 99 percent of the Nevada Limited Partnership may be owned by a limited partner—the same individual who owns 100 percent of the general partner, LLC. Since the single individual controls the Nevada Limited Partnership through ownership of the general partner, LLC—which holds a minority interest in the partnership but controls it entirely—the individual's exposure to potential loss is only 1 percent.

Meanwhile, the same individual is also the sole limited partner of the Nevada Limited Partnership owning 99 percent of the company. While owning little (1 percent, general partner, LLC) and controlling everything (99 percent, limited partner), the person has little at risk.

TRUST MANAGER PRINCIPLE

One high-level privacy tactic that has been used successfully is the *trust manager principle*. A trust is formed for the purpose of "managing" the Nevada Family Limited Partnership and the Nevada General Partner, LLC. Privacy advocates prefer using a manager rather than a member as the contact for the general partner, LLC.

The general partner of the limited partnership must be listed on the Nevada secretary of state records. The trust manager is the manager of the general partner, LLC, and is listed as such on secretary of state records. The trust manager actually is the "manager" for both the LLC general partner and the limited partnership.

Because only the manager is required to be listed on secretary of state records, and the manager may be located anywhere in the world, your privacy is assured when you use only the trust of which you are the trustee as the manager of both the general partner, LLC and the limited partnership.

For maximum privacy, the trust should be in a name with no similarity to your true name, and the address on record should be in a foreign country. Since the trust has no registration requirements, you as trustee remain anonymous. No one will ever be aware of your involvement in the Nevada Family Limited Partnership.

ADMINISTRATIVE TRUSTEE CONCEPT

When a trust is formed for the purpose of functioning as the "manager" of both the general partner LLC and the Nevada Family Limited Partnership, a person with very limited duties, powers, and responsibilities may also be designated in the trust as the administrative trustee. The purpose of the administrative trustee being listed in the trust (which functions as the manager of record on the secretary of state filing) is to have someone capable of doing very limited duties for the trustee(s) and the company manager who wants anonymity.

When privacy-oriented investors structure their companies this way, the manager of record on the general partner LLC is the trust manager, with an administrative trustee's signature on the filing record. The administrative trustee may again sign on behalf of the general partner for the limited partnership—for the trustee(s), whose name(s) and signature(s) will not be required.

Your attorney can phrase the administrative trustee provision of the trust in this way. Currently, only a signature is required, without clarification of who is signing on behalf of the trust manager. So by using an illegible signature, the administrative trustee does not reveal his or her identity. You, as trustee of the trust (the manager of the company on public records), are now completely anonymous as the controller of all investments held by the Nevada Limited Partnership.

RESIDENT AGENT

All legal entities registered with the State of Nevada require someone on record who can be served a summons in the event any party has a complaint against the business. Such a person or company is known as a *resident agent*. Your attorney will act as your resident agent, or you can retain any number of others who offer these services. Only the general partner, LLC and the limited partnership will be required to have a resident agent. The trust manager will not, as the trust is not a registered entity but a totally private one without registration requirements.

BUSINESS BANKING PRIVACY

As you manage investments privately, you will naturally want to convert paper assets into cash and will want to use the services of a commercial bank for normal business banking purposes. The purpose

of opening a business bank account is to access your cash through normal withdrawals or Automatic Teller Machines (ATMs), deposit business checks as they are received, send and receive wire transfers, utilize Automatic Clearing House (ACH), write business checks, buy cashier's checks as necessary, and use other banking services offered by the institution.

The account should be opened in the name of the Nevada Family Limited Partnership which holds assets under your control. In some cases, you will receive resistance from banks that will not want to open an account outside of the area where your business is based, or registered—in this case, Nevada. Keep in mind that even though the Nevada Limited Partnership is registered in Nevada, it can legally do business any place in the world.

Furthermore, the partnership only holds assets—and goods and services are not provided to the outside world. So this is important for your bank manager to know as you call and make inquiries about opening a bank account in the name of the limited partnership. No business licenses or permits will be required of your "business," as the sole function is to hold liquid assets under the name of the limited partnership. However, Nevada now charges an annual fee in addition to the registration fee on business entities.

Most commercial banks based in the United States will require your personal appearance when you open a bank account in the name of the limited partnership. You as the manager and signer should use a U.S. passport as your primary identification and one other form of acceptable I.D. to open the account. Insurance cards—or a school I.D.—have been used as a second form of identification.

The *partnership agreement*, plus the tax identification number (EIN) will need to be seen by commercial banks. An IRS form SS4 will need to be completed, perhaps by the administrative trustee of the trust manager, in order to obtain a tax identification number for the limited partnership. If you structure a Nevada LLC as the general partner, the articles of organization of the LLC will need to be shown to the bank manager as well.

When the trust manager principle is used, trust papers outlining this agreement will also need to be shown to the bank manager. Carefully consider what information you want the bank to have pertaining to the Nevada Limited Partnership. The only requirement the bank has is to assure itself that they are dealing with a legal entity. The bank will need to know that the EIN is legitimate. Also, all state registration paperwork needs to be up to date, and the company formation must be legal. Everything else they want to see and keep in their files is negotiable.

So negotiate and keep you business banking as private as possible.

Some banks will want to collect your Social Security number and run it as well as your name through the ChexSystems or other company database to make sure you have no negative history with other banks. Review Chapter 15, "Anonymous Banking," and make your own decisions about how to handle such inquiries.

SEPARATE LEGAL ENTITIES

Keep in mind that the Nevada Limited Partnership which you control will own the bank account. Therefore, you and the partnership are totally separate entities. For example, an attorney has advised me that no one or any agency can lawfully make a claim to any partnership assets or sieze any partnership assets of a limited partner, who is liable as an individual for such a debt or a monetary judgment—providing, of course, that the individual did make timely transfer of the assets from himself to the partnership and without an intention to defraud.

However, just because something is illegal does not prevent it from happening, especially when government and quasi-government agencies are involved. Today, for example, the Federal Bureau of Investigation (FBI) is using their "administrative" powers to obtain search warrants instead of obtaining them the old fashioned way—by presenting their case to a judge and receiving a search warrant on the merits of the individual case.

Government agency powers are superseding laws all over the United States of America. Recognize this and protect yourself accordingly. While the partnership under your control may not be liable for your debts as an individual, a judge may be convinced that you are the partnership, for whatever reason, and the assets of the partnership may be seized, at least temporarily, until you have retained legal counsel to prove otherwise.

In view of all of the possibilities and potential for unlawful seizures of assets, it is now, more than ever before, imperative that your privacy measures are at the highest level possible. This will help to thwart unwanted inquiries and snooping by government officials, federal and state income tax collectors, investigators, child support enforcement agencies, identity thieves and others.

IS IT POSSIBLE TO OPEN A BANK ACCOUNT WITHOUT A SOCIAL SECURITY NUMBER?

The claims are all over the Internet. People claim to be able to open a bank account without providing the bank with a Social Security number or other tax identification number. Essentially, the claim is made that such a requirement is illegal, based on one not having to obtain an SSN under current laws—and further claims are made that it is illegal to deny one the opportunity to bank without the tax identifier.

Some may have convinced a bank to open an account without an SSN or a taxpayer I.D., although I am not aware of any individual cases. Your author has researched this option extensively, and at one time, it appeared that this possibility existed in the form of an "association bank account" through an organization known as Americans for Lawful Financial Independence and Information (AFLII).

This association has a contract with the Interactive Currency Interface System (ICIS), which, according to AFLII representatives, offers members the ability to open bank accounts without any identification documents—a Social Security number of taxpayer I.D. Further, the ALFII website at www.alfii.com informs members that no Social Security numbers or other such identifiers are required.

The author is aware of dissatisfied ALFII members. Several e-mail correspondents state they made contact with the association prior to joining and were advised that no identification—SSN or taxpayer I.D.—would be required to deposit or clear checks made payable to either a member individually or to a company name. Also, they were advised that the ICIS bank account allowed ICIS members to print out money orders, utilize a Palm debit card, and bank confidentially through the use of the association's bank account.

However, AFLII has now instituted new policies requiring their members who use their ICIS banking services to furnish photocopies of government identification. Therefore, this option—which I recommended in the manuscript of this book prior to publication—I can no longer endorse. All members, according to ALFII representatives, must—as of late 2006—comply with these new identification requirements.

Does this mean, then, that there are no alternatives to traditional, privacy-invasive banking? Not at all. For example:

1. You may utilize the dual trust account principle, as explained in Chapter 15, "Anonymous Banking." Receiving checks made payable to yourself or to the trust's name assures you of the ability to deposit these negotiable instruments in the "public trust account." Once the checks have "cleared," withdraw the funds in cash, convert them into money orders, and deposit them in the "private trust account." Those issuing checks to you or to the trust always have the capability of tracing the check issued, to

your "public trust account," since the checks clear through this account. However, the "private trust account" remains your secret, as only non-traceable money orders and cash go into this account. For further explanation of this principle, see Chapter 15.

2. Your author has opened trust bank accounts, using only the EIN of the trust, while ensuring that the accounts are titled only in the trust's names and that statements are mailed to the trust address provided.

3. Check-cashing stores offer financial privacy, providing they are used correctly. Those who use the services of these stores may cash checks made payable to themselves or to a company or trust of which they are authorized to receive payment. Finding the right store and using "people skills" will result in one giving up little privacy-invasive information. For example, your author has utilized these pseudo-banking operations to cash checks made payable to entities other than himself, while presenting the appropriate documents only—without allowing the store to make photocopies of any personal or business entity information. Refer to Chapter 15, "Anonymous Banking," for more information.

4. Instead of stashing your cash in a bank, you can store it instead in a safe deposit box at 24-7 Private Vaults, which requires no I.D. of any kind. You will never be asked to provide your address, phone, Social Security number, employment information, driver's license, credit card numbers, or even your name! See Chapter 18 for more details. Privacy seekers have also utilized bank safe deposit boxes held in business entities—a Nevada Limited Partnership, for example—for the purpose of storing cash prior to making an investment decision.

5. You can keep your liquid assets in the name of a Nevada Limited Partnership—cash included. Cash may be held in either a bank or brokerage account under the name of the limited partnership. Keep all information concerning the partnership accounts confidential.

CHECK-CASHING STORES

These check-cashing operations may be used to service your business banking needs by presenting a check made payable to the Nevada Limited Partnership which you manage. Typically, your U.S. passport and the portion of the partnership agreement that names you as the manager of the partnership—who has authorization to receive money on behalf of the company—is sufficient to present to the check-cashing store as evidence that you have authority to cash checks made payable to the company.

Although their fees are high, check-cashing stores offer a business manager a completely private way of cashing business checks. Since the only records kept by the store are the copy of the check and your illegible banking signature, your privacy is assured.

For added security and privacy, certain check cashing stores don't require either your Social Security number or a partnership Employer Identification Number in order to cash a check made payable to the partnership. Advise the store manager at the check-cashing store that you do not want them to make a copy of your U.S. passport or any of the Nevada Limited Partnership operating agreement paperwork.

You may be required to present the company paperwork and your identification each time you cash a company check. These stores are regulated by the government, but to date, their policies are far more customer friendly than are those of banks. There's a tremendous difference among these companies as far as their quality of services is concerned. The reader is advised to do his or her own research by telephoning the managers and corporate officers of various check-cashing stores for information on business banking services.

STOCK BROKERAGE BUSINESS ACCOUNT

Once a Nevada Limited Partnership has been properly formed, you as manager will want to open a stock brokerage account for the purpose of holding company liquid assets. Managing assets and making proper decisions as to how to invest capital are necessary decisions the investor/manager will need to make once all the facts have been gathered and the information has been evaluated.

It is the opinion of the author that all investors should hold financial assets in a stock brokerage account and make their own investing and trading decisions. In the event you feel incapable of this and do not feel inclined to undertake the study necessary to learn to handle assets under your control, enlist the services of a highly recommended fee-based financial planner.

You may choose not to give the person you hire to manage assets a blanket "power of attorney" over the account. Instead, you may want to maintain full control yourself, while considering the financial planner's expert recommendations as they are made. Financial assets, including cash, bank certificates of deposit, treasury bills, notes and bonds, corporate bonds, stocks, and mutual fund shares of all types, may be held in the Nevada Limited Partnership stock brokerage account.

You as an individual, and your spouse, if you are married, will be required to transfer assets held in your names into the partnership account by signing appropriate transfer authorizations which give new ownership of your assets to that of the partnership under your control. This transfer of assets is done at the time the application is completed with the stock brokerage company of your choice.

The most time-efficient way to shop for a brokerage company is to do your research online, followed by telephone calls to managers of various offices which you consider good candidates. Handle your inquiries much as you would when dealing with a bank—speak only to managers, and insist that they answer all relevant questions about the account requirements for a limited partnership account.

Carefully screen companies based on your requirements for privacy, as well as on services they offer. You'll need to provide proof that the partnership is up to date in terms of registration requirements and is properly formed. The Employer Identification Number (EIN) number will be required to open the account. The general partner, limited partner(s), and resident agent information will also be required on the application.

Some companies will ask for the manager's Social Security number, just as do banks, but others will let you open the account without providing it. Given the choice, don't provide it, although this may be difficult and may require your best people skills, as well as persistence.

BROKERAGE ACCOUNTS FOR BANKING

While your intention of using a stock brokerage account is for the purpose of holding, buying, and selling liquid assets and securities, you will find some firms that offer services similar to a bank.

Banks and brokerage companies are regulated by government agencies. Brokerage companies are more inclined to provide good customer service, in my experience. I have found brokerage companies to be more flexible than banks when asked to provide extraordinary customer services. For example, in some cases, a stock brokerage account held in the name of a Nevada Limited Partnership may be the only financial institution account necessary, as some firms will provide full-service banking services for a business account as well as the usual brokerage services.

Some brokerage firms will accept checks for deposit made payable to the brokerage firm's name, the partnership's name, or the partnership manager's name. Typically, banks will not accept checks for deposit into a business account that are made payable to the signer, while brokerage companies, in some cases, provide this service for their best customers. When you find a stock brokerage firm with these services, you may not need the services of a commercial bank.

Other banking services which some brokerage companies provide include wire transfers, Automatic Clearing House (ACH), checking account services, collateralized loans on assets held in the account— known as margin account loans, Automatic Teller Machine (ATM) services, cashier's checks, and MasterCard or Visa debit cards.

COMPANY NAME DEBIT CARDS

Regarding ATM services, I've found that brokerage companies are much more likely to provide the MasterCard or Visa debit card with only the partnership or other entity name on it, than are commercial banks. With a Visa or MasterCard debit account in only the partnership's name, you as the manager will have the use of an "anonymous" debit card, which may be used in conjunction with your alternate name for privacy and security purposes.

You can use the business debit card as necessary to purchase those services that are necessarily purchased with a MasterCard or Visa card. Since the card provided by the brokerage company is a debit card tied to the stock brokerage account held by the partnership, transactions are not reported to any credit bureaus, and only you and the brokerage company and the company at the point of sale will be aware of these purchases as they occur. Also, only the brokerage firm will be aware of the identity of the signer on the account. Be sure to use your illegible signature on all purchases.

FOREIGN BANK AND BROKERAGE ACCOUNTS

The U.S. investor who spends substantial time out of the country may benefit by keeping assets offshore. Others may choose to open foreign bank or brokerage accounts for the jurisdictional advantages— or for investment opportunities offered by these institutions. Checks from U.S. sources deposited into a foreign account may be subject to long hold periods before funds are made available for use. Some foreign banks will accept checks for deposit into the account, as well as other negotiable instruments, but do not offer check-writing privileges on the account.

By and large, however, foreign banks offer a full array of services to foreign investors and business account holders. Those who qualify as residents of foreign countries can receive tax advantages on a portion of their income. Consult a competent Certified Public Accountant or Enrolled Agent for advice on your tax liabilities.

I do not recommend avoiding your income taxes, but rather educate yourself on applicable tax laws specific to your individual case. For those who do substantial business out of the country or reside offshore for a portion of each year, offshore accounts may offer convenience and opportunity for foreign investments. You'll find that certain banks based in Switzerland, Liechtenstein, and the Isle of Man offer excellent services to foreign customers.

Many foreign banks are full-service institutions that offer customers the opportunity to hold all asset classes under one account. Banks based in Belize, Panama, the Cayman Islands, Austria, Gibraltar, and Nevis also are popular with foreign investors. Foreign brokerage houses are sometimes used by companies and individuals to buy and sell stocks and mutual fund shares worldwide.

When dealing with any foreign institution, you may be best served by obtaining bank and brokerage referrals from those who have been satisfied with the customer service of these companies.

MERCHANT ACCOUNTS

Merchant accounts are tied to business bank accounts for the purpose of accepting customers' credit cards for the payment of goods and services. A merchant account is an added feature on a business checking account with a commercial bank.

Typically, businesses based in the U.S. accept Visa, MasterCard, Discover Card, and American Express as payment for goods and services. As a business manager, you will find that many banks utilize third-party companies to service their merchant accounts, while some larger institutions have their own companies in house. The ability to accept credit card payments is necessary for a business, although institutions require a great deal of privacy-invasive information from the manager of the account, due to the amount of fraud committed on these accounts, especially in businesses deemed to be high risk.

Banks—and companies handling merchant accounts for banks—want a personal guarantee from you, the manager, as well as all of your confidential information, including your credit reports, Social Security number, and business references prior to giving your business a merchant account. These requirements, of course, are unacceptable for the privacy-conscious individual.

In order to overcome these hurdles and still have the sales advantages associated with accepting credit cards for the business you manage, consider utilizing either a foreign bank for your business, or use a third-party vendor to process your credit card purchases. Foreign banks may have strict requirements as far as deposits maintained to collateralize the merchant services account. However, if you establish a foreign business account, particularly when opened in Panama or Belize, your privacy is assured.

Fees, quality of service, and availability of funds depend on the institution you select, so compare prices and bank policies prior to settling on a company to handle your credit card transactions.

SUMMARY

1. Privacy seekers may utilize legal entities to hold liquid financial assets for privacy and asset protection. You as the manager can control everything, while owning very little property.

2. A Nevada Family Limited Partnership is the preferred entity of many privacy-conscious investors for holding liquid assets and offers privacy and asset protection.

3. A Nevada L.L.C. may be the partnership's general partner.

4. The "trust manager principle" allows the human manager to remain anonymous.

5. An administrative trustee may be used for high-level privacy purposes.

6. The Nevada Limited Partnership owns the financial assets, while the manager controls and makes management decisions concerning the property held by the partnership. Both are separate legal entities.

7. Those desiring to open a bank account without a tax identification number or a Social Security number should occasionally check the www.PrivacyCrisis.com website for updates on the availability of this option. Also, review the five suggestions on pages 222 and 223 of this chapter.

8. Check-cashing stores can be used to cash checks held in the name of a business entity, once the company manager provides proper documentation to the store.

9. Stock brokerage accounts held in a Nevada Limited Partnership's name are often recommended for holding liquid assets. Additional business banking services may be provided to the manager of the partnership by the brokerage firm.

10. Foreign banks and brokerage companies may be useful for those investors who spend substantial time outside of the U.S.

11.   Merchant accounts allow businesses to accept major credit cards for the purchase of goods and services. American banks will require the manager to personally guarantee the merchant account as well as require privacy-invasive information. Third-party merchant account processors require less personal information from the business managers and signers.

12.   Foreign banks will allow the business owner more privacy for his merchant account and may require a substantial security deposit.

EIGHTEEN

Real Estate and Hard Assets

"If you're never scared or embarrassed or hurt, it means you never take any chances."—Julia Sorel

REAL PROPERTY, PRECIOUS METALS, AND COLLECTIBLES

The privacy-conscious investor will face the most challenges for complete secrecy of investments as he or she invests in and manages real estate holdings. "Real property" is defined as real estate holdings of all types, whereby the actual property is owned.

Single-family homes, apartments and commercial buildings, undeveloped property, farm land, and any other such property may be bought, held, and sold by the investor.

Managing to conceal any ownership ties to the property is necessary for individuals who desire to privately hold these properties. As with liquid investments, hard assets and real estate require the structuring of registered entities as well as confidential buying and selling and management of these properties. You can either manage the property yourself or utilize the services of a management company or hire a manager to perform those duties required to service the real estate holdings.

Investments in real estate, gold, silver, platinum, rare coins, and all types of collectibles will comprise the asset classes of real estate and hard assets for the purpose of this chapter. Real estate and collectibles are considered illiquid and require a willing buyer and seller in order for a transaction to occur. Illiquid investments are less convenient than liquid assets and require ongoing management and effort to sell or buy the property.

Precious metals, including gold, silver, and platinum are liquid and can be converted to cash once the physical metals are presented to a dealer. These metals can be purchased from gold dealers as well during every market day. Rare coins, while considered collectibles, are also liquid and can readily be bought and sold through dealers. Extremely rare coins will require time and effort to acquire as well as sell, however.

Although the reader should consult his attorney for expert advice concerning proper entities for holding real property and hard assets, the author will present information which has been recommended by attorneys who specialize in asset protection and privacy.

REAL ESTATE INVESTMENTS

For confidentiality and protection from personal liability, many investors have formed a Nevada LLC for holding real property investments. The LLC could be 100 percent owned by another entity under your control—a Nevada Limited Partnership, for example. Some attorneys recommend that real property investments be held in separate entities from liquid investments. Consult your own attorney for expert advice in view of your individual circumstances.

Be certain to explain to all real estate agents and other professionals with whom you deal that you are bidding on property and buying and selling on behalf of the LLC—the company that will be the legal owner of the property. It is not imperative that you provide your true name unless you choose to do so. You may in fact use only the LLC's name during the course of your business dealings or perhaps have an understanding with a senior real estate broker that your name as manager of the LLC is to remain confidential and not to be revealed to anyone. Real estate agents and brokers want your business, and they will honor your request for privacy as you make your property deals.

You may want to review Chapter 17, "Private Investments," and utilize the trust manager principle and the administrative trustee concept as you register your Nevada LLC for holding your real estate investments.

REAL PROPERTY OWNERSHIP AND TITLE COMPANIES

While real estate agents and brokers are easily convinced to honor your privacy requests, you may—using only your company name in relationship to property transactions—approach the title company your broker uses to make certain that your privacy will not be invaded

during the title search. You may elect to use a title company other than the one your real estate professional normally uses for purchases.

Speak to title company managers and explain that you, as manager of the LLC, want no mention of your name on any searches or title registration in any county, government agency, or private company whatsoever. Title companies are restricted by their internal company guidelines, so you will need to deal with a manager or experienced representative who guarantees that the procedure will be completed your way. Meet them in their office if need be and obtain a signed written agreement stipulating your personal privacy requirements.

Typically, when you use the trust manager principle and administrative trustee concept in conjunction with the LLC as the owner of the property, a search of both the LLC and the trust names is done on county records only. It is possible to have only the company name and trust's name revealed on all records pertaining to real estate transactions. Avoid having your name placed into any database, because a remaining paper trail in the county records could come back to haunt you at some future date when you have the greatest need for privacy.

The LLC must be registered with the Nevada secretary of state, and the trust manager principle can be used as well to preserve your privacy as the manager of the company. County records will reflect the LLC as the owner of the property. The administrative trustee can sign on behalf of the trust manager whenever signatures are required on government forms.

Preliminary research of title companies, real estate agents and brokers, county recording documents, and any other requirements for property ownership will provide you with the information you'll need to plan your private real estate transactions. Because of the variations in laws and policies of both private companies and government agencies that will be involved in your real estate business, you are advised to complete your research and make appropriate privacy planning prior to the time real property is purchased or sold.

Regardless of where investment property is purchased, business-friendly Nevada can be used as a business base for real estate ownership.

PRECIOUS METALS AND RARE COINS

The most private way to buy gold, silver, platinum, and rare coins is by cash and carry. Find a reputable precious metals dealer, go to your trusty ATM and make your cash withdrawal, and place your order for whatever investments you wish to buy. Pay the man, pick up your precious metals and rare coins, and be on your merry way. Have the receipt made out in the name of the Nevada Limited Partnership, LLC, or other entity that holds your investments.

▶ Gold bullion may be held in a variety of ways. American Eagles, Canadian Maple Leafs, South African Krugerrands, Australian Kangaroos, and Swiss 20 Francs are some of the preferred bullion coins investors use to hold gold. In addition, gold bars may be purchased for investment purposes.

▶ Silver bullion is purchased and sold by investors. Junk silver coins, silver bars from five to 100 ounces, and one-ounce rounds are typical silver investments.

▶ Platinum, the most rare of the precious metals, may be held in coin or bar form.

▶ Rare coins, depending on their scarcity, liquidity, the expertise of the individual investor, and his or her tolerance for risk, may be suitable for investment purposes. Those who invest in rare coins should study the market prior to making use of these collectibles as investments.

Grading services such as Professional Coin Grading Service (PCGS) provide investors with assurance that the quality of the coin has been independently certified by a rare coin expert. Precious metals and rare coins may be held in the name of the Nevada Limited Partnership, and you as the controller of these investments can remain anonymous by following the procedures previously outlined pertaining to the registration of the partnership.

SAFE DEPOSIT BOXES AND SAFES

While precious metals and rare coins may readily be bought and sold and are considered liquid, the one drawback to ownership is the storage requirements of these investments.

Silver is the most cumbersome and will require the largest space to store in an amount that will equal a substantial value when the time comes for it to be converted into cash. Gold, platinum, and rare coins, on the other hand, can be stored much more efficiently. Many coins can be stored in a large safe deposit box.

Home safes come in a variety of sizes and shapes and are popular among those of means, though they are considered dangerous if and when someone with criminal tendencies learns of their existence. The more popular bank safety deposit boxes serve the average investor just fine, though they cannot be accessed on a whim but require normal banking hours for you to visit your gold.

A bank safe deposit box can be opened in the name of the Nevada Limited Partnership. Keep in mind that the banker will want all the information he asked for when you opened the partnership business checking account. Keep your personal Social Security number off of the account and supply only the tax I.D. number of the business. Also, remember to restrict access to the account to yourself and your spouse, if you are married.

As with a business bank account held by the Nevada Limited Partnership, the contents of the safe deposit box are owned by the partnership, not you as the manager and signer. So in the event you or your assets are being hunted by identity thieves, an ex-spouse's lawyer or investigator, or others who make a claim to your money, the partnership's holdings are not vulnerable for seizure to satisfy personal debts of the manager or signer on the account.

Just the same, don't test the law. Lay low, so to speak, telling no one of the partnership's holdings or of the location of the safe deposit box if you decide to rent one. Obtaining a safe deposit box in a bank where you do no other business is a high-level privacy idea. Paying for the rental fee with cash and money orders will leave no trace of who is paying the bills for storing the precious metals.

HOW TO OPEN A SAFE DEPOSIT BOX WITHOUT A NAME OR SOCIAL SECURITY NUMBER

For those who really want to privatize their investments, there is a way to do this without leaving any paper trail whatsoever. Would you like to have a totally secret way of storing your precious metals and rare coins? Do you need a secure vault to sock away your excess cash, jewelry, private documents, and other valuables? Are you facing a nasty divorce and/or a child support and custody battle? Have you been a victim of identity theft and need a totally secure and private way of storing cash, gold, credit cards, documents, and other valuables?

Perhaps you need to disappear and leave no trace of any asset or account belonging to you or any company under your management or control. Maybe you're ready to convert all of your holdings into cash, for whatever reason, and stash the cash and other valuables until you make a plan for the future of your money.

You can open a safe deposit box in complete privacy by using the services of a Nevada company that offers complete secrecy to their safe deposit box holders. This company will allow anyone to rent a safe deposit box without any identification and without providing any name or Social Security number or Tax I.D. number. You do not need a driver's license, a U.S. passport, or any identification to open a safe deposit box with this company.

24/7 Private Vaults uses iris recognition technology to identify their customers instead of traditional government identification documents. Customers' eye scans provide a foolproof way of identification so no other identification or documents need to be produced in order to obtain a completely private safe deposit box. Also, unlike a bank, the customer keeps both keys to his or her box. Banks give the customer one key and keep the second key.

Safe deposit boxes may be rented from 24/7 Private Vaults in a variety of sizes ranging from 3 x 5 x 22 inches to 10 x 15 x 22—and prices for yearly rental fees vary. You can access your private safe deposit box at 24/7 Private Vaults any time of day or night, 365 days a year. Contact them at:

Website: www.24-7PrivateVaults.com
Telephone: (702) 948-5555
Email: contactus@24-7privatevaults.com
Address: 24/7 Private Vaults
3110 E. Sunset Road, Suite H
Las Vegas, Nevada 89120, U.S.A.

COLLECTIBLES AS INVESTMENTS

Collectibles of all types may be used for investment purposes and may be held in a Nevada LLC. Consult your attorney for advice on what entity he recommends to hold ownership of this special asset class. While the ownership of collectibles, by the very nature of the product, is private, special knowledge will be required in order to become a successful investor in these illiquid investments.

Collectibles may include but are not limited to cars, baseball cards, rare coins, furniture, stamps, dolls, books, paintings and other artwork, guns, and other specialty items. Markets vary according to the collectible, as do the storage and maintenance requirements and costs of each class of collectible.

SUMMARY

1. Real estate investment property will present challenges for the investor who chooses to remain anonymous.

2. A Nevada Limited Liability Company (LLC) may be used to hold investments in real estate.

3. The trust manager principle and administrative trustee concept allows the manager to remain anonymous on Nevada secretary of state records.

4. When dealing with realtors and title companies, make certain to form agreements of confidentiality prior to transacting business. Only the trust which will manage the LLC—and the LLC which will own the property—need to be searched by title companies. Make sure you as the trustee and manager do not have your name entered into databases when buying property.

5. Research ownership documentation requirements in a given county prior to making real estate purchases and sales.

6. Precious metals, rare coins, and other collectibles may be purchased with cash to preserve your privacy. When selling hard assets, have the check made payable to the entity which owns the property or other entity under your control. Payments for sales may also be received in cash.

7. Safe deposit boxes may be held in the name of a Nevada Limited Partnership.

8. 24/7 Private Vaults, Las Vegas, Nevada, offers confidential safe deposit boxes and does not require customers to provide a name, identification, Social Security number, or Tax I.D. number.

9. Collectibles of all types can be used for investment purposes and will require specialized knowledge and information.

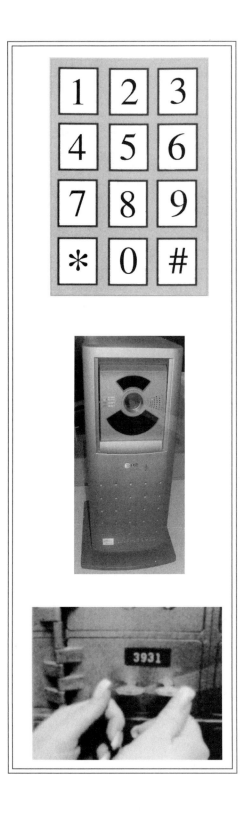

Your personal (PIN) access code, assigned privately and retained exclusively by you.

An iris (eye) scan—a proven safe, irrefutable identification system.

Two keys—in all the world, there are only two keys to open your small, medium, or large security vault unit, and you keep BOTH of them.

NINETEEN

Credit Bureaus

"We at Chrysler borrow money the old fashioned way.
We pay it back."—Lee Iacocca

FREE MONEY

In early 2003, credit lines under the name of the author were accessed and money was borrowed at 0 percent interest. This "free money" was used to capitalize on the uptrend in stock prices at that time. Without a squeaky clean record of paying bills and loans on time, one will not be offered money at low interest rates or, in some cases, interest-free loans, when the cost of borrowing money is low. So in order to be eligible for such opportunities when they do arise, it is important to learn about those companies that store and share the records of your bill-paying history—the three major credit bureaus.

CREDIT BUREAUS: CORPORATE BIG BROTHERS

Three companies—TransUnion, Equifax, and Experian—plus many smaller, less-significant local credit bureaus, keep personal record files on all U.S. residents who utilize the American system of borrowing and buying goods and services requiring creditor and consumer historical, financial records.

Historical records are stored in credit bureau files on all whose names make it into their databases, which includes virtually everyone who buys products and services "on credit" while giving their true name to companies who utilize the credit bureaus for establishing credit or for screening applicants for the purchase of essential goods and services.

Contact information for the three major credit reporting agencies is as follows:

Equifax
P.O. Box 740341
Atlanta, GA 20274
(800) 685-1111
www.equifax.com

Experian
P.O. Box 2104
Allen, TX 75013
(888) 307-3742
www.experian.com

TransUnion
P.O. Box 1000
Chester, PA 19022
(800) 916-8800
www.transunion.com

THE THREE MAJOR CREDIT BUREAUS

Companies that report their customer's payment history will provide information to one or all three major credit bureaus. This reporting, done electronically, provides information for a file that contains information for your credit report. In-depth financial and credit and personal information is contained in one's credit file and will be made available to those who receive your credit report. Identification and employment information, including your name, birth date, Social Security number, home and business addresses, employer, and spouse's name are routinely noted.

Additionally, the credit reporting agency also may provide information about your employment history, home ownership, income, and previous addresses. The accounts held under your name are listed, showing how much credit has been extended and whether you have paid on time. Other events, such as referral of an overdue account to a collection agency, may also be noted.

Credit bureaus maintain records of all creditors who have asked for your credit history within the past year—or in some cases, two years—and a record of those persons or businesses requesting your credit history for employment purposes for the past two years as well. These "inquiries" may reduce your credit score—a numerical assignment calculated by proprietary credit bureau formulas.

Public record information, including bankruptcies, foreclosures, or tax liens, appears on your credit report. Negative credit report information will remain on your credit report for a period of seven years. However, exceptions are made for certain "offenses," which include the following:

▶ Bankruptcies will be reported on credit reports for ten years.

▶ Information reported concerning an application for a job in excess of $75,000 may remain on your credit report indefinitely if the prospective employer provides it to credit reporting agencies.

▶ Life insurance application information for a policy exceeding $150,000 has no time limit.

▶ A judgment entered against you will remain on your credit report for a period of seven years or until the statute of limitations runs out.

"We do not want to avoid being in the credit bureau databases..."

While on the surface it may seem that this privacy-invasive storage of your personal information and credit history is a huge disadvantage, let's use it to your advantage to improve your ability to disappear while using other people's money. You don't want to avoid being in the credit bureau databases, lest you become ineligible for the financial leverage advantages of buying certain expensive products and services on credit.

Also, you want to be in a position to be able to borrow money when it is beneficial to do so. With these objectives in mind, it is imperative that your credit report reflect accurate, up-to-date information, as well as a record of timely interest and principal payments on loans and credit lines at various banks and credit card institutions and other companies where credit has been granted. You want to create a credit bureau file that increases your privacy, and, in order to do this, you must learn how to gain control of your individual credit report. To accomplish privacy objectives through the use of credit reports, review current data on your credit reports at each of the three credit bureaus.

MONITORING YOUR CREDIT REPORTS

In order to effectively "disappear" from anyone you might not want to find you, or those who may want to cause you difficulty at some future time, regardless of what the motivation may be, it is prudent to begin by obtaining a copy of your three credit bureau reports from Trans-Union, Equifax, and Experian. You'll be asked to supply information verbally, once you finally get through on the telephone, a time-consuming task in and of itself.

Once you provide the personal information necessary to obtain your credit reports, you may obtain them via mail or online. Carefully review all of the information and be prepared to dispute any late payments or incorrect addresses, misspellings of names, or other incorrect data on your credit reports. In view of the class action lawsuits filed and judgments entered against credit bureaus in recent years—as well as the weight carried by The Fair Credit Reporting Act, enforced by the Federal Trade Commission—credit bureaus will work with you to correct information that has been inaccurately given to them. But you will need to contact them and provide documentation, then wait out the dispute period prior to removal of incorrect information from your credit report.

However, it is well worth the effort. You will discover that in the world of business, a good credit report will enable you to accumulate high credit lines from banks and credit card companies, and these funds can be accessed whenever you choose. Or you can leave the accounts dormant until an opportunity presents itself for utilizing your borrowing power to purchase personal items or to make a timely investment, providing the institution which has extended credit to you allows for the use of funds for investment purposes, of course.

CREDIT REPORT DISPUTES

Whenever you discover payment mistakes—late payments, for example—on your credit bureau report, complete the necessary paperwork provided by the credit reporting agency with a cover letter explaining their inaccurate information. Usually, routine late-payment errors require no more than completing the dispute form or advising the credit bureau company by telephone.

The company that provided the inaccurate information to the credit bureau has a thirty-day period of time in which to counter your dispute, and if they do not, the late-payment "ding" is removed from your report. In the event the problem is serious, documentation on your part—including payment records, signed statements, and the like — may be necessary to convince the credit bureau of the legitimacy of your dispute claim.

Sometimes a telephone contact with a manager at the bank or business who made the false report of your payment history will work wonders. Always call the head of the department. This means the equivalent of the CEO of the credit department. Generally, he or she has staff to take their calls, and when you sound convincing enough over the phone and quote the Fair Credit Reporting Act—the law that requires creditors to treat consumers fairly, and note that your next phone call will be to 1-877-382-4357, the Federal Trade Commission, followed by the Better Business Bureau—your adversary will likely be amenable to a fair and timely settlement of the problem.

If not, call a different manager, the CEO, and then the chairman of the board of the parent company—and you will eventually get your way, providing that you're right, of course. Refer to Chapter 25, "People Skills," in this book and wait a day or two between calls for best results and to replenish your energy. Such tasks are stressful, and you want to be at your best as you make your case for cleaning up mistakes on your credit report.

The executive with whom you speak will, in most cases, see to it that you receive the proper documentation—in writing if necessary—to have credit bureaus remove incorrect credit report information.

OFFSHORE RESIDENCY ADVANTAGE

While the three credit bureaus service only U.S. residents, you can be officially based offshore and still receive the benefits of having a credit bureau report at the American credit bureau companies. In fact, you gain a high-level privacy advantage by "residing" offshore, and you can take full advantage of keeping the credit you currently have, as well as increasing your credit with American creditors, as you receive all your bank and creditor statements at your offshore address.

You could establish and use an address in a state as your last address on record, thereby allowing you to access your report online while you keep the credit report "frozen" and still maintain your primary address offshore (see section on "Freezing Credit Reports: A High-Level Privacy Tactic," on the facing page).

PANAMA CITY, PANAMA—A POPULAR OFFSHORE RESIDENCY CHOICE

The offshore address needs to be stated in the "consumer statement" or "personal statement" on the credit report, as U.S. credit bureaus will not place it in the personal data section, nor will they normally service your report when you "reside" outside of the country. Exceptions can be made when you make direct contact and establish a rapport with high-level managers at the credit bureau companies.

The consumer statement on a credit report allows for the consumer to include a personal statement as part of the file. In this case, it could include the offshore address. It could also serve to provide explanations of a judgment, bankrupt spouse, or other items—either already in the file, or as an addition to it.

Privacy advocates have advised their banks and credit card companies that have extended credit on their behalf of their correct offshore address, and they will begin sending statements to the address requested. Once their creditors have sent statements to their out-of-country address, privacy seekers have advised the credit bureaus of their off-shore address, with a supporting statement.

By placing a statement indicating your actual foreign address in the "consumer statement" of each of your three credit bureau reports, you will let all those inquiring eyes who sneak up on you by viewing your credit report know that you live far, far away from your last place of residence—the U.S.A. You will appear to be out of reach by anyone who wants to trouble you, for whatever reason, because the distance, travel time, costs, and inconvenience of chasing you down offshore is an extremely effective buffer—in most cases, shielding you from those who may want to bring unwanted court papers or the like into your life.

Certainly the jurisdictional disadvantages and red tape associated with pursuing anyone outside of the country will slow down the most ambitious of private detectives or lawyers working on behalf of claim-ants with intent to defraud and who pursue civil cases without merit. Stalkers and enemies of all sorts who have spent the time, energy, and money to view your credit report also will contemplate carefully before beginning the complicated task of finding you, if you are believed to be out of the country. Remember that creating a location illusion is para-mount for your successful privacy plan. It is no one's business where you live, and your privacy and security are virtually guaranteed when no one has links to your true home address.

So long as you are careful to pay your bills on time and keep your creditors apprised of your correct foreign address, they will not, for the most part, object to keeping you as a potential debtor while you live out of the country.

Having an official offshore residence, with documentation that you ac-tually live there—evidenced by having the address on your credit bureau reports and by having creditors' statements sent to you at this address—is a high-level privacy and security measure worth your consideration.

FREEZING CREDIT REPORTS: A HIGH-LEVEL PRIVACY TACTIC

At the time of publication, certain states allow residents to "freeze" their credit bureau reports with all three credit bureaus. California, Louisiana, Nevada, Maine, Connecticut, New Jersey, and North Car-olina currently allow consumers to freeze their credit bureau reports with credit reporting agencies. In addition, Illinois, Texas, Vermont, and Washington permit victims of identity theft to place a freeze on their credit bureau files.

Twenty-seven states have filed security freeze bills, including California and Texas, which filed bills to strengthen existing freeze bills as of this writing. If you live in these states and want to prevent individuals or companies with whom you do not have a credit relationship from accessing your credit files, you can complete the proper form with each of the credit bureaus (there is a nominal fee for this service).

Once done, each credit bureau sends you a password, and only those with password authorization can access your reports. Those not currently reporting to your credit bureau reports cannot. So you can essentially lock up your credit bureau files to prevent those with whom you have no credit account, thus preventing inquiries—whether "soft" or "hard" (the two types of credit report viewings, based on the relative detail of the inquiry)

Are you in danger of having a predator, in the guise of a legitimate creditor but eager to make off with your money or identity, pawing through your credit file? Are you at risk of investigators—or even business or financial entities—accessing your files without your knowledge or permission and then using the information against you? Freeze your credit report file, and these snoops will have no idea of your bill-paying history, creditors, available credit, current and past addresses, or other identifying information contained in your credit bureau reports. Consider using this high-level privacy measure as you place yourself out of the view of all those who want to know your personal business.

CHOOSING YOUR STATE OF RESIDENCE

Whenever it is to your advantage to "reside" in a location that provides suitable privacy measures or the potential for added personal security, it's prudent to take the necessary steps to create such a location illusion. As you study the principles in the "Behavior" section of this book and exercise those "people skills" discussed in that section, you'll learn that whatever you may require to ensure your privacy is available to you if you properly research and utilize all available information.

Improve and use your communication skills to accomplish your goals and objectives, because it is through people that you gain privacy and the advantages of having your personal credit profile presented in the best possible way. For example, in the event a particular state offers residents the ability to "freeze" credit reports, an advertisement can provide resources for accomplishing your objective.

Privacy advocates use mail nominees to secure mailing addresses in states offering credit bureau privacy advantages. Then, following the receipt of several mailings to that address, the companies that subscribe to credit bureau services will surely advise the big three credit bureaus of the "new address." The "resident" of a given state can then take advantage of everything this new home has to offer, including the ability to have their credit bureau files "frozen" and kept away from those who threaten to damage them or their pocketbook.

PRIVATE INVESTIGATORS USE CREDIT REPORTS

While reviewing his credit reports two to three times yearly had become a habit during his years of being hunted, our friend Alex Corbin made it his business to monitor these files with compulsive regularity to keep apprised of the efforts of his enemies.

Since no "freeze" laws were in effect at that time, he had to take the steps necessary to create a distance barrier—at least on paper—between him and those who wanted to drag him into court. Private investigators from four states attempted to locate him by tapping into credit bureau databases. But their efforts proved futile, because his trail of long-abandoned mail drops and his offshore residency left Gumshoe without much to go on, especially since there was little information in the personal data section of the report—information which he was careful to dispute and have deleted if it offered any leads to his history or whereabouts.

You should have no previous driver's license numbers or records of states that have issued state identification cards or driver's licenses to you, no telephone numbers, or e-mail addresses.

Naturally, your Social Security number will need to remain on it, but other than this piece of information—a necessary and required identifier—all other information is subject to change, including your name variations. You can use two initials in lieu of a first and middle name, which will give you a nonspecific name and create more work and paper as your adversaries pull multiple reports searching for you, especially if you have a common surname.

In all cases, remember that you, as a hunted individual, have a distinct advantage, especially when using the credit bureaus as tools for privacy, because you will be able to change and manage your report to suit your fancy while providing more work and confusion for anyone seeking to pry into your private affairs.

And with the "freeze" tactic now available to "residents" of certain states, folks whose addresses are in those progressive consumer credit-protecting states now can opt to just saying "no" by "freezing" their reports to prevent anyone whatsoever from breaking into their private credit bureau report files.

For the reader who follows the information in this book, credit bureau reports no longer hinder your efforts to become "invisible." In fact, the credit bureaus, when used correctly with the tactics described herein, will make it easier for you to "disappear."

THE INVISIBLE DEBTOR: BORROWING MONEY PRIVATELY

The use of financial leverage is always attractive to the astute business person who has a structured plan for his venture capital. When you can borrow money privately, with only immediate associates, if any, knowing of its use, the prospect of borrowing money when offered at a low cost is even more compelling.

Privacy advocates reportedly have been able to obtain money while also retaining their privacy—by restructuring debt in such a way as not to reveal their actual intentions for use of the funds.

For example, the "balance transfer" is popular among credit card companies who attempt to entice consumers to shift their debt from one source to another—essentially "borrowing from St. Peter to pay St. Paul." The credit card institution will typically send out promotional offerings at low introductory interest rates—or even no interest at all—to customers with average to above-average standing, to entice them to borrow funds to pay off an existing creditor by transferring their debt balance to the new lender at an attractive interest rate.

For example, Alex Corbin expected to owe Pennysavers Garage $3,500 for extensive repairs to his old jalopy and was to be charged 12 percent per annum on the balance if he chose to finance the bill with the garage. Along comes First Finance Credit (a fictitious name) with a Visa card promotional balance transfer teaser rate of 2.99 percent for nine months, plus a $25 processing fee. By agreeing to transfer the debt from Pennysavers Garage to his Visa card account, Alex would save 9 percent in annual interest charges, while paying off the car repair bill and shifting the debt to the First Finance Visa credit account.

First Finance Credit is in business to make money, of course, so they were counting on him making minimum payments over the long haul and extending the payments well past the nine-month period so they could charge 17.9 percent, beginning on the tenth month following the agreement to the balance transfer "loan."

Since Alex is an astute consumer, he wanted to pay off his debt quickly, while gaining the advantage of a low rate of interest for the use of the $3,500, plus be able to convince all who viewed his credit bureau reports of his credibility.

Alex did not, however, want anyone to know of his business dealings with Pennysavers Garage—a credit bureau subscriber—because this business is located in the same city as his employer, and this revelation, if discovered by an alert private investigator, could bring a casing crew to his neighborhood in an attempt to serve him with those dreaded court papers—the summons which his attorney had instructed him to avoid at all costs in order to legally avoid any future court appearances.

With all of these facts, knowledge of how the system works, and careful planning to detail, Alex began to set forth a plan of action which would enable him to use other peoples' money—his Visa account— while concealing the actual debt and restructuring it to another entity under his control.

This plan was laid after he reviewed his credit agreement with the finance company, which did not prohibit him from following his plan.

First, Alex determined the actual projected debt for the car repairs from the garage service manager prior to his authorization of the repair job. This amount, he was told, would be near $3,500 and would not exceed this amount. Next, he held a company meeting for an entity registered as Desert Sand Valley Limited Partnership, which he manages and controls and which holds liquid assets of stocks, mutual funds, bonds, and cash. He then borrowed the sum of $3,500 from this Nevada Limited Partnership. A meeting was held, and a written company agreement with the manager, Alex, was signed and filed to document the transaction.

Now, Alex was in debt to the tune of $3,500 to Desert Sand Valley Limited Partnership and wished to transfer this debt to his First Finance Credit Visa account. Appropriate calls were made to the finance company, the debt terms were discussed and agreed upon by both parties, and soon a check in the balance transfer amount of $3,500 was received at the mailing address of the Limited Partnership by manager Alex's mail-drop nominee, who forwarded the check to Alex. He then stamped it with the Limited Partnership bank account information and mailed the check to the bank holding the Partnership business checking account.

Repairs had begun on the car to be rehabilitated for distance driving, and Alex paid for the job entirely with cash in hand—borrowed from the partnership—and now paid in full by his personal creditor, First Finance Credit. Their records—as well as the credit bureau reports on Alex Corbin—now revealed his debt to the Visa account, with no one the wiser as to how Alex had creatively financed his car repairs—and without revealing the location of the "real' creditor," which would lead to Alex's true locale.

Other ways are available to creatively manage debts without revealing all of your business to those who have access to your credit bureau reports. Personal credit lines have been used to loan money to companies under a manager's control—money that is then borrowed back again from an entity. And there are other methods, depending on one's individual circumstances and needs for privacy.

As always, the goal is the same: to access credit or use other people's money at a favorable interest rate, while preserving privacy of an individual's affairs. Read and study the contracts with the lending institution, while making certain that every transaction is legal and ethical so as not to jeopardize the credit line or compromise yourself.

In the event one elects to manage debt this way, always carefully document the steps taken, as well as the transactions executed, in the company files and keep all payment activity up to date so that the company is in compliance with all regulatory requirements. Also make sure that money is really owed to the company under your management when requesting that a loan transfer be made to it. Loans to corporate officers and managers are made all the time by companies, although the careful documentation of this activity is crucial so that personal and business assets remain separate.

CREDIT MAINTENANCE

Once you gain credit worthiness in the banking and lending community, you'll be able to increase your personal credit lines and credit card limits, which will serve as available money for use whenever you choose. Business managers have created a number of ways to use business entities as creditors, in order that legitimate debt is shifted from one entity to another for the interest rate and privacy advantages to be gained through these financial maneuvers.

Many individuals have substantial credit lines available in the form of bank credit lines and credit tied to credit cards, notably MasterCard, Visa, Discover Card, and American Express. Over time, through timely payments of bills and loans, anyone can accumulate credit, which can be used when opportunities present themselves for the use of borrowed money.

Keep in mind, however, that creditors with whom you currently do business are most likely to allow you to increase your levels of potential indebtedness, so you're best served by cultivating relationships with banks and institutions that know you and will love you when you pay off your bills on time—especially the large loans.

Once you have amassed a substantial amount of available credit—usually in the neighborhood of $300,000 to $500,000—in most cases new creditors will be reluctant to offer credit business to you. They will be scared off from taking you on as a potential credit risk once they view your credit report and see your high credit lines with available banks. Some institutions may even cancel your credit cards when they learn you have a large amount of available credit.

However, the larger banks, your preferred credit choices, will want to keep your business once you build a sound, timely bill-paying record. Your established creditors will increase your credit limits to their ceiling levels as you prove your credibility by paying them their principal on time. At times, new applications will be required, whether by telephone or written application, and you will have to weigh the advantages and disadvantages of providing personal information to your lenders in exchange for additional credit.

As always, keep as much information about yourself as private as possible and always provide accurate information to the institutions that have extended you credit, while making timely payments a priority.

CREDIT BUREAU CONTACTS AND DOCUMENTATION

As you continue monitoring, maintaining, and tweaking your credit report and discover how much value is associated with having spotless credit, you'll find it is advantageous to keep a diary of your calls to the credit bureaus. Also, you will find that when you really need changes made, it is advantageous to speak to and communicate in writing with high-level managers. Not customer service "supervisors," but regional and home office high-level mangers whose decision-making power and business expertise will save you time, effort, and money.

Build a file on each of your credit reports, complete with names, addresses, direct telephone numbers, and copies of important letters and completed forms you collect over the course of doing the part-time job of keeping your credit bureau reports in top shape. This type of organization will enable you to fully document your credit report activity and communicate with those individuals in the industry who have the power to assist you in making necessary corrections on your credit report. It also will improve your ability to utilize other people's money while taking advantage of the privacy you gain with full control of your credit profile.

YOUR CREDIT REPORT AND PRIVACY

Inquiries or viewings of your credit report are made when one person or any number of people gain authorization to see all of your personal and financial data contained in the report. In any case a "soft" inquiry or a "hard" inquiry will be made, with the differences being the security level of the observer and the information contained in the report.

Once you take advantage of "freezing" your report, you will be able to keep the snoops out of your business and will have no concerns about anyone spying on you and your most personal and confidential information file. When the opportunity for a business purchase or investment presents itself, you may need to verify your personal credit history—not an uncommon request among business professionals, investors, and others who want to know a lot about you before allowing you access to capital or business responsibilities.

Be extremely careful not to authorize anyone to "pull" your credit report. Rather, keep your credit file frozen, pull it yourself from the Internet or receive it by mail, and hand carry or mail it to the person to whom you want to show it. Be sure to mark out the Social Security number and other personal information that you do not want revealed about yourself, while leaving all the important historical payment records—the pertinent information to any entity that wants to evaluate your credit history in order to gain an understanding of how you have managed your personal finances over a long period of time.

The privacy advocate should not allow his or her credit report to be viewed for the purpose of obtaining consumer items such as telephones or automobiles. Nor should the report be pulled to obtain home loans or to rent property. When finance companies and prospective landlords tap into your credit report, you have given up essential parts of your privacy.

For financing consumer items, privacy-conscious individuals have been able to structure the debt to shield the actual reason for borrowing, as explained through the examples of Alex Corbin's privacy challenges. And when renting, privacy-conscious people use an "alternate name"—never their true name. Never obtain routine services such as telephone, Internet services, and the like in your true name, and don't allow any service provider to obtain a copy of your credit report.

IDENTITY THEFT CONSIDERATIONS

Preventing identity theft is an ongoing process for all of us, and because it is the fastest-growing crime in the U.S. today, it's critically important that you increase your privacy, both personally and as you do business, if for no other reason than to prevent crooks from stealing your personal identity information.

Freezing your credit reports is an effective way to thwart identity theft. Once this is done, no one will be able to obtain credit under your name when access to your credit report file is attempted. Once you have frozen your reports, the password given to you is the only key that can open it. And you should carefully guard the lock on this door to your credit bureau report.

Until you are able to go through the steps required to freeze your credit reports, place a "fraud alert" on your file. This can easily be accomplished when an explanation is given to the credit bureau companies that someone may have attempted to steal one's personal information. Then you can place a confidential password on the account, which adds a medium-level security feature on your file until such time as you can freeze your report.

In your normal business and personal correspondences, limit the number of correspondences received under your true name. Use an alternate or nickname or first name only as you correspond via snail mail and email. Utilize the privacy principles described in the section on "Finances," and don't hold assets in your own name. Instead, use a trust with no name similarities to your true name, with its own tax identification number for holding a personal checking account.

Consult your legal advisor for the best choice of entities for holding businesses, if you are a business owner, and consider using a business name other than your true name. Investments, both liquid and illiquid, should be held in entities other than your true name, and each entity—whether a limited partnership, LLC, or other business formation type—should have its own separate tax identification number, when an EIN is required.

Following the above recommendations will eliminate a paper trail back to you individually, providing that you carefully follow the other privacy considerations outlined in this section so that your true name will not be associated with any statements or registration of entities under your control.

And when the correspondences to all businesses, trusts, and the like under your control go to faraway mail drops with no association to your physical address, it makes it extremely difficult for anyone to steal meaningful personal data from you in order to accomplish identity theft.

To further ensure against the problem, store only necessary hard copy and computer files containing personal information, utilize coding to increase your security, and store important files off site. Shred paperwork you do not need to file. This will prevent any passing of information in the event of a random break-in at your residence, office, or place of business.

Other precautionary steps to help keep your private information out of the wrong hands include carefully screening all mail nominees and business people who come into your business life, as well as the careful selection and trust of personal friends. Passwords or fraud alert messages can be included on all of your credit card and financial institution accounts for an added layer of security.

As a consumer, you should know that the credit reporting agencies or credit bureaus sell portions of the personal data contained in your credit report file. Contact them in writing, advising them you wish to "opt out" of all of their mailing advertisements—and strictly prohibit them from sharing any information whatsoever about you or your report.

BUSINESS CREDIT

Establishing business credit will be necessary to some extent, depending on the type of business you manage or operate. When the operator of a body shop, for example, purchases paint and supplies "on account" from a wholesaler and pays the bill when it comes due, he has begun building a business credit profile that may become a bona fide business credit report under the name of the body shop.

This is not at all a bad idea, since all prudent business people want the advantage of buying something with only a promise and agreement to pay for it later, while collecting money for services rendered or goods sold prior to the time the original bill is due. Whenever this type of "short sale" (selling something before it is actually owned) is accomplished, financial leverage is effectively used, while using other people's money for business working capital.

Business credit agreements should be limited to pledging assets of the business and a guarantee to pay back the money owed by the business. Officers and managers should not personally guarantee loans, as many banks will request when credit is sought for companies under their control.

A personal guarantee will result in your personal credit report being pulled, thereby alerting the world of your involvement in the very business you want to make anonymous.

Also, do not co-mingle business assets with personal assets, as this may result in compliance violations, and the company may be determined to be invalid in the event of an audit. Avoid personal guarantees for business credit. Instead, either obtain credit under the business name entirely, without reference to your personal holdings, or restructure debts to entities under your control to fund business operations, as outlined previously—providing this is in accordance with your agreements with the financial institution, of course.

BUSINESS CREDIT REPORTING AGENCIES AND BUREAUS

A number of business credit reporting agencies in the United States are used by businesses and financial institutions: Dunn and Bradstreet, Experian Business, BusinessCreditUSA, FDInsight, Equifax Business, and ClientChecker. Two of these—Equifax Business and Experian Business—are extensions of the credit reporting agencies with like names.

▶ **Dunn and Bradstreet**, the largest business credit reporting agency, is almost a brand name within the industry, with over seventy million businesses registered with D&B. A DUNS rating is issued by Dunn and Bradstreet to businesses.

▶ **Experian Business**, with approximately fourteen million subscribers, grants credit scores based on business payment history.

▸ **FDInsight**—a NASDAQ-listed publicly traded company—is relatively new to the business credit reporting arena.

▸ **BusinessCreditUSA** provides cost-effective business reports and is a division of InfoUSA.

▸ **Equifax Business** provides credit scores for businesses, which include Small Business Financial Account Acquisition Scores, a Management Score, a Principal Score, and a Non-Financial Generic Risk Score.

▸ **ClientChecker** is a business credit company dedicated to serving small businesses. They grant a PayQuo Score and create profiles based on the reporting of vendors only.

Some of these business credit companies will want to include your personal data on their credit reports, and the reporting done may cross-reference the personal credit reports contained, so be extremely careful what personal information you share. A good rule to follow to avoid having your personal credit and privacy compromised is to refuse to give your Social Security number to any business credit reporting agency, while instead furnishing the business tax identification number (EIN) *only* as an identifying number.

State your position as "manager" or other job title, while explaining that your role as an operator is not to guarantee any debts incurred by the business. By effectively separating yourself, credit wise, from the business you control, operate, or manage, you will not risk having your personal privacy invaded by those with whom you do business, and your personal information will not be revealed to those who access the business credit report.

Unless you cannot prevent your personal information from being made available as part of a business profile, you may elect to forego building a business credit report altogether and instead, restructure debts by loaning money to the business under your control by accessing personal credit resources, while carefully following the privacy guidelines outlined herein and, of course, adhering to the policies of the institutions that have granted personal credit to you.

PAYING IT BACK

At the very heart of every credit system is the honesty of the borrowers and creditors behind it. Without morality and a willingness to pay back what is owed, the advantages of financial leverage, as well as the convenience of it all cannot exist, because those possessing the capital to loan cannot loan money at prevailing market interest rates without reasonable assurance that the principal will be returned when the debt becomes due.

Also, the lender must have the ability to command a fair return on the invested capital, which will be earned from the borrower in the form of interest on the money loaned. Your author discovered the advantages of risk-free investing early on while a student, when Discover Card—a well-known consumer credit card company—began offering incentives in the form of 0 percent interest rates and a nominal processing fee for cash advances as well as rebate-type refunds on purchases.

At the time, money market rates in banks and savings and loans were paying 8.5 percent, as I recall. So, being an enterprising student, I quickly opened accounts at several institutions and began making "risk free" investments with the money of Dean Witter—the owner of Discover Card at that time.

Deposits were made late Thursday afternoons, sometimes within minutes of closing time at an institution, allowing me to make full use of the float time to earn interest on the money in both the bank holding the money from which the check was written, as well as the receiving institution where the deposit was made, as immediate credit was given on the check when the deposit was made, although a three-day hold was placed on the funds.

The receiving institution did not have time to receive clearance from the other bank for several days, due to the weekend, so interest was earned on each account. Now, of course, I had maxed out my credit with Discover Card, which at that time was $70,000, as I recall, and each cycle, a check was written on the full credit limit, deposited into one account, and moved each Thursday afternoon.

When the money became due each cycle, I paid it back in full, waited for the payment to post with Discover Card, and repeated the process. This served as a part-time job for me at the time and, unknown to Dean Witter or Discover Card, provided money for my tuition and other expenses during my college days. Prior to undertaking this small business venture, the "business plan" was met with approval from my business law professor, an attorney, and a professor of business who taught my finance course. And because the lending institution had no restrictions for use of funds at the time, I proceeded to use "free money," minus my labor, travel, and processing costs.

Also, other companies began granting me credit and were anxious to give me substantial credit lines due to my wonderful payment history with Discover Card, so soon I was devoting Thursday afternoons to driving to banks and making deposits in person, while using other people's money "risk free" with the full faith and credit of the United States of America, the FDIC and FSLIC agencies—the bank and savings and loan insuring agencies—backing my short-term investments.

Today you can do the same with other people's money by paying bills on time as you access credit lines and use institutional money for either the purchase of high-ticket items or using cash from credit sources for investment purposes.

Whenever you borrow money without pledging collateral, it is unsecured credit. You are responsible for repayment of money you use, so remember to have a repayment plan and the discipline to stick to it. For high-level privacy, use the dual trust account principle while using the public trust account to receive and clear checks from creditors who extend you personal credit when cash is received and checks are made payable to you.

Keep the balance low in the public trust account. Remember that the primary reason for having it is to clear personal checks while keeping your name off of bank account titles and statements. Likewise, repay the creditors from this account. You may send and receive payments via bank wires, ACH transfer, or cashier's check.

Checks drawn on the public trust account may be used to pay debts as well. This account will be known by those creditors who receive funds from it, and they will—without a doubt—store it in their database.

Cash and money orders are too time-consuming for the payment of large debts. The private trust account will not be known by creditors, and you may withdraw and deposit personal money into it in the form of cash and money orders to keep its location a secret.

SUMMARY

1. A favorable credit report with a timely repayment history will boost your credit rating and enable you to use other people's money at attractive interest rates.

2. The three major credit bureaus store consumers' personal and financial histories and receive relevant credit information and other personal data from creditors.

3. Your credit reports should be monitored and received thrice yearly. Corrections should be made to obtain low interest rates and substantial credit lines and loans.

4. Dispute incorrect credit report information with credit bureau managers, not customer service staff.

5. Offshore "residency" enables privacy by distance, while still keeping U.S. credit sources. One may choose an English-speaking country with a reliable mail service system.

6. Certain states enable you to "freeze" your credit bureau files. A record of "residence" in one of these states is advantageous for personal privacy.

7. Privacy advocates structure personal debt into company debt and borrow from these entities to effectively become an "invisible debtor," while preserving personal privacy. They document all loans and repayments, while making certain to adhere to the credit agreement with the creditors.

8. When establishing credit relationships with banks and credit card companies, request increases of credit limits over time with the same companies rather than obtaining many smaller lines of credit with numerous creditors. Quality relationships with fewer financial institutions will result in more available credit. Timely repayment of large loans will convince financial institutions that you are a good credit risk and lead to increased credit limits.

9. Build relationships with managers at credit bureau companies.

10. Rather than authorizing inquiries to your personal credit bureau file, access your reports online or receive them by mail and provide them yourself to companies who need to see your credit report.

11. You can "restructure" consumer purchases into debts owed to companies under your control, rather than charge them directly on personal credit lines, when this type of restructuring is permitted per the contract or credit agreement with the financial institution.

12. Use the dual trust account principle for privacy. Receive personal deposits and pay bills with bank wires, ACH transfers, cashier's checks, and trust account checks from the public trust checking account. Keep balances low in this account.

13. Shred all confidential information that is not necessary to store. Store all highly sensitive files off site for privacy.

14. Business credit may be established when one's business requires the services of business vendors. Do not guarantee business loans and credit personally. Separate yourself from the business.

15. Establish the discipline of paying bills and loans on time and make a repayment plan at the time a loan is received.

TWENTY

Retirement Accounts

"There is only one success—to be able to spend
your life in your own way"
—Christopher Morley

NOT-SO-PRIVATE MONEY

Money and investments held in retirement plans and checks received from these plans—and all payments from other third-party sources—are, in almost all cases, payable to the individual and are traceable to the recipient by his or her name, date of birth, mother's maiden name, and Social Security number.

Monies relevant to this chapter include:

▶ Retirement funds of all types

▶ Long-term disability payments

▶ Worker's compensation checks

▶ Medical insurance reimbursements

▶ Medical supplemental insurance policy payments

▶ Automobile insurance medical coverage checks

▶ Social Security disability payments (SSDI)

▶ Supplemental disability insurance (SSI)

▶ Medicare payments

▶ Veteran's Benefits

▸ All other funds received from private insurance companies or government sources

Consider these funds as your non-private money, as any investigator, identity thief, or other person who completes a thorough search on your name and Social Security number and has access to the right database will be aware of these accounts and your receipt of funds when you receive your payments.

For the most part, the sources of these funds cannot be hidden, nor can they be made payable to another entity, as can be done with investments and payments from business sources. Follow the recommendations in Chapter 15, "Anonymous Banking," and cash the checks at a check-cashing store or use the "public trust bank account" for the deposit of these checks.

Also, when the issuing bank is within a reasonable distance of your location, you may present the check there for your cash. Once your check has cleared, you are free to make your cash as private as you wish, by utilizing the privacy measures discussed throughout the applicable chapters on Finances in this book.

RETIREMENT PLANS

One portion of your asset list—which you will be unable to conceal, in most cases—includes your retirement plans. These include the following:

▸ Individual retirement plans (IRAs)

▸ SEP IRAs

▸ Teachers retirement plans

▸ Federal, state, and local retirement plans of all types

▸ KEOGH Plans

▸ Payments from vested plans from all sources

▸ Retirement payments from life insurance policies and other insurance plans

▸ Social Security retirement benefits

▸ All other age-qualified payments received during retirement

Of all of these retirement plans, only the KEOGH plan may be held in a company name, "for the benefit of" the individual for which the plan is made. All other retirement plans must be held under one's personal name and Social Security number, and the KEOGH plan too will reference the person's name and Social Security number.

If you are going to have a retirement plan, you should realize that these assets will be open to prying eyes that have access to databases which contain names and Social Security numbers of those under the particular plan. Realize that retirement benefits are subject to seizure, in certain cases.

The KEOGH plan offers the most safety, and the protection or exceptions for seizure vary greatly, depending on the type of litigation or lien against you as an individual. Consult your attorney for your individual questions about the safety of your various retirement plans.

Receiving your retirement checks at your offshore mail drop and cashing the checks at U.S. check-cashing stores may be an option and will keep bank accounts under your control a secret from all who choose to snoop into your financial affairs. Cashing the checks at the issuing bank's branch office is another viable option to preserve your privacy.

INSURANCE PAYMENTS

Insurance companies investigate their policyholders periodically. The priority list for being investigated will include all who become beneficiaries of the policy under which they are insured. If and when you are injured or become ill and are covered under the provisions of a worker's compensation policy, other work injury or illness-related insurance coverage, or a long-term disability policy—whether a group plan or an individual plan—expect to be investigated by the insurance company which issues the checks.

Major medical insurance policy claims and all medical supplemental insurance claims may also trigger an investigation by the company. Social Security disability insurance coverage is provided to all who have worked long enough in the United States and have contributed enough to Social Security to be eligible for benefits. Total disability is required in order to receive it, so you won't have a great deal of fun if you receive SSDI, but be assured that the Social Security Administration's investigators will investigate you from time to time anyway.

Unemployment insurance payments are paid to those who, under certain conditions, lose their jobs, are direct employees of a company, and are otherwise eligible for it. Claims made under this insurance are carefully reviewed, both prior to the issuance of the first check as well as when ongoing claims are made for unemployment benefits. Be sure and follow the rules as you make your claims for unemployment.

Once you have occasion to claim benefits under your insurance policy, the value of your distant mail drop will become evident when you are not required to be a local—as in when you are required to actively seek employment in a specific area. If your location is not an issue, your faraway mailing address will stump Mr. Investigator at least temporarily and throw him off your trail. You are assured some privacy and freedom from bothersome snoops when your address in Gumshoe's file leads him to a South Dakota bookkeeper's home office while you are recovering in your Miami hospital bed.

Of course, you will be able to be tracked by your medical treatment records, so do not expect a high level of privacy during convalescence from injury or illness. Instead, do the best you can, and above all, take special precautions to avoid having any investigator find your home address.

Regardless of where you choose to deposit your third-party checks, those issuing the payments can pull the cancelled checks and determine where your account is held. With this in mind, a check-cashing store or the use of the "public trust bank account" are your best options for privacy.

You may present the check to the issuing bank with your identification and demand your cash as well, when the bank is located in your area. However, many times, your disability claim filed from California will be serviced by an East Coast office, and your checks will come to you drawn on a bank which has no branch offices in your area.

Also, sometimes insurance drafts are issued which require much more hold time than do normal checks in order to clear. These types of delay tactics are practiced often by the insurance industry, so you may have to use either your own public trust account or a check-cashing store to cash your benefit checks. Expect to have all aspects of your life investigated in the event you become disabled, and be assured that your finances will be at the top of the investigator's list.

GOVERNMENT CHECKS

As a taxpayer and citizen, you will on occasion be issued refund checks and other payments from government and quasi-government entities, and you will want to use financial privacy tactics as you convert these checks into cash. Social Security retirement benefits, Veterans' retirement payments, state and federal retirement checks, and other government payments for which you qualify by age only may be handled as you normally handle your personal receipts—the public trust bank account or a check cashing store are reasonable options.

Other checks may require more attention, to make sure that Big Bureaucrat and others know as little as possible about your financial affairs. Checks received from the Internal Revenue Service and State Franchise Tax Board should be cashed at a check-cashing store or at the bank from which they are issued. The paper trail stops at the bank where the check is cashed, so your bank account and any activity on it will remain a secret and will not become fuel for a tax investigation at some future point in time.

Refund payments received from the Department of Transportation, the Department of Motor Vehicles, or other automobile registration state agencies, should be handled as discreetly as possible. By utilizing a trust to hold title to the automobile, you assure yourself of anonymity, as the state will issue a check to the trust without mention of you as trustee on it. A check-cashing store is a private way of converting these checks into cash.

Business license refunds from city or county government, sales tax overpayment refunds, and all other checks received and made payable to either you or the business or trust you control, should be presented to a check-cashing store for cash.

If you are not concerned about government knowing certain aspects of your business, your low-balance public trust bank account can be used for depositing government checks made payable to you individually. However, remember that whenever you utilize a bank—whether this be the public trust bank account or other account—the issuing agency, company, or individual can learn where your account is held simply by checking the deposit stamp on the back of the cancelled check.

Also, the payer gains information as to the account number, bank routing number, and signature of the account holder, unless you follow the author's recommendations and only stamp your checks rather than providing a signature on deposited checks. Be especially careful with all government checks, as they can open a door of information to the people you least want to know anything about your financial affairs.

OTHER THIRD-PARTY PAYMENTS AND CHECKS

Alimony, child support payments, court-ordered judgment awards, insurance settlement checks, and other payments which are the result of litigation may come to you from a government agency or from your attorney. Consider the ramifications of the other party knowing your financial business as you receive these checks.

When an individual owes you money, elect to have the payment issued to a trust or a company that you manage. In all cases, when you receive a check payable to you individually, whether from government, any insurance company, or from any other company, agency, or individual, you may insist that the issuing bank cash their own check by presenting acceptable personal identification at the teller's window.

Sometimes the bank is out of the area, and this method of cashing the check cannot be done without devoting substantial time to traveling to that particular bank. Attempting to handle cashing the check by mailing it to the issuing bank and requesting the funds be sent via a money order, minus the processing costs, has been suggested, but this is a slow and risky way of attempting to get your money due, and your author recommends you not cash your checks other than in person.

You may elect to clear certain, less-sensitive checks by mailing them to your public trust bank account or by depositing them via the automatic teller machine or in person. Check-cashing stores offer high-level privacy for cashing sensitive checks.

SUMMARY

1. Retirement accounts are necessarily held in the individual's name and are linked to the person's Social Security number.

2. Insurance policies, Social Security accounts, retirement benefits, and other private and public benefit and retirement plans are held under the beneficiary's name—and claims and benefits are made payable to the individual.

3. Payments received from all public and private sources and made payable to the individual who is eligible for these payments are less private than are non-entitlement and non-retirement payments. The individual must receive these payments in his true name.

4. Checks received in one's true name may be cashed at the issuing bank, a check-cashing store, or deposited into the public trust account.

5. Distant mail drops may be used to preserve privacy when receiving third-party payments and retirement benefits.

6. Special care should be taken when cashing all government and tax agency checks.

♦ TWENTY-ONE ♦

Business Entities

"The ideal man is his own best friend and takes delight in privacy."—Aristotle

INVISIBLE PAPER MAN

Lawrence Randall Worthington (an alternate name) is a man obsessed with privacy. Indeed, his own mother and father know little about his life. He tells no one except his attorney, bankers, brokers, and other professionals on a need-to-know basis of his numerous Nevada Limited Liability Companies (LLCs) which hold title to various businesses, investment properties, and other ventures designed to shield him—the true controller—from all who might want to know who is really behind all that paper.

Trusts are used to hold his personal bank accounts, his primary residence, and two cars—and serve as "managers" of entities registered with the Nevada secretary of state. A living trust will keep the estate out of probate and assures the private distribution of assets to heirs upon his demise. A Nevada Limited Partnership is the sole owner of all the LLCs and is used to hold his portfolio of stocks, bonds, mutual funds, and precious metals. And an *offshore asset protection trust (OAPT)* based in the Cook Islands owns the limited partnership.

Our "invisible paper man" has insulated himself and his business from the outside world and remains anonymous to potential identity thieves who would love to be Lawrence. Private investigators may search for him to serve him a summons, and two ex-wives might also want to continue their extortion games of years past—if only they could locate Mr. Worthington.

Our boy Larry, known to those around him as "Barry White," does not use his true name for any purpose except when official business and the law requires him to do so. Otherwise, he operates anonymously through the use of many carefully concealed business entities and trusts, while preserving his privacy.

You may or may not want to duplicate the privacy measures used by Larry or "Barry"—his more common alternate name—through the extensive use of paper documents for privacy and asset protection, but depending on your individual needs, business entities and trusts can be used to enhance your privacy, eliminate your name on public and private records, and assist your exclusion from many databases. Consult your attorney for the purpose of obtaining answers to your legal questions and to obtain advice on all business entities and trusts.

TRUSTS

A trust is a written agreement under which property and assets are held and managed by one person for the benefit of one or more other people. Various types of trusts may be used to accomplish different goals. A trust offers a means of controlling or administering property with the added benefit or privacy. A trust, unlike other legal entities, does not have registration requirements with government agencies.

Necessary elements for the creation of a trust include a trustee,

trustor, beneficiary, trust property, and a trust agreement. The individual who provides property and forms the trust is known as the trustor. This person or other entity is sometimes referred to as the grantor, donor, or *settlor*. The trustee is the individual, institution, or organization responsible for management of the property held by the trust. Beneficiaries are those who receive the benefits of the trust. Trust property is any form of property held by the trust. A trust must hold some form of property in order to be valid.

How does one make a trust fulfill the property ownership requirement, when the trust is formed specifically for the purpose of becoming a trust manager for privacy purposes? One innovative attorney has recommended stapling a $10 federal reserve note to the original trust document.

A trust agreement is the contract that formally states the understanding between the trustor and trustee. A trust's name should have no relationship to the grantor or trustee, in order to preserve the privacy of those who form and control the trust. For example, Lawrence Randall Worthington forms a trust, which will serve as manager of certain Nevada Limited Liability Companies under his control. The trust is called The Northern States Valley Irrevocable Trust.

No one who learns the name of the trust manager will have a clue who formed the trust or who has been appointed as trustee(s). Mr. Worthington's attorney, Barton Arnold Kensington (an alternate name), agrees to be the administrative trustee and will scrawl his illegible signature on Nevada secretary of state registration documents each year when the companies file their list of officers.

Through the use of the "trust manager principle" and the "administrative trustee concept," Lawrence Randall Worthington has fulfilled all state government requirements to register his companies, while establishing a high level of privacy. A $10 federal reserve note is stapled to the original Northern States Valley Irrevocable Trust document to fulfill the trust's requirement of owning property, thereby eliminating the need for a tax identification number and a bank account or the titling of other property in the trust's name.

THE LIVING TRUST

A living trust is formed during the lifetime of the trustor. Property held by a living trust is not subject to the court-supervised process of probate. Living trusts are usually revocable and will not protect assets from judgments and seizure to satisfy judgments. Generally, a revocable trust is formed when the trustor does not want to lose control of the trust property. Any income generated by the trust will be subject to taxation.

OFFSHORE ASSET PROTECTION TRUST

Popular offshore asset protection trust jurisdictions include Nevis, St. Kitts, the Cook Islands, and the Bahamas. These jurisdictions have a long history of recognizing asset protection trusts. Foreign jurisdictions do not require locating the assets held by the trust in the country where the trust is formed. An offshore asset protection trust will not eliminate taxation for income earned or generated by those entities it owns.

The primary reason for an offshore asset protection trust is to protect assets from seizure. An offshore asset protection trust in Nevis, for example, has significant advantages over domestic asset protection trusts established in Delaware or Alaska. Nevis laws protect the transfer of assets except in the case of factually proven fraud. Nevis will not recognize a foreign judgment. Instead, a creditor must file a new lawsuit in Nevis and prove the case in a Nevis court.

Investors and business owners who require bulletproof asset protection have utilized a Nevada Limited Partnership as the owner of all liquid assets and as sole owner of LLCs that hold business interests and real property. A revocable living trust has been used to hold title to the private residence, and other irrevocable trusts have been formed to privately hold title to automobiles.

An offshore asset protection trust is then formed to protect all assets, with one offshore trustee and one U.S. trustee. This asset protection trust (APT) provides the settlor with jurisdiction advantages in the event the Nevada Limited Partnership assets are threatened by a U.S. court judgment.

Although privacy is the focus of this book, and the tactics recommended throughout will ensure one the anonymity required for business and personal privacy, these tactics do not eliminate liability from civil actions and judgments. True, being properly served a summons is necessary in order to be brought into court and become liable for a judgment, and the goal is to be so anonymous, so secretive and private in one's business and personal life, that Gumshoe has no traceable evidence of your involvement in any of your business dealings nor any evidence of where you live or any means of tracing your whereabouts.

However, in the event that you and your business assets are discovered, and meaningful assets are owned by an offshore asset protection trust, pursuing you will be less than fruitful for the other side. This lack of ownership of any assets and full control of all assets is the ideal position for business people, professionals, and high net worth individuals.

THE NEVADA LIMITED PARTNERHIP

A limited partnership, also known as a family limited partnership, is an entity like a corporation and is used for the protection of assets. The partnership is owned by the partners. A general partner or partners have a percentage of ownership and have control of the partnership. General partner(s) are also held responsible for any liabilities that may be incurred by the limited partnership.

A Nevada Limited Liability Company (LLC) may be formed for the purpose of being the general partner of the Nevada Limited Partnership and given a minority interest in the partnership of 1 percent, which limits the liability of the general partner to this small partnership interest.

Creditor protection is inherent in the interest owned by a limited partner in a Nevada Limited Partnership. A limited partner's creditors cannot take his or her interest in the limited partnership to satisfy a personal debt, even though his interest in the partnership may be the remaining 99 percent of the Nevada Limited Partnership.

This is providing that the partnership—or any entity for that matter—was formed prior to any legal actions being brought against a partner or other controller, grantor, or other person transferring the property. When one has knowledge of any such action and transfers property in order to avoid actions of future creditors, the new entity may not be able to withstand the test of fraudulent conveyance—the transfer of property that is made to delay or hinder a creditor and place such property beyond the reach of any creditor.

A charging order is allowed by law and allows for monetary or financial payments from the partnership to a particular partner, to be given to the partner's creditors. The partnership may respond to this order by documenting the reinvestment of earnings instead of making distributions to the limited partner.

Attorneys often recommend using Nevada Limited Partnerships to hold passive and "safe" investments such as liquid financial assets.

These assets are considered "safe," due to the unlikely possibility that they could cause damages. The partnership can also become the sole owner of Nevada LLCs, which are often used for the purpose of holding "risky" investments such as service businesses, investments in real estate, and other property that may be capable of causing damages.

The separation of entities for holding different businesses and investments restricts the damages for liability to the business entity liable for the damages. Thus, the passive liquid assets held in a Nevada Limited Partnership cannot be used to satisfy a judgment against a car wash held by a Nevada LLC, for example, even though the Nevada Limited Partnership owns 100 percent of the LLC that owns the car wash.

Nevada Limited Partnerships are required to name a resident agent on secretary of state records. In the event the company is sued, the resident agent will be served on behalf of the partnership. Income produced by the partnership flows through to the partners. The partnership files federal tax returns and distributes K-1s to individual partners so that their shares of partnership income and deductions are shown on their individual tax returns. Of all business entities, Nevada Limited Partnerships may be the most difficult to pierce if a limited partner becomes liable for damages.

TRUST MANAGER PRINCIPLE

For maximum privacy, form a trust that is totally private and has no government registration requirements or any taxpayer identification number requirements. The trust will become the "manager" of the Nevada Limited Partnership as well as the Nevada LLC, general partner when high-level privacy is required. Use of a trust as manager of the partnership ensures the privacy of the human manager, who is the trustee of the trust that will manage the partnership and satisfies the requirement of listing officers on secretary of state records, which is done annually.

ADMINISTRATIVE TRUSTEE CONCEPT

An officer or manager will sign registration documents generated by the secretary of state each year. Appoint an administrative trustee—who is limited to only one responsibility and power by the trust—to sign on behalf of the trust manager on government registration documents. An illegible signature by an administrative trustee assures the trustee and manager of anonymity.

ANONYMOUS CONTROL AND MANAGEMENT

The Nevada Limited Partnership is registered with the Nevada secretary of state, but may be located anywhere in the world. Only the general partner is required to be named on public records with the office of the secretary of state. However, the general partner may be another entity, such as a Nevada LLC, and a trust may be formed to be manager of both the limited partnership and the general partner, LLC, thereby creating an entity without registration requirements, Social Security number, or Tax I.D. number.

The trust manager is used to replace an actual person as the named "manager" of the registered entities. Since a signature is required on secretary of state records by an officer of the limited partnership and general partner, LLC, and a trust is only a paper document and incapable of signing forms, a trustee must sign on behalf of the trust manager.

The trustee(s)—who really do the bidding for the trust manager and manage the limited partnership—will want to remain anonymous and not sign any government registration documents. Therefore, use of the administrative trustee concept may be an ideal way to satisfy privacy requirements while registering entities. The administrative trustee has limited powers and authority—only that of signing on behalf of the trust manager on government registrations for the general partner, LLC and the limited partnership.

Thus the trustee(s) retain full control of the trust while retaining their privacy. The controller(s) gain complete business privacy and personal anonymity through the use of this structure. Neither the Nevada state government nor those viewing secretary of state public records will have any information about who really controls the Nevada Limited Partnership. Neither will anyone know who is behind the general partner, LLC, when one is used to hold a minority interest and take the small fall for the partnership—limited to its 1 percentage ownership, of course.

Furthermore, when an attorney is appointed as the administrative trustee to sign company registration forms, the attorney-client privilege applies, and the lawyer is bound to protect his client's privacy. The use of the "trust manager principle" and the "administrative trustee concept" provides the actual controller and manager anonymity as he/she operates businesses.

These high-level privacy tactics eliminate the need for the use of "nominees" as front men on state government records. Nominees will reveal the true manager's identity when pressed for information by investigators and when bribed or told to do so by government officials—often with very little coaxing. Also, shifting ownership interests around from true owner/controller or manger to a nominee willing to be a temporary manager may compromise the company in any number of ways.

Always make certain the company follows proper compliance guidelines. Seek expert professional advice from your attorney when you have questions on these matters.

THE NEVADA LIMITED LIABILITY COMPANY (LLC)

An LLC is a hybrid between a partnership and a corporation. It combines the "pass-through" treatment of a partnership with the limited liability allowed to shareholders of corporations. Advantages of a Nevada LLC include no state tax on profits generated from the LLC and no state personal income tax.

Single-member LLCs may be formed in Nevada, and the company may be managed by either a member or a manager. Ordinarily, only the LLC is responsible for the company's debts, thus shielding the member(s) from personal liability. The articles of organization must be filed with the secretary of state. Annual fees must be paid to keep the company legitimate.

In addition, a resident agent must be retained and on record with the office of the secretary of state. The LLC and the manager may be located anywhere in the world. In order to accomplish anonymity as the manager of a Nevada Limited Liability Company, the "trust manager principle" and the "administrative trustee concept" may be utilized as previously described for the Nevada Limited Partnership.

Nevada Limited Liability Companies have been used for a variety of business purposes. An LLC can become the general partner of the Nevada Limited Partnership, which owns liquid investments under your control. A Nevada LLC may be suitable for holding investments in real estate, businesses, or other property. Consult your attorney for professional recommendations on how to best use a Nevada LLC for your individual purposes.

PROFESSIONAL ADVICE

The use of trusts and business entities is an important aspect of business and personal privacy. Of paramount importance is the use of experienced professionals who are experts in this field, mainly attorneys who specialize in wills, trusts, probate, and asset protection.

Since this chapter is merely an overview of some entities that have been used to make one's life private, the reader is advised to retain the services of a competent professional capable of providing advice based on individual requirements. This chapter is not meant as a substitute for professional advice.

Consider the use of trusts and business entities included in this chapter, while obtaining legal counsel capable of advising you, based on your current and future needs.

SUMMARY

1. The use of appropriate business entities and trusts for personal and business privacy are high-level privacy tactics. One may operate anonymously, without his or her name being on secretary of state records, while still controlling business entities.

2. For the ultimate in business privacy, tell professionals only on a need-to-know basis of your business interests.

3. Trusts are the most private of all entities, and registration of trusts with U.S. government agencies is not required. Use names dissimilar to your true name for trusts.

4. An offshore asset protection trust based in Nevis or the Cook Islands has jurisdictional advantages over similar trusts established in the U.S.

5. An asset protection trust must be formed prior to knowledge of any claims against the grantor, in order to withstand the test of fraudulent conveyance. One offshore trustee and one local trustee are required for offshore asset protection trusts formed in Nevis and the Cook Islands.

6. The Nevada Limited Partnership is one of the most difficult of all entities to pierce. It has been used effectively to hold liquid assets.

7. The Nevada Limited Liability Company may be suitable for owning investment real estate, businesses, and other property and may be used as the general partner for a Nevada Limited Partnership.

8. The "trust manager principle" is used to eliminate placing the company controller's name on secretary of state public records.

9. The "administrative trustee concept" is used to eliminate the need for the company controller to sign secretary of state registration documents each year.

10.   Obtain professional advice when considering the use of trusts, a Nevada Limited Partnership, a Nevada Limited Liability Company, an offshore asset protection trust, or other entities that may be suitable for your business and personal needs.

TWENTY-TWO

The Invisible Student

"I have never let my school interfere with my education"
—Mark Twain

INNOCENT STUDENTS TRACKED BY POLICE

Virginia's colleges and universities are now required by law to turn over tens of thousands of students' names and Social Security numbers to the state police.

The same law, passed in 2006 and signed by Governor Timothy M. Kain (D) also requires Department of Motor Vehicles officials to release personal information to police any time a Virginia resident applies for a license or a change of address. The law, passed under the guise of a crackdown on sexual-offender crime, makes it possible for state police to monitor a vast number of citizens throughout their lifetimes.

PUBLIC SCHOOLS

School records offer identity thieves, government, investigators, and others a great deal of information about students over an extended period of time. Public school students—past and present—are vulnerable to having their permanent school records stolen, as "officials" will turn over all student records once they receive a signed, written authorization to do so—and sometimes authorizations are fraudulently submitted.

Government's invasion of your career privacy begins as you enroll in public schools. Public schools are supported by those property taxes

of 1 percent to 3.75 percent of the most recent sale price of your house, which Americans pay for the privilege of "owning" their homes.

The majority of children in the United States—whether American citizens or illegal aliens from Mexico or elsewhere—are educated in public schools. That's right. Those who come across the open borders of the United States of America can get a free education at the expense, in some cases, of those who pay the taxes.

Don't understand a word of English? That doesn't matter. Big Bureaucrat will in some cases provide a Spanish-speaking, bilingual teacher for you, as well as school supplies, transportation, and free school lunches and other related educational expenses. Is it any wonder most of the population's children are educated in the "free" public education school system? Or are they really being educated? Forty-two percent of those attending public schools in grades 1 through 12 in California do not speak English (source: Jim Dallas, KDWN radio, "Wake Up America" program, July 28, 2006). Twenty percent of Clark County, Nevada, high school seniors did not graduate in 2004 but instead received a certificate of attendance (source: Las Vegas *Review-Journal*).

Once an elementary student enters the public school system and until high school graduation, he or she is required to provide the school—

an agent of the state—with all identifying personal information. In addition to having each student's Social Security number, date of birth, birth certificate, and home address, the school will weigh and measure the students, test them for intelligence and academic achievement, grade them, and write subjective essays about their behavior. The subject matter is approved by the state—the educational staff are credentialed, hired, and licensed by the state.

HOME SCHOOLING

A home school education movement has been forming within the United States for the past three decades. Essentially, parents assume the responsibility of educating their children in the home. Curriculum information and supplies are available from a number of sources that specialize in home school education.

Although statistics are limited to document the superior education received through home schooling, many satisfied parents and students have benefited from this personalized, private means of education. In view of the available tools online and the growing number of students being educated at home, this method of education is increasing.

Privacy advocates who wish to keep their children out of the government school system are advised to consider home schooling as an option for educating their children. Parents' personal information is collected by public schools if their children attend these state-sponsored institutions. An added benefit of home schooling is the elimination of this information becoming a part of state school records. Some websites that are recommended for additional information on home schooling include:

1. www.homeschool.com
2. www.homeschooling.about.com
3. www.homeschools.org
4. www.independent-learning.com
5. www.exelhighschool.com
6. www.calvertschool.org

POST–HIGH SCHOOL EDUCATION

People enroll in colleges, trade schools, technical training courses, and work training programs for the purpose of gaining skills and knowledge necessary to qualify them for employment. Depending on the vocational or professional objective, the choices are many in terms of how to secure the education necessary to obtain the qualifications and credentials for a career.

Today, more education options are available to students than ever before. Many colleges and technical schools offer online courses, and there is wide acceptability of educational training received via the Internet. Fully accredited colleges offer bachelors, masters, and doctoral degrees in a variety of disciplines, with complete programs available online.

A student can, in some cases, complete all degree requirements without ever setting foot on a college campus. Some websites that provide information about post-secondary colleges and technical schools that offer education and degrees in a variety of fields include:

1. www.elearners.com
2. www.trade-schools.net

The advantages of receiving an education online include flexible scheduling as well as control over personal contacts made with those involved in the educational process. Additionally, personal records are best controlled through enrolling in online colleges and technical courses.

This is particularly true when dealing with private institutions, as opposed to state colleges and universities. It is possible to never have to provide any information to an online school that could compromise your privacy. A true name would naturally be provided, because the diploma(s) or course certificate(s) necessarily need to match your "official" identity. However, aside from providing your true name to the school, no other privacy-invasive information is necessary.

A nominee's mailing address can be used as an address on school record files without being questioned. Substitute numbers can be used for a Social Security number and, in fact, this should be done to avoid anyone accessing school records to obtain this information. All other information, including telephone numbers and historical information normally collected by schools can also be provided as per your discretion, depending on the privacy level you desire.

By carefully controlling what information is in your school record files, you will keep your personal and confidential information away from all sources that may have intentions of stealing or misusing it.

INDEPENDENT STUDY AND SELF-EDUCATION

Many individuals have achieved their education largely through correspondence study, independent study, or by being self-taught. Self-teaching is perhaps the most effective of all, as adults who study on their own through reading are the most motivated. It is sometimes difficult to gain credentials for given fields through self-learning, although some accredited schools give students college credit for life learning experience and work experiences.

The Internet, with all its resources for learning through research and making contact with websites offering books, CDs, and other tools for learning, enables anyone to learn and study independently in their spare time. Libraries provide the individual who wants to gain knowledge the ability to do so through the use of books available to the public.

Government, under the provisions of the U.S. Patriot Act, can now spy on you, however, so be aware of the books you read. A reader writes that he is offended by this invasion of his privacy and has obtained a library card under an alternate identification to thwart the efforts of Big Bureaucrat and keep what he reads his own business.

DEGREES, CREDENTIALS, AND LICENSES

Colleges and institutions that confer degrees maintain permanent records of all students' academic coursework. These records can be obtained from the institution from which the degree or courses were taken.

Obtaining a copy of your transcripts from your alma mater with its "certified seal" is a good idea, as is advising the registrar's office of your preference for privacy. You can instruct the records department head not to release any of your transcripts or permanent records without a letter from you with your notarized signature.

Anyone who elects to enter into one of the professions that require a license or credential issued by the state can expect to undergo a great deal of privacy-invasive questioning and will be required to surrender in-depth personal information. Medical doctors, attorneys, certified public accountants, nurses, public school teachers, chiropractors, psychologists, marriage and family therapists, medical technicians, real estate brokers, stock brokers, and others are required to provide personal, educational, and career information in order to obtain their license or credentials.

Some licensed professionals, such as attorneys, are fingerprinted prior to being admitted to the state bar, although their fingerprints supposedly are not entered into the various databases used by law enforcement to search for criminals.

Once credentialed and licensed, you have the same privileges and freedoms as anyone else in the workforce and are able to practice all the privacy tactics outlined in this book. Occupations, businesses, and professions will each be unique in terms of the privacy and freedom allowed for those practicing and working within them, and you can also structure your work environment to suit your individual privacy requirements.

SUMMARY

1. Public schools require students to furnish sensitive personal information about themselves and their parents. This information will be kept permanently in state-sponsored school databases.

2. Home schooling provides students and parents with private alternatives to traditional education. Many online resources are available for home schooling students at all grade levels. Home schooling learning aids are readily available as well.

3. Post-secondary education can be obtained privately online with less risk of a student's privacy being compromised. Technical fields of study, as well as college degrees and graduate degrees, are offered through reputable online institutions.

4. Independent study and self-teaching offer the privacy-conscious student alternative education options.

5. Degrees, licenses, and school records should be kept in a safe place. Institutions can be advised not to release one's permanent records without a notarized signature. Academic credentials and records are sought by identity thieves and others who wish to pry into your confidential business.

♦ TWENTY-THREE ♦

Career Privacy Options

"The biggest mistake we could ever make in our lives is to think we work for anybody but ourselves."—Brian Tracy

TRADITIONAL EMPLOYMENT

This chapter is *not* about breaking employment laws, working under the table, falsifying taxpayer identification documents, or doing business off the books. Several privacy articles in magazines and a few books advocate doing just that in an attempt to become a "private" employee or business person.

Unfortunately, failing to follow the laws of the land makes the whole business of living and working an anxiety-producing, paranoid, and sleepless affair, which in turn, makes one spend time worrying unnecessarily instead of concentrating on business and career success. Besides, once you have enough information, implement the correct business structures, and add some creativity to the mix, you will find it unnecessary to work or operate a business except as a law-abiding employee or businessperson.

This chapter is about just that—operating as a career professional and business person while doing it privately and by following all applicable labor and tax laws.

When you are hired by an employer to sell your work skills and time in exchange for a wage or salary and other employment benefits, you are generally given few options for personal privacy. This traditional method of hiring is done through personnel directors and area supervisors who interview you, assess your job skills, and check your references. Personal information, including date of birth, a birth certificate, Social Security number, and other intrusive information is filed by employers.

All new hires' information will be accessible by certain government databases, providing that key information—mainly the SSN, date of birth, and name—is accurate. To avoid being researched, do not provide a date of birth or SSN until actually hired—if at all. Leave these boxes blank on the application while explaining that a previous "privacy challenge" is the reason for deferring on this personal information.

In lieu of the Social Security number, an Employer Identification Number (EIN) can be substituted—along with its "owner"—the LLC or trust for which you "work" when such an employer/employee relationship is agreed upon. More employers than you can imagine will be amenable to structuring employment relationships this way, providing they, too, get something out of the deal—a break on health insurance benefits or a reduction in sick-leave days have been used as incentives.

Some employers or personnel managers will not do it your way regardless of how big a carrot is dangled in front of their noses, however. Once the new applicant is hired, his or her employment location becomes available to a number of government agencies' databases— if the SSN and date of birth has been given to the employer.

Which government agencies will receive this information? Just about all of them who have any possible reason for knowing anything about you. High on the list are the child support enforcement agencies in all fifty states, of course, and state tax revenue boards, the department of treasury, and others which no one will tell you about, because no one knows for sure due to the constant changes made and the additions of new agencies being on the receiving end of the new hires lists every so often.

Just be advised that when you work as a traditional employee for an employer and furnish your date of birth and SSN, *they* know about it, and *they* know exactly where to find you. Just in case you forgot to pay your child support. Or *they* forgot to credit your payments.

Maybe you are attempting to escape your ex-husband or a stalker. Perhaps you just want the security of not making your name available in any employment-related databases. Identity thieves tap into those, too. Or you may have any number of other reasons. You get the idea. You are easily found, and you may not want that to be the case. So decide what to do about it. You do have career privacy options—learn to use them.

EMPLOYMENT AGENCIES AND REGISTRIES

Skilled office workers, computer technicians, registered nurses, licensed practical nurses, nurse aids, medical technicians, and others often "register" with an employment agency or registry that acts as a middle entity between the employer and employee.

Typically, the agency or registry is called by an employer, and positions are filled as per the employer's current needs for personnel. Policies vary from agency to agency and are different for the various positions and industries, but essentially, the worker is paid by the agency and is not under the direct employ of the employer, in most cases.

TRUST OR LLC AS EMPLOYER

Form either a trust or an LLC for the purpose of receiving payment for services on your behalf as you work either for an employer, employment agency, or registry. The LLC is my first choice. See your attorney for expert guidance and advice for your individual case.

You will need to explain your employee relationship with the LLC to the director or manager at the registry or agency where you make yourself available for work. Generally, little resistance is encountered when there is a demand for your services. It also helps to have an open minded and flexible personnel manager or employment agency manager to deal with when you need something accomplished.

You may need to pitch your story to several managers in order to get things done your way. Do not despair—it is doable. Many use this employee structure with LLCs for privacy purposes, as well as to shift liability from themselves onto another entity. You just need to present it to the right person and at the right time. As in when he or she really needs you and your services. Then they will be amenable to doing whatever has to be done to fill positions.

The purpose of using the LLC as your "employer" is to have another entity besides yourself receive payments for your labors. See to it that the agency does not record your SSN, as the LLC—your "front entity"—is his "employee" or subcontractor, actually, and you work for the LLC.

Naturally, a tax identification number will need to be obtained for the LLC, and the LLC articles of organization will need to be shown to the manager in charge of hiring or the employment agency or registry manager. The manager is hiring the LLC, and you work for the LLC.

This structure will enable you to be essentially self-employed while receiving the referrals for work from the third party. And your true name and Social Security number will not become a part of any new-hires database records. Read Chapter 25, "People Skills" in this book prior to making your presentation to the various employers, registries, and agencies that become candidates for employment.

INDEPENDENT CONTRACTORS

Today employers love to outsource their work to offshore companies, which are able to do it for a fraction of the cost of U.S. businesses. However, many opt for the cost-effective and high-quality performances of independent contractors, who are really self-employed people or companies that provide necessary services to an employer.

Employers, particularly smaller companies, cannot justify having a full-time employee to provide many services that are necessary for their company to function. These positions may include bookkeepers, accountants, tax preparers, computer programmers, computer service technicians, maintenance personnel, janitors, clerical staff, mechanics, auto body repair personnel, financial planners, actors, writers, directors, sales people, and other independent contractors who may market their skills individually to prospective companies or elect to work for a company or an employment agency that refers them to employers.

Either arrangement will usually be conducive to using a trust or an LLC to receive the wages or salary, instead of receiving direct compensation for privacy reasons.

UNIONS

Various unions exist for worker support and other employment services related to the jobs of various businesses, occupations, trades, and professions. Some unions are most active in placing the employee on a job, such as the carpenter's union, while others set policy, wage scales, and provide other regulatory functions, such as the Screen Actors Guild. In some cases, the union member will need to approach his union to arrange for wages or salary to be paid to an entity other than himself, such as a trust or an LLC.

PLANNING FOR WORK PRIVACY

Those who have marketable skills in an occupation, business, trade, or profession, have the potential to work independently and utilize another entity such as a trust or LLC to receive payments on their behalf. This work arrangement may come through the referral of employment agencies, registries, or unions.

First, identify your prospective employers and seek out representatives who will be involved in referring you or placing you on a job. Explain that you have, for privacy reasons and per the recommendation of your attorney, formed an LLC or a trust to receive your wages or salary in lieu of you receiving the checks individually. You may have to present your case with the assistance of your attorney's written correspondence or enlist him to provide telephone support on your behalf.

This type of work arrangement can be accomplished. In fact, it is necessary if you want to work privately and use a business entity in place of yourself to be on record with the employers who retain your company for services. This is also absolutely necessary in order for you and your SSN to remain beneath the radar of the new-hires in databases that are tracked by many government agencies.

Consult your attorney for expert advice on the best entity to receive payments on your behalf. Use your people skills, and exercise persistence to accomplish this non-traditional, important, privacy employment goal.

SELF-EMPLOYMENT

Only one in five businesses that start up today will make a profit during the first five years of operation. While these are not great odds, if you have an entrepreneurial spirit, by all means go for it, once you have tested the marketplace for your prospective goods or services to be sold.

Be certain you have written a viable business plan and have adequate financing in place. Self-employment offers the privacy seeker the best opportunity for strategic work privacy and planning. A separate entity will be necessarily used to do business, while you—the individual who forms the company—will manage the business. Seek the advice of legal counsel and your tax-planning expert to determine which, of a number of available entities, are best suited for your particular business or profession.

THE ANONYMOUS MANAGER

Once you form a company and manage it, you become the most anonymous of all employees, in that your company will operate as an LLC, corporation, limited partnership, or other entity. Consult your attorney and tax adviser for the proper entity to be used for your particular case. Also, use the trust manager principle and appoint an administrative trustee in order to keep your true name off all state government registration records. See Chapter 21, "Business Entities," in this book for clarification of these concepts.

As a manager, you can keep your business anonymous by using either an alternate name or a first and middle name only. Always use a separate mailing address for your business correspondences for confidentiality. As the manager, you can control your privacy.

The privacy afforded you as the business manager will be dependent on your business. Professional practitioners will naturally have a higher profile as compared to computer programmers, website construction businesses, automobile mechanics, carpet cleaners, roofers, and other service businesses.

KEYS TO EMPLOYMENT ANONYMITY

Keep your work relationships separate from your personal relationships, and if and when you let work friends into your personal life, think carefully prior to inviting someone into your personal residence. Provide coworkers and employers with your voicemail number only, unless you have to be on call for a work commitment—and in this case, provide your cell phone number only to the person who must have it, with the instruction of not giving your number to anyone else.

When traveling to and from work, always be cognizant of those who are behind you, and if you suspect someone is following you, take several turns to rule out being followed to your place of work or tailed by someone into your home neighborhood. Do not hold parties or work-related meetings at home. Instead, use an office or other neutral site.

Despite what you may have heard to the contrary, work friendships and personal friendships are ideally separate, though one will naturally make exceptions during his or her career. Be careful, and screen people carefully and think it over prior to mixing the two relationships.

THE CASE OF JAKE MANSFIELD

Jake Mansfield, Ph.D., (an alternate name) is a licensed psychologist certified by his state's medical board. He begins to seek employment with his own and his family's personal privacy as a consideration. Jake is trustee of the Business Associates Irrevocable Trust, which is the manager of David Jose Williams, LLC, formed specifically to be the company which provides the testing and other services offered by himself.

The LLC will receive payments for those services provided by Jake Mansfield, Ph.D. Jake interviews with private and government agencies and pitches his employment arrangement to directors, who are in charge of making hiring decisions for their new psychologist position. He advises the prospective employers that they can save on employment-related benefits such as health, worker's compensation, and life insurance—and pension costs—by hiring David Jose Williams, LLC, which is managed by the Business Associates Irrevocable Trust, of which Jake is the trustee.

An enterprising director of City Wide Counseling Services, Inc. pushes the numbers and determines that substantial monies can be saved by doing it Jake's way and agrees to retain the services of David Jose Williams, LLC, instead of hiring Jake individually as a company employee.

Jake works privately by cashing the checks issued to the LLC, which has its own employer identification number (EIN) for tax purposes, and he receives the benefits of being "self-employed," including the tax write-offs associated with self-employment.

Dr. Jake escapes having his name and SSN included in the new-hires database normally provided to government agencies and others once new workers are hired. Additionally, he is not under the employ of City Wide Counseling Services, Inc. and is allowed work time flexibility and has the ability to structure his work hours to accommodate his latest research project—a self-help book. His group sessions and individual testing sessions are scheduled according to his own determined work schedule. In this example, both the employer and employee win, as each benefits from this fictitious, non-traditional employment relationship.

SUMMARY

1. Traditional employment offers minimal privacy benefits for the employee, as new hires' names, dates of birth, and Social Security numbers are entered into a new-hires database. Many government and some non-government entities have access to the names in this database.

2. Using a trust or an LLC to provide services provides a privacy shield for the individual who desires privacy at work. Consult your attorney and tax advisor for your best available choices.

3. Independent contractors provide employment savings to employers and offer workers' privacy benefits. Employment agencies, registries, and unions may refer the independent contractor to the employer, or the individual may be self-referred. LLCs or trusts may receive payment on behalf of the employee, while the actual worker remains anonymous, in these non-traditional employment relationships.

4. Plan for work privacy by writing a business plan and employment agreement that benefits both the employer and employee. Present this plan to employers and managers responsible for hiring personnel.

5. Self-employment is the most risky employment venture and provides the highest level of work privacy. An anonymous manager can effectively make all decisions for a company formed under a fictitious business name.

TWENTY-FOUR

Nominees:
Invitation for Disaster

"Common sense ain't common."
—Will Rogers, American cowboy humorist

AUNT MARTHA

Francine McCord and her husband, Billy Bob (fictitious names), divorced following a long separation and a violent relationship during which she was physically abused on numerous occasions. Following the divorce, she still could not live in peace. Her husband stalked her constantly, so she began taking steps to privatize her life.

Billy Bob had used a private detective to locate his ex-wife through her bank accounts, which were held in her own name and under her Social Security number at both a money center bank and a regional banking institution. Believing that her money was her one weak link to being located by her threatening husband, Francine sought advice on how to remove her name from her bank accounts while still owning her money.

Several authors have recommended using "nominees" to hold bank accounts, for the purpose of concealing one's money from asset searches. Francine decided to use this method to hide her money, to escape from her abusive ex-husband.

Francine's Aunt Martha, who lived in a distant state, had always kept in touch following a close, loving relationship throughout her childhood. She decided to approach Auntie with the proposition of requesting her to become her "nominee" for banking purposes. Francine knew her aunt only as her aunt—and many times when relatives have relationships, the "social and family" side of the personality is known, rather than the all-important business side and other facets of one's personality.

Suffice it to say that Francine based her trust in Auntie on a long-standing "social and family" relationship, and she had never really had occasion to know her aunt otherwise.

Aunt Martha agreed to help her niece out of her predicament and came for a visit. Accounts were opened in two separate banks. Approximately $50,000 was placed in each account under the name and SSN of Auntie—now the "nominee" for Francine. Auntie spent hours signing blank checks that were to be used by Francine for the purpose of using the money on deposit.

Once this was concluded, Francine removed herself from her money—the problem in her desired private life—and she now believed Mr. Ex's private investigator would be unable to locate her through asset searches as before, because she now no longer held assets.

Months passed without any sightings of Billy Bob or his private eye, and Francine began to believe she had conquered her devil of a husband. While checking the bank accounts online, however, she noticed significant withdrawals and became most alarmed, as her savings were now being depleted by Auntie. Auntie failed to take Francine's phone calls, and Francine sought remedy by paying the bank a visit—all to no avail, as it was explained to her by a bank manager that she, Francine, had no rights to any information or funds held in the name of someone else.

Francine had no legal claim to her money. It was now owned by Aunt Martha. Such is the danger of following the advice of storytellers who write privacy books, rather than people who actually practice financial privacy in real time while under fire.

Aunt Martha had a penchant for gambling, and while her intentions may have been only to "borrow" from those accounts she controlled as nominee, the casinos failed to cooperate with her repayment plan, and, after eleven months, Francine was entirely free of her problem with her money. The funds she had entrusted to Auntie were now completely exhausted and gone forever.

It is this author's opinion that nominees should not be used to hold money or other assets. Do not trust a friend, a relative, or a business associate to hold your assets. Review the "Finances" section chapters in this book to gain an understanding of how to anonymously manage banking and investments.

NOMINEE THEORY FOR PRIVACY

Privacy authors have recommended the use of a nominee—one nominated to stand in or substitute, for the purpose of acting on behalf of another to preserve privacy. In theory, the use of another person to perform duties for the person who is making the decisions has validity and appears to be a valuable and worthwhile solution for the privacy seeker.

However, in actual practice, you should be extremely careful about those you use for any purpose. Do I recommend using a nominee? Perhaps. But in certain cases only. Your author has used nominees for opening accounts with utility companies, high-speed Internet service providers, and for the receipt of mail. On the occasions when a nominee was necessary, I used a business person I screened — just like any other subcontractor or employee—and we made our agreement via a written contract.

I believe it's risky to use just anyone for a nominee, as one privacy author suggests in his writing. First of all, imagine what you risk if you pick someone who is not trustworthy or who is sought by law enforcement or any state or federal government agency. Want to have a bounty hunter breaking down your door in search of a fugitive? Your nominee—if selected without knowing a whole lot about him or her—could be someone who is wanted. Having this person's name on a utility company account, residential or office lease, or title of any account of value could lead the agency or the cops straight to your door, where the nominee supposedly lives or works.

On page 158 of his book, *How to Be Invisible*, Mr. Luna writes (concerning the selection of nominees):

> "Who might be an ideal candidate? You may already have someone in mind, but, if not, here are a few suggestions:

> ‣ A homeless person who has not filed a tax return since Truman beat Dewey.

> ‣ That illegal Guatemalan whom a friend uses to take care of the kids.

> ‣ The town drunk, who sobers up just long enough to sign some "papers" in return for a case of Thunderbird.

> ‣ A relative or close friend who will do this as a favor.

▶ Someone who owes you money, is not in a position to pay you back, and would act as nominee in exchange for clearing the loan.

Do you really want to retain a homeless person, who obviously does not have the funds for the basic necessities of life, to hold your bank account? Want to entrust an illegal alien from Guatemala to stutter and stammer around while attempting to open an account for gas, electricity, and cable TV at an address where you are going to be living? Did you know that in 2004, some 90 percent of all arrest warrants in Los Angeles were for illegal aliens?

How about granting the town drunk signing power on your bank accounts? Be advised that close friends and relatives are the most dangerous of all to use as nominees to hold your bank accounts, in the author's opinion.

Would you really want someone who owes you money and has not cleared the loan as agreed, to have control of your finances, or to open and maintain your utility and other important accounts? Serious privacy seekers should use business people for nominees for services such as utilities, but always, without exception, maintain control of their accounts, while retaining their privacy though the use of business entities and trusts as described in this book, in the opinion of this author.

Still not convinced it is a bad idea to use relatives to hold your money? The following actual case history is buried somewhere deep in the archives of microfiche files of an unnamed insurance claimant—a "professional claimant" who stole from the rich and gave to the poor. The problem is that he intended to have his gifts returned—always a bad idea—especially when fraud is involved. Who does a fraudster complain to when he is defrauded?

SPOUSE AS NOMINEE: THE CASE OF DOC LAIRD

Early in your author's career, while I worked for a Fortune 500 company, an associate who suffered from illness took a leave of absence, and yours truly inherited some of his cases. Among the files placed on my desk one Monday morning was the case file of a man I will call "Doc" Laird.

Being a manipulative sort, this man nicknamed "Doc" attempted to hide assets by first liquidating everything of value. Many insurance claim checks were cashed, followed by his purchase of assets such as gold, guns, travelers checks, and money orders. Following the accumulation period of his believed-to-be secret stash, he filed a petition for bankruptcy, claiming his funds had been exhausted and that he had no money with which to pay his huge medical bills.

Doc was an insurance claims wizard who amassed a good-sized fortune through claiming benefits on many insurance policies that he accumulated over time. When his illness did permit him to file for benefits, he refused to assign policy benefits to medical providers, instead agreeing to pay them once he received payment under the terms of the policies.

But when payments were received, he took the money and ran, so to speak, straight to the gun stores, the precious metals dealers' shops, and convenience stores, where he bought items of stored value for hunkering down during hard times. Having amassed nearly three quarters of a million dollars, Doc Laird sought diversification and thus added cash in the form of $100 greenbacks to his untraceable asset collection.

Soon the bankruptcy process began, as a lawyer was retained, forms were completed, and a hearing and court date were set. When testimony time approached, the sweat began to pour, as medical providers, insurance claims people, and investigators began to call him on the phone and appear at his door.

Wanda, Doc's wife, was given about a third of the booty collected, in the form of $100 bills, a confidant was told. The intention was to have Wanda hold the cash for safe-keeping as Doc attempted to use a nominee—his wife, no less—to hold his funds until the storm passed. It has been said that illness begets marital problems, and this is probably so. Doc's funds given to Wanda were never seen again, because they separated and later divorced.

Doc lost nearly $250,000 by trusting his own wife with a secret—albeit illegal. That's not to mention the affect on his credit, because a bankruptcy is, indeed, a serious matter to have on one's credit report. Don't ask about whether this unscrupulous character was ever found out and prosecuted. I don't know. The last I heard, he was seen traveling east with guns and gold packed in a U-Haul, while trying to avoid the doctors, hospitals, and others screaming for their money. Moral of the story: Do not trust your relatives or others to hold your money—no matter how you got it.

PROPER USE OF NOMINEES

When you own shares or have voting power in a company, you may elect to allow another to vote on your behalf by designating a nominee.

In the event your signature is required on a document, a tax return, a contract, a company meeting record requiring a signature, or other important writing, you may elect to ask your attorney, tax preparer or CPA, or business associate to sign on your behalf, thereby making that person a nominee.

For certain utilities—including water, gas, electricity, cable television, trash, or other services—it may be a good idea to use a business associate or self-employed office manager or business person whom you believe to be credible, to obtain the utilities and services in their name. A contract should be made for this service, and the nominee should be paid for his/her time.

When and if you choose to trust another person with something of value—property of any kind, for example—some may choose to use an attorney with whom they have a long-standing relationship, because he is bound by law and risks being disbarred if he mishandles their affairs.

NOMINEE SERVICES

Successful and serious privacy seekers do not use a nominee for obtaining a rental residence. If a nominee represents that they will be living in an apartment or house, when in actuality you will be residing there and they will not, this improper use of a nominee may cause future problems for you. Do not use someone else to sign a residential lease unless they, in fact, will be living at the residence. Property owners and managers are very much aware of their tenants, and you will not want to be in the middle of such a caper.

Reread the "Home" section of this book for information on how to preserve your privacy.

As previously demonstrated by the case studies cited in this chapter, it is not only dangerous but also poor judgment to use another person to hold your money or other assets in their name, in your author's opinion.

Suppose the person you select is a fugitive from justice, has a monetary judgment entered against him or her, becomes divorced, falls into arrears on child support payments, decides to feed his undetected drug addiction, or gambles with and loses the money you entrust to him or her. You have no recourse.

A contract between the nominee—and the one giving power to the person to hold assets—may be of value. However, consider the chances of collecting on a judgment from one who breaches the contract in the first place. In the author's opinion it is not a prudent business decision to use nominees to hold assets.

When you require a nominee for a utility service or other day-to-day necessary service, remember to select that person as you would anyone on your payroll. Obtain background information and do an online investigation, or hire a private investigator to provide this information to you. Form a contract with all nominees in order to document your business relationship and the provisions of the agreement. Contracts are not perfect. They are breached every day. But a well-written, clear business agreement signed by all parties prevents a misunderstanding at a future point in time.

SUMMARY

1. A nominee or person acting on your behalf should be a business person under contract, whom you believe to be credible.

2. Using a nominee to hold bank accounts in his or her name and Social Security number gives control to the nominee. Successful privacy advocates have recommended using business entities to hold assets anonymously, while avoiding the use of nominees for this purpose.

3. Authorizing a professional or businessperson or associate to be your nominee to sign documents on your behalf offers convenience and privacy to the person who needs anonymity or who must be absent.

4. Do not use nominees to obtain living quarters for you, unless they will be living with you.

5. Utilities and personal and business services may be obtained by nominees.

6. Be extremely careful when selecting nominees, and screen them as you would other employees and contractors.

♦ TWENTY-FIVE ♦

People Skills

"The most important thing in communication is hearing what isn't said."—Peter F. Drucker

A BROKEN SYSTEM

A large portion of this book is devoted to information that will allow you to form a plan to privatize both your personal and business life, so that identity thieves and others will not know anything about you. In fact, when you follow the steps to privacy presented throughout the eight sections, you will have essentially "disappeared."

Because America has changed so drastically during the past three decades, and because so many facets of your personal life and business are regulated by government and controlled by bureaucrats, your privacy is now more important than ever before.

Compound all this by the current strict controls on your finances, your vehicles, your business, and other aspects of your life and an estimated 5,000 to 10,000 illegal alien Mexicans crossing the border each day and competing for your jobs—and often getting those jobs ahead of you, the English-speaking, legal U.S. citizen—and you have chaos instead of what was once a first-world, service-oriented, United States of America.

Within this broken system, you can naturally expect to encounter more difficulty than ever before in getting what you need to function as an anonymous, law-abiding citizen. With such an influx of illegal aliens storming our borders, a demand to service them is naturally created. And the language with which to service them is, of course, Spanish, not English.

Hence, the broken borders have a snowball effect, as language and culture fall by the wayside, causing a lower standard of living and an unacceptably poor quality of customer service. You, the law-abiding American, have no choice but to stand in the unnecessarily long lines created by those who do not belong in our country, listen to phone messages in languages you may not understand, and tolerate the abuse imposed on you by a government that has facilitated the invasion and encouraged it all to happen.

Due to all the difficulty in obtaining basic services—as well as the regulatory barriers, many of them gray areas, and near-constant changes occurring through either policy or statute and subject to interpretation by those with whom you deal—your "people skills" become a most important factor as you strive to keep yourself and your assets anonymous.

This chapter is worth your review from time to time so you can improve your results in obtaining what you need from those who have the control to help you make your life private. By exercising your best presentation and communication skills, you will be better served by those bankers, government agencies, credit bureaus, and others who can provide a clear path for you to keep your important information private.

WORK FORCE DECLINE IN AMERICA

Twenty-four-hour customer service sounds great, doesn't it? How great is it if you spend five minutes going through a phone menu with Spanish being spoken as your first language choice, followed by nearly deafening music for another five minutes, prior to being connected to a representative you cannot understand?

The decline to third-world status of America's once-great work ethic and excellent service to customers—now, customer "no service"—has many ramifications for the privacy seeker, so learn to make the adaptations necessary to deal with those first in line to service your inquiries.

ACTUAL CASE EVENT

Recently, Jill spent an hour in the office of the manager of a stock brokerage firm. The woman with whom she met, did not—repeat, did not—know the meaning of an "LLC." Throughout the course of the meeting, she referred to the LLC as the "limited liability corporation" rather than limited liability *company* and made reference to "corporation" and shareholder meetings—and other irrelevant conversation totally unrelated to any requirements for opening a brokerage account in the name of the Nevada Limited Partnership of which the LLC is the general partner.

When asked a simple question about having the ability to deposit and clear checks through a brokerage account, she mumbled some meaningless doubletalk that made her appear even more ignorant about her own business. Soon, it became evident to Jill that this woman was dodging her questions regarding the requirements to open an account in the name of the business entity.

Keep in mind that this woman was the manager, not a clerk or an entry-level broker. She was, in fact, the highest-level broker at the office of this brokerage firm. But she knew nothing about articles of organization, operating agreements, or resident agents.

The meeting was spent with her wiping beads of sweat from her forehead as she called her "back office" repeatedly for the answers to Jill's questions. Back office apparently knew nothing about business accounts either, and after an hour in this embarrassing situation, Jill was promised that the manager would be calling her within a couple of days with the answers to all of the questions she could not answer during the meeting.

Jill never heard from her again. As this is written, your author is even more discouraged about the service in America today than when the book project began more than one year ago. Call your bank, call your credit card company, call the DMV office, the credit bureaus, or any government agency office, and you will be, almost without exception, dissatisfied with the service you receive.

The level of service provided by American businesses and government offices has deteriorated to such a low point that one cannot justify the time spent in using the telephone to call them at all. In fact, unless you have a plan to deal with the customer "no-service" personnel of today, you will be frustrated beyond the point of being able to be productive—and we don't want that. Instead, make a plan for dealing with those who can help you accomplish your privacy goals in the "New America."

Supervisors at various agencies and offices are the "experienced" ones who are supposed to know the business. However, those so-called supervisors in customer service "boiler room" operations are merely clerks with slightly higher pay scales and are really of no value to you as a customer seeking answers to policy-related questions. Your best approach is to ask for a supervisor as soon as you are connected, and once he or she comes on the line, ask for a home office telephone number. Believe it or not, some will ask what a "home office" is, so have your polite hat on as you explain that this is where the CEO works.

Asking to speak to whoever takes the CEO's calls is a good idea, though you can expect resistance from the supervisors. Persist, and you will obtain the names and telephone numbers of those who can make decisions. Going to a high-level manager is a shortcut to someone who can service your call. Build a file with names and direct telephone numbers, and you will save time in the future as well.

In fact, once you make contact with a high-level manager or executive at a given company or government office, expect excellent service. Upper-level management, in both the private sector and in government, knows the importance of good communication and generally has the skills to provide you with the services you require. This is an extremely important step to take whenever you need something important accomplished, so find out who runs the company or agency and place your calls to that person's office when you have questions related to policies and procedures.

NEGOTIATIONS

During your quest for confidentiality and privacy in everyday living, remember not to accept what others tell you at face value. Learn to think outside the box and question everything pertaining to information others collect on you for their files. Negotiating for what you need in order to maintain your personal privacy is just like any other deal. Each party makes an offer as to their satisfaction, with consideration given to the other party as well. Then, the two parties meet somewhere in the middle to strike the actual deal.

ACTUAL CASE EVENT

Robert, a privacy advocate who was living a low profile life, returned to a dentist who had performed dental work to correct trauma suffered during athletics fifteen years earlier.

"We need your Social Security number," said the dental office manager as she handed him a form.

"I don't have it memorized," he replied, handing it back. During Robert's next dental office visit, Dr. Dentist explained, "The dental board requires us to identify all of our patients in case of an emergency—such as an automobile accident—in which dental records would be used to verify a victim's identification."

"Fine," replied Robert. "I want to be identified in the event of an emergency. I will provide your office manager with my U.S. passport number. That, along with my name and date of birth, which you already have in your file, will prove my identity in case of an emergency."

"Okay," said Dr. Dentist. The passport number was placed in Robert's file in lieu of his Social Security number. This actual case illustrates what the author stresses throughout this book—the proper use of communication and people skills is of paramount importance as one deals with those who make decisions relevant to preserving your privacy.

Properly and effectively dealing with the office manager and dentist enabled Robert to keep his Social Security number private. His offer and compromise caused him to sacrifice little privacy, while still giving up what was necessary. The dentist was able to meet his requirement by obtaining a means for satisfactory identification of his patient, which could be used in the event of an emergency. By compromising and negotiating, both parties were able to gain satisfaction and continue with the ongoing dentist-patient relationship.

THE COST OF CUSTOMER "NO SERVICE"

Have you been offered a "free" checking account? A great deal on a cell telephone? Be careful. Those free bank accounts and great phone deals may become extremely expensive. How much does your "free" checking account cost if your bank makes you listen to Spanish recordings and music for fifteen minutes before they answer your call?

Still think your cell phone is a great bargain, when you are shifted around the world to call centers where broken-English-speaking representatives repeat back every word you say and then place you on hold and ask someone else what to do about your routine inquiry?

Recognize that the price of goods and services is directly proportional to the quality of goods and services received for the money expended. And expect to pay a fair market value for all products and services.

When you demand good customer service from your service providers, you have established a starting point from which you can begin to utilize effective communication to get what you need. Do business only with the best companies, as measured by their products, services, and customer service.

ACTUAL CASE EVENT

Richard was on vacation when he returned a telephone call to the automobile insurance company that insured the trust-owned car he drives. The representative informed him that his policy had been cancelled two months earlier (without his knowledge).

Being certain that the mistake could easily be corrected, Richard asked to speak to a "supervisor," who was of no help. In fact, the remainder of Richard's vacation was spent dealing with this insurance problem, and the company demonstrated it had "no service" as it failed to resolve the very mistake they had caused their customer.

Following nearly two days of frustration on the telephone with various "boiler room supervisors," Richard obtained the CEO's name and address, wrote him a detailed summary of the event, and began shopping for another insurance company to provide automobile insurance coverage.

Though he disliked spending his vacation buying insurance, Richard learned the importance of having reliable business people with whom to deal. After interviewing representatives from several companies, he settled on a company that provided the coverages necessary and worked directly with a company representative to "bind" his coverage within two hours of making telephone contact.

Having paid 15 percent more for his coverage with the new company, Richard nonetheless obtained a bargain on his automobile policy. His new company answers the telephone, has minimal hold time, and keeps his records straight, thus preventing him from spending his valuable time correcting their internal mistakes.

Six weeks later, a home office manager from the original insurance company called Richard and apologized for all the misunderstanding and mistakes their uninformed personnel caused him—and an offer was made to reinstate the policy. Richard, having long since placed the unfortunate event behind him, informed the company manager that he was now very satisfied with his new company and refused the offer.

YOUR EFFECTIVE PRESENTATION

Your "presentation" is the sum total of all the personal resources you bring to the table as you communicate and negotiate for what you need. While it is beyond the scope of this book to quantify the actual effectiveness of your presentation, the author believes that the total subjective concept of presentation is a valuable consideration as you attempt to improve your abilities in dealing with people.

Present yourself as best you can to those who can provide you with a gateway to your business and personal privacy goals. By presenting yourself in the best manner possible, you will maximize your effectiveness with those who have the ability to assist you reach your goals and objectives.

ATTITUDE IS KEY

You are best served by maintaining a positive attitude when dealing with those who have the power to provide key ingredients for your privacy program, or who have the ability to steer you in the direction of those who can make exceptions to their normal customer policies. In either case, making sure that your mental attitude is positive will ensure that you have optimized your capabilities when dealing with individuals who can affect your ability to enhance your privacy.

Be prepared and aware of the topic you are calling to discuss. Avoid taking unexpected calls, being unprepared, or being caught off guard. Prior to making a call—to a bank, for example—know the party to whom you wish to speak, remind them of who you are, and be fully prepared with all pertinent numbers, facts, and dates relevant to the discussion. Taking five minutes to review the file and your notes will save you a great deal of time and effort, as well as enable you to appear in your best frame of mind as you deal with your bank manager.

DRESS WELL

While clothes may not make the man or woman, a well-dressed person will be more pleasant to view than one poorly attired. Packaging to suit the occasion, or dressing for it, may influence the party with whom you are meeting, albeit ever so slightly. Also, when you feel your best, are totally comfortable with yourself, and are confident that you are well dressed, a better aura is projected, thereby setting the stage for more effective communication.

For business meetings, dress appropriately, and those in attendance will form a positive first impression of you. A pleasant visual impression, even prior to the first word being spoken, is an advantage. Sport coats and neckties or business suits for men and the equivalent business attire for women should be worn for meetings with the bank manager.

Appear in casual dress attire for your department of transportation or DMV dealings. Jeans are fine when you stop in to join the health club. People make judgments about you based on your haircut, your watch, and your shoes.

MANNERS

Good manners convey caring and understanding for those to whom your communication is directed. An unpleasant conversation, for example, tempered with courteous verbiage, is much more pleasant when spoken with true conviction in polite terms.

Remember always to separate yourself from the business at hand as well. For instance, even though Mr. Banker lied to you over the phone when he said he would open that trust checking account with only the tax identification number and now wants your Social Security number as well, telling him of his "lies" (which have cost you a half day's time) will not be productive.

Show real character by telling him how disappointed you are by his "misunderstanding" of your clear statement of the requirements for opening the account, prior to your travel to his bank. Leave the door of communication open, even though he was at fault. He, as a manager, knows he made a mistake but does not have the class to admit it.

Managers usually fail to do what they promise to do because they were not able to make the decision on their own in the first place and had to verify it with their "supervisor" after they made it. And guess who overrode the original decision? And then he did not call you back and explain it to you prior to you driving into town to do the deal. In spite of the mistakes made by others, confronting them directly, especially on their own turf, will do little to reverse their decision. Realizing that others will not always give you what you need, even when the most careful plans are laid, is important to absorb as you strive for optimum communication to assist you to enhance your privacy.

Even the best communicators will be humbled as they experience repeated strikeouts with bureaucrats and business people alike in today's highly regulated America. Prepare, gather all the information required, and make the best contacts possible, while being insistent on dealing only with policy makers, and your chances of getting what you need for privacy will be greatly improved. And always, without exception, be polite.

TALK IS NOT CHEAP

Your ability to speak well is the single most important personal trait for effective communication. Speak with clear diction at medium speed and use sentences that are "on point" to the discussion. Do not run sentences together, and do not ramble. Practice speaking into a tape recorder and in front of a mirror.

The best training for becoming a competent speaker is speaking in front of others. Acting classes and Toastmasters clubs may be good resources for improving your speaking skills. Listen to the professional voice quality of a few radio announcers for pointers on how to best communicate.

While meeting in person, you have your personality to assist you, but when speaking on the telephone, you must rely entirely on your verbal skills, so the effective communicator must have a rich, energetic voice as well as a good command of the English language. Speaking clearly in order that the other party fully understands what is said, is important, so take your conversations seriously as you attempt to deal effectively with business and government on your privacy matters.

LISTENING

Years ago, your author took a one-day college course entitled, "Listening Skills." Principles taught in this simple and effective course emphasized tuning in to the other person's emotions or developing "feeling level" rapport during the conversation. This is accomplished by making eye contact during the verbal exchange and through having a genuine interest in what is being said.

Concentration and focus on the discussion will enable your memory bank to store the important points for later recall. Visualization of key words used by the speaker will assist in the retention of key facts conveyed during the discussion. While working toward the improvement of listening skills, it helps to do exercises that facilitate memory.

For example, as someone states the numerals 1, 3, 5, 7, 8 to you, visualize these numbers and form a mental picture that will enable you to repeat the numbers, using this "memory script" to read back and verbalize what was recited to you. This type of exercise can help you remember key points, which are necessary for favorable first impressions.

For instance, Mr. Banker walks up to meet you and introduces himself as "John Morris." While smiling, shaking his hand, and looking into his face, mentally picture "John Morris" in written form, and the name will be imprinted in your memory for future reference.

It also helps to meditate on communication. Positive affirmations reinforce your belief in your speaking and listening abilities. Such affirmations could include, "I am a very effective speaker who makes a dynamic first impression on all business and government people I meet, through my energetic, rich, voice, and I remember everyone's name and the important information we discuss during our business meetings."

Placing these positive suggestions into the subconscious mind will enable you to become what you feed into your subconscious. However, you must believe what you tell yourself.

PHYSICAL APPEARANCE

Grooming, physique, and personal hygiene are key points for effective communication. Maintaining a healthy lifestyle through a regular exercise program and a healthy diet will allow you to make a better presentation at important meetings. Close attention to hygiene, particularly one's hair and nails, enhance appearance and are indications of good grooming habits.

The trained manager and professional business person will see all of your physical attributes during your meeting, so do not neglect your appearance as you use your people skills to get what you need. Also, taking care of your body, teeth, hair, skin, and nails automatically commands respect from others, thereby creating a favorable first impression.

PUT IT IN WRITING

The written word remains the most powerful of all modes of communication, due to the permanence of a letter, e-mail, or other document. Develop effective writing skills for those times when it becomes necessary to provide letters of confirmation and other forms of business writings. Practice writing "on point" when composing written communications, while also remembering not to sign letters.

PATIENCE

Patience can be learned, so if you don't have it now, don't despair—you can make improvements. First, recognize that it is no small feat to accomplish a high level of privacy in your business and personal affairs. You will naturally encounter resistance during the process, but with ordinary intelligence, the information contained in this book, and a true desire to make your life private, you too can fly beneath the information radar system.

Recognition of the changes occurring before your eyes in the "New America" is the first step in understanding and coping with a broken system. Preparing to devote triple time to a simple telephone call, due to the incompetent service people of today, is no doubt a difficult adjustment for many—particularly those who remember when a great deal could be accomplished with a single three-minute telephone call.

Patiently dealing with the non-communicators, while keeping your own standards high, all the while seeing the humor in it all, is a healthy way to handle your new culture and the third-world service now available to the population.

Always remember that there are new ways to approach a problem whenever one method does not yield a favorable solution. There are new institutions to approach, when one fails to do business as per your requirements. New managers with more flexible attitudes are hired each day, so be optimistic and patient.

MAKING ADJUSTMENTS

Throughout this chapter, the need for you to recognize and understand that your country has changed a great deal over the past several decades has been emphasized. A less-literate population, with neither the cultural esteem to expect a high level of service nor the education and English fluency to deliver it, makes up a huge segment of the American workforce. Practicing your best people skills, while understanding that things are not like they used to be nor as they ought to be, will be positives as you continue to live and work in America. The following events really did occur in the United States of America.

ACTUAL CASE EVENT

Mike Bolesta, a resident of Baltimore, Maryland, paid for stereo installation services at a Best Buy store with $2.00 bills in the amount of $114.00 in April 2005. The clerk at Best Buy did not know the bills were legal tender and refused to accept them as payment. Managers at the store did not authorize the clerk to accept the bills as payment, because they too did not know the bills were legal tender.

Police were called to the scene—they were unfamiliar with the $2.00 currency as well and arrested the man and chained him to a nearby fixture. Eventually, Secret Service agents were called. They verified that the bills are legal tender for the payment of debts. (Source: Americanvoiceradio.com radio program, Bo Gritz, host, April 8, 2005.)

ACTUAL CASE EVENT

Believing that the above incident might be an aberration, rather than a reliable indicator of whether the current workforce in America really does not recognize our own currency, Barry, an e-mail correspondent, decided to perform his own small sample study.

A fast-food restaurant in Los Angeles, California, was the location for his first inquiry. A clerk at this establishment was asked if she would accept $2.00 federal reserve notes as payment for lunch. She said "No" and turned to another employee for confirmation of her answer.

Employee number 2 also said "No" but turned to a third employee, the assistant manager, who also said "No." So don't try to spend your two-dollar bills at certain restaurants in Los Angeles.

ACTUAL CASE EVENT

Continuing his informal survey, Barry visited two separate check-cashing stores, money business service companies that are regulated under the Bank Secrecy Act and the U.S. Patriot Act.

Two tellers were asked if they would accept $2.00 federal reserve notes as payment for money orders. Both tellers said, "No." A third check-cashing store was visited and asked the same question. The teller did not understand the term "federal reserve note," and when Barry advised her it was money, she said she believed the bills could be accepted, but to be sure, he would have to come back the following day and check with her supervisor.

SUMMARY

1. America's changing population has resulted in the decline of customer service.

2. Poor literacy and lack of fluency in English is evident in many customer service departments in both government agencies and the private sector.

3. These conditions make the development and use of "people skills" more important than ever for the individual who desires to make his or her life private.

4. Negotiate for privacy measures in order that each party can meet his or her requirements and continue with the business relationship. Question everything clerks and "officials" request whenever your business or personal information is requested.

5. Poor customer service is expensive.

6. One's personal presentation will facilitate obtaining the best possible service from all providers.

7. A positive mental attitude, combined with appropriate dress for the occasion, good manners, clear speech, and listening skills enable one to function at a peak level during business meetings and over the telephone.

8. Business letters are the most powerful form of communication.

9. Patience is a key personal attribute when dealing with people.

10. Use "people skills" to reach managers and executives to provide services and manage time effectively.

♦ TWENTY-SIX ♦

The Personal Side of Privacy

"In the end, we will not remember the words of our enemies, but the silence of our friends."—Martin Luther King, Jr.

NOT HIS BROTHER'S KEEPER

Houston's phone rang in the afternoon as he was preparing to leave his house and return to work. The man on the other end of the telephone identified himself as being "assigned to your brother's case"—and Houston, Alex Corbin's brother, being the average bird that he is, willingly began to answer each and every question asked by the unverified caller.

Later, the story was told to Alex about how his brother provided his personal information to the alleged investigator, including the verification of his name, address, and Social Security number, employer, and home and work telephone numbers. All of this was done without ever confirming the other person was actually the investigator from the state government agency.

Later, Houston faxed photos of Alex to the investigator, which were used to create a "flyer"—you know, the kind you see in post offices on the walls with the word "WANTED" on them. Alex was being hunted by investigators for the purpose of being served a summons for a civil case filed for an increase in child support payments. He was being hunted by agents of the state, even though all payments were current, and the payments exceeded the amount required for the support of his children.

Alex's income had risen the past few years, and the state was attempting to penalize him for his success by forcing him to pay additional money in child support—never mind that the current amount was more than enough for his family. But Alex, whose attorney had advised him to avoid the serving of a summons in this matter, had adopted a high-level style of privacy living—and was avoiding the state's investigators.

No summons was ever served—and no court appearances were ever required or made.

UNCLE

Alex and his Uncle Ben used to go hunting together when Alex was a kid. Alex was taught to wait patiently for game to come into range, then to carefully aim for a proper "kill shot" before harvesting the various wild animals. Uncle Ben taught Alex how to aim, while fixing only the very tip of the front sight of his rifle on the target—and to slowly squeeze the trigger.

Uncle and nephew were close and remained in contact, and their bond strengthened as Alex entered adulthood and beyond. Alex grew up believing his Uncle Ben—a veteran of two wars—was a tough nut and would always be on his side, if for no other reason than that blood is thicker than water.

First, a "location and support" specialist—one of those state-employed child support investigator types who tries to track down "deadbeat dads," even though Alex was not a "deadbeat dad"—called Uncle Ben and asked a number of questions. Next, Uncle Ben was visited unexpectedly by a local man who claimed to be an investigator working with distant state agents searching for Alex. The questions ranged from asking for the description of Alex's last automobile to his last-known address—as well as personal and business telephone numbers, banking, and other information.

Alex was told the story by his shamed Uncle about how he had answered all questions without providing any resistance whatsoever. Uncle Ben even provided old photographs of his nephew to the man who claimed to be an investigator.

MORAL OF THE STORY

Neither relative verified the identity of any "investigator" with whom they dealt in the above-described interviews. Either relative could have simply refused to talk to the parties who contacted them. However, as this true story and many others demonstrate, people easily forget about past promises made in confidence. They forget fastest when approached by anyone who claims an affiliation with law enforcement. Your most trusted relative and your closest friend will in most cases give you up to anyone who even claims to resemble a law enforcement official. So keep your private life a secret. Tell no one your business unless you expect it to be repeated.

Alex Corbin had not shared any personal information with either relative that would lead investigators to him, except a telephone number—a standalone voicemail number provided by an independent communications company.

He began receiving telephone messages from "loan officers" offering him the opportunity to take advantage of interest-free loans.

According to the phone messages, Alex had already been preapproved, and the money would be available as soon as he activated the account by pressing the appropriate telephone keys. Realizing that his voicemail phone number had not been supplied to any bank or finance company, Alex recognized the ruse the investigators had designed to locate him through a telephone tracing system. He tolerated these messages for a period of time prior to changing his number—thereby eliminating any links to himself.

No harm was done by his relative's full cooperation with those claiming to be investigators. Although his popularity increased, and many began to see his photograph over the next few years, he was never served a summons, nor did he have to appear for any court hearings.

The statute of limitations ran out when Alex's youngest child turned 18, and he continued to pay support payments at the court-ordered amount set more than a decade earlier. This amount was excessive at the time the original judgment was entered and continued to be more than adequate for the living comfort of his children until they each reached their eighteenth birthdays.

FAMILY TIES

In my experienced opinion, you—the privacy seeker—should not provide many people, not even relatives, with your personal and confidential information. Relationships change over time, as do an individual's privacy requirements. Remember, a close friend or relative will be the first resource tapped by identity thieves or investigators when they attempt to locate you and your property.

So keep even those with whom you have close relationships guessing as to your most private matters. Relatives and friends may sell you out in a New York minute—sometimes unintentionally and innocently—and you will bear this risk when you tell too many people too much about your personal business. If and when it becomes a great risk for you to reveal pertinent information about yourself for whatever reason, total secrecy becomes the best policy for remaining anonymous.

SOCIALIZATION

Can you justify using all of the privacy tactics outlined in this book? Hopefully, you will not need to cut ties with family and friends to fly beneath the information radar system. Discretion as to whom you allow into your circle of friends, relatives included, will prove to be the most sensible way of living a private life.

A wise man once advised me to think ten times prior to inviting someone over for dinner. That was good advice then and remains so today. One can live normally and socialize regularly and still keep his business to himself. When few, if any, know the particulars of your home, business, money, and personal data, your risk of having this information fall into the wrong hands at any future point is minimized as well.

TRUST

If you believe you must trust *someone*, trust your attorney. He will have the most at risk in the event he should breach the attorney-client privilege. He is bound by law to keep your secrets and risks disbarment and his professional practice in the event he sells you out for any reason. Do not use family or friends to preserve your business or personal privacy. Generally it is the best practice not to do business with family or personal friends. Use business and professional people instead, and always form written contracts.

FAMILY AND HOUSE GUESTS

Children, spouses, and significant others who learn privacy tactics and practice the privacy lifestyle will become accustomed to keeping your home location a secret. For example, depending on one's goals, the home may be off limits entirely for those who do not live there—or be open only to a few selected guests. Grandparents and siblings may be the only visitors into your home for those desiring to live a low-profile life.

Others can be seen at neutral locations, including event sites, restaurants, coffeehouses, the gym, office, church, public libraries, parks, and other places. Your home address is the most sought-after secret for those who wish to locate you. Such hunters will use any method possible to obtain this information, including use of a "pretext" to convince those close to you to show them the way to your front door. Sometimes "none-of-your-business lies" become necessary to preserve your privacy and security. Don't be afraid to use them to keep your business private.

Privacy, while necessary for security, is not always pleasant or convenient and is always more expensive than the "normal" lifestyle. You must consider your individual circumstances in order to make necessary adjustments once all the information is available. Family and friends must be educated about your individual privacy requirements. Reread the chapters under the "Home" section of this book for important privacy information.

POSSESSION ADDICTION

Life becomes more pleasant for the individual who chooses to live privately, once a sensible separation between self and personal possessions is accomplished. Do you have trouble packing your suitcase? Struggle to get every last item inside, even for a weekend getaway?

You may be able to better manage your accumulated personal "stuff" once you recognize the significance of it all. In all cases, adjustments to the private way of living are most pleasant when you or your family keeps only personal items that are of use for normal living requirements. This comes down to a matter of taste, but from a behavioral standpoint, personal items not used for everyday living will slow you down and perhaps impair your ability to make the adjustments necessary to acquire a high level of privacy should the need arise.

When you have collections that require significant storage space, an organization of the items, as well as an up-to-date inventory, will reduce difficulties associated with segregating throw-away or donation items from keepsakes and heirlooms.

SELF-AWARENESS

Knowing yourself, as well as recognizing your own behavioral tendencies when under the stresses of making the adjustments necessary to live a more private lifestyle, will assist you in the development of a suitable plan. Establish privacy objectives based on your needs, and prioritize according to their importance in your privacy program.

A significant amount of time, effort, and money must be allocated to achieve a high level of personal and business privacy, particularly in the beginning of your program. So start with a review of the various sections of this book and refer back to appropriate chapters that will enable you to decide on your requirements. Personal adjustments are necessary as well, although this is generally very positive and painless when one weighs it against the alternatives.

Behavioral aspects of privacy are significant, and satisfaction is gained when you are able essentially to build a shield around yourself, your immediate loved ones, and your business affairs. Above all, establish a comfort level that will not drain your energy, time, and pocketbook.

The development of a more secure and private style of living can be adventurous and is certainly a valuable insurance policy against identity theft and other crimes, so recognize the positive aspects of it all once you seriously apply yourself to making lifestyle changes.

The development of a highly confidential lifestyle does not mean suddenly switching from being an extrovert to a hermit. On the contrary, you can continue associating with family and friends, while making moderate changes over a period of time—or you can pick up and start a new life entirely without leaving a trace of yourself.

These are choices you will need to make according to your experiences, desires, and individual circumstances. With moderate effort, reasonable time expenditures, and limited expenses, everyone can make positive changes.

RELATIONSHIPS

Marriages, friendships, and partnerships are built and maintained on love, understanding, trust, and contracts. Emphasize "contracts." Establish contracts in writing, and use an attorney for the most important agreements, whether these be of a personal or business nature.

For the most peace of mind, do not mix business and personal relationships without considering the risk of doing so. This is a difficult rule to abide by, and exceptions are justifiably made. The best guard against privacy breaches is to have contractual protection.

When you form business relationships with individuals and private businesses, you will have far more flexibility than when entering into agreements with banks and other businesses closely regulated by the government. In spite of your best efforts, expect the human factor to weigh heavily in all your privacy efforts and recognize that your best efforts and caution only cover your side of the equation.

THE PRACTICE

Over a period of time, refinements in your business and personal privacy will be made whenever your circumstances change significantly or when you desire additional measures of security. Living and practicing a high level of privacy does not begin on the day after you read this book. However, you can make changes almost immediately that will become the foundation of your total privacy program.

Obtaining a mailing address without any connection to your residence location is a very important first step, for example. Changing from a personal checking account with your Social Security number and name as the identifiers of the money, to using a trust and tax identification number for anonymity, can be accomplished within a reasonable period of time and for a moderate sum of money.

Graduate slowly and make changes according to your needs and budget, while gaining an understanding of what is available to you in your quest for privacy and security. Your success will depend in large part on your ability to deal with people. Bankers, brokers, realtors—even DMV personnel—will do things your way when you approach the problem with all the facts, utilize your best manners, and persist in having documents prepared as you require them for your personal and business privacy.

People have the power to give you what you need, so do not accept the psycho-babble from uninformed clerks and bureaucratic types, which will not normally be correct when you begin your inquiries.

This book emphasizes using your communication and people skills to accomplish what you need in the world of privacy. Your author has either practiced all the methods and tactics outlined in this book or is aware of the success of each principle and concept described herein as being successfully used by privacy seekers. Some of these privacy tactics will require persistence as well as time, as you accomplish your privacy goals.

SUMMARY

1. Do not expect relatives, friends, and associates to keep your secrets private in the event law enforcement or investigators question them.

2. No one is obliged to provide information unless ordered to do so by a court order.

3. Friends and relationships are important for normal behavior and socialization.

4. Trust your attorney with your confidential information.

5. Make all agreements of significance with written contracts.

6. Family and friends play important roles in your privacy and security program. Educate family about the necessary precautions for family privacy.

7. Keep the accumulation of personal possessions under control and efficiently organize your home environment.

8. Being comfortable with yourself and understanding your needs will enable you to establish a suitable privacy program based on your individual requirements.

9. Relationships, while important for normal behavior and socialization, require discretion and careful thought in order for you to establish business and personal privacy.

10. Practicing privacy will enhance your knowledge and skills pertaining to the measures available to make your life private. Continue to improve your skills in dealing with the people and agencies that provide services and control certain aspects of your private life.

♦ TWENTY-SEVEN ♦

Coping With Government

"For in reason, all government without the consent of the governed is the very definition of slavery"—Jonathan Swift

CROOKED COPS: A CASE OF STOLEN PROPERTY

Yvonne Schmidt, a West Coast resident and real estate investor/ entrepreneur, rented an office for business use during her planned three-month stay in a major Southeastern city. A nearby storage facility offered rentals and the security of an iron fence, a code-operated gate, and a full-time watchman.

Yvonne, believing it was prudent to store her valuables, business documents, and other property in a secure facility—off site and away from her hotel and office—paid storage fees to the storage rental company for peace of mind and safety.

Eight days after signing the month-to-month rental agreement with the storage company, Ms. Schmidt received a voicemail message from the property manager. He advised her that the police had presented him with a search warrant, removed her secure lock from the door of her rented storage room, taken all the contents, and were holding everything as "evidence."

As she questioned the manager by telephone, she learned that during her move-in, the video cameras on the property had recorded her every move. The video showed her removing several case-enclosed hunting rifles and a shotgun from her car. Other items in her rented storage room that were confiscated by police included personal and business files and records, original trust documents, an automobile title, company registrations, bank credit cards, checkbooks for business and personal use, family heirlooms, gold coins and silver bullion, jewelry, novelty/alternate identification cards, books, handguns and ammunition, hunting equipment, automobile accessories, and other property.

When Yvonne asked the storage manager why her rental storage property had been violated by the police, he explained that the police believed she was a drug dealer, because their dog had smelled contraband at her storage room's door. Knowing that nothing could be farther from the truth, Yvonne began searching for an attorney.

Following several days of down time and $3,500 in expense, a reputable criminal and civil attorney began the process of negotiating with the police detective and district attorney in charge of the case against Yvonne. It took thirteen months, $5,300 in legal fees, 4,700 miles of travel, and six weeks of missed work for Yvonne to receive her property from the thieves who stole it—the police who are supposed to protect people and property from criminals.

When asked about compensation, the attorney who represented her said he would sue the police for damages under a civil rights statute for unlawful search-and-seizure. But when push came to shove, only an underling associate was available for her long-distance calls to the attorney's office, after she was cleared of any wrongdoing and the police agreed to return her property. Yvonne was advised that a substantial retainer—plus the advancement of fees for legal expenses that could total six figures before trial—would be required in order to pursue the civil rights action against the police department.

Witness the "good ole boy" syndrome at its best. No charges were ever filed against the falsely accused Ms. Schmidt. No evidence of drug or any other illegal activity was ever linked to her.

GUILTY UNTIL PROVEN INNOCENT: "COUNTERFEIT PASSPORT"

Do you remember when people could walk the streets freely in America, and tax-paying citizens were able to enjoy their free time and public property without worry of interference from the police? Are you old enough to remember when the neighborhood cop was respected and held in high esteem? Once upon a time in America, citizens could depend on their civil servants to uphold the laws while arresting the bad guys—not instead, the very people who pay their salaries. Sadly, the country is different today. Now, every citizen is threatened with the police state of a government gone mad.

Michael O'Donoghue loves to donate his time and money to a volunteer project that feeds the homeless in his community—a city in the western U.S. Michael feeds people on holidays and on a regular basis at parks and other public places. There were no statutes or ordinances against this practice in Michael's city.

Following one of his visits to a park, where he provided meals to those who needed them, Michael and several of the homeless community were chatting on a bench in the city park. Along came a police car. Then two. Finally three police cars arrived on the scene. Meanwhile, in the eastern and south-central parts of this same city, Crips, Bloods, and MS13 gang members and other criminals were plying their trade, threatening taxpayers—who are prohibited from carrying defense weapons by guarded politicians and judges who sit in their towers of power ruling all who would dare to disobey. Illegal-alien Mexicans flood the streets, committing felonies just by entering the United States unlawfully for the second time, while the police pounce on Michael O'Donoghue—feeder of the homeless.

Michael was handcuffed, unlawfully searched, held without cause, and questioned for nearly six hours. He was called a liar by the lead police officer, who did not recognize his U.S. passport as being an official identification document. Apparently, the policeman had never seen a United States passport and believed it to be counterfeit—or at least said he believed it was counterfeit.

Following hours of being held in handcuffs without being arrested, Michael requested that he be charged or released. A police sergeant was eventually called to the scene, where a total of seven policemen and three police cars had come and gone over the past several hours. The police sergeant told Michael that they would like to photograph him and take his fingerprints.

Michael said, "No." He told the police sergeant that he would not allow himself to be photographed or fingerprinted unless he was arrested and charged. He repeated his earlier statement, telling the policeman either to charge him or let him go. Soon the sergeant advised the lead police officer to release Mr. O'Donoghue.

Following his release, he told the sergeant that he had been unlawfully searched following his request to the officer that he not have his person searched. The officer lied to his superior, saying he had been given permission to search Mr. O'Donoghue. Following the collection of the names of all officers who had been on the scene, Michael O'Donoghue, feeder of the homeless, was released without being arrested or charged with any crime whatever, and allowed to go home.

DUMBING DOWN AMERICA

These two case histories of citizens' abuse by police actually happened. The names were changed, and the locations are not specified, to protect the anonymity of those involved. These cases illustrate what is happening in the United States today. The U.S. is now a "police state," with nearly unlimited yet unconstitutional powers given to local law enforcement officials, judges, and Homeland Security and FBI agents—all under the guise of a War on Terror.

All of this is for the protection of the citizens, of course—those who buy all of it or most of it. Or at least enough of it so that they can't be disturbed from watching their all-important ball games as they lounge in front of their televisions, listen each evening to the talking heads fronting for the conglomerate-controlled media, and accept most everything dictated to them.

People will continue to accept the current state of affairs, so long as they are not interrupted from their football games. Or baseball, basketball, hockey, soap operas, favorite prime-time shows or other distractions that keep them sedated and out of touch with the real happenings—the police state in action—designed to steal property and freedoms from a desensitized America, once the land of the free.

Americans are so busy working and borrowing from Peter to pay Paul that they don't have the time or energy to resist government's increasingly tight stranglehold on citizens. Many workers who do manage to achieve business and career success are so heavily taxed that their actual take-home pay—their true net income—becomes a living wage only, with minimal savings left over for emergencies and investment.

Overburdened by high taxes, runaway inflation, and a now "near third world" currency in the form of the U.S. dollar, Americans, for the most part, are becoming slaves of the state—both career-wise and when charged with breaking laws. Thus, the cycle of working for and bowing down to Big Bureaucrat continues—a disgusting existence, if you participate in it. The slaves—worker bees—repeat each day their hurried routine: rushing to dress, commuting to and from work, buying their $3-plus gas, rushing to lunch, and then rushing to keep paying their taxes, obvious and hidden.

Rush. Rush. Rush. All to fund a government—federal, state, and local—that gains increased powers over citizens at its every whim.

FELONY GUILTY-UNTIL-PROVEN-INNOCENT CASES

Not all suspects get off as easily as Yvonne Schmidt, who lost time, money, and property, only to reclaim it eventually following thievery committed by lying cops intending to justify their salaries as well as boost their property inventory. Nor are all allowed to return home like Michael O'Donoghue, following hours of fear and discomfort as he was being falsely imprisoned by a gang of cops acting like thugs, who evidently haven't the guts to chase the real criminals, so instead prey on a man who innocently attempts to enjoy his public-funded park while contributing to the homeless community.

Today in the United States of America, citizens who pay the salaries of the police and are law abiders may sometimes become the targets of the officers sworn to protect them. Innocent citizens may be smart to establish a high level of privacy in order to avoid having soldiers of the state knock on their door—or kick it down, as they do in "reality" TV programs—and to prevent government and police from finding their car in DMV databases, locate their money through Fin-CEN and other searchable databases, find cell phone records, or discover where they work.

I'll bet Dennis Brown wishes he had been invisible to police and able to escape the court system, as he struggled through nineteen years of jail time after the State of Louisiana falsely convicted him of rape, burglary, and crimes against nature. Brown, sentenced to life, was convicted in 1985 and exonerated in 2005 but has yet to be compensated for Big Bureaucrat's mistakes.

How about Jimmy Ray Bromgard? He's the Montana man who was sent to a Big Sky big house at age 19 to do a forty-year stint for a sexual intercourse without consent rap, of which he, too, was exonerated in 2002—but not before he had his best fifteen-plus years stolen from him by Montana's court system. Of course, a few cases fall through the cracks, right? Some mistakes are bound to be made, even in the fairest judicial systems, right?

How about the cops who lie routinely while on the witness stand to compensate for their inadequate skills in catching the real criminals? Some have. Sometimes they've planted evidence. District attorneys have suppressed evidence, even when it would have proved the convicted person was wrongfully serving time. Witnesses have lied, too, of course.

Maybe it is time for the innocent to minimize their risk of being wrongfully convicted. Perhaps the best defense against government—all government—is to become "invisible" on paper.

Phillip Leon Thurman probably wishes he had been able to implement a bullet-proof privacy plan back in 1985 and "disappear" before he spent twenty years rotting away in a Virginia prison hell-hole where he was scheduled to do thirty-one years—prior to his exoneration in 2005.

Alan Crotzer lost one third of a normal lifespan as he spent twenty-four years in a Florida jail for a crime he didn't commit—until he was set free in 2006.

Kenneth Adams spent eighteen years of his seventy-five-year sentence in an Illinois penitentiary cell, prior to proving his innocence.

Chester Baur lived for nine years behind bars in Montana before being let go in 1997. He has received no money for the state's mistake. If the right jury were ever assembled, he and Jimmy Ray Bromgard might become the co-owners of a good piece of Montana state government property. They should.

How much is a year of your life worth when you have it stolen from you by government and are forced to live like a caged animal; fight off the real rapists; lose access to decent medical and dental care; and lose your career, family, friends, and reputation? What's it like to struggle to be heard by a rigged system, while losing your faith in the system and the rule of law, your country, and your state government, with no hope of ever regaining normalcy during a lifetime?

The case list goes on and on of wrongly accused, falsely convicted citizens who are later forced to prove their innocence. It's an upside-down circus without the laughter, but in far too many cases, with plenty of government clowns dressed up in their uniforms, suits, and black robes, ready to arrest and convict someone—anyone—in order to satisfy the bureaucracy, qualify for pay raises, build their political reputations, and obtain votes and support from the public. No matter that an innocent man or woman is falsely convicted and forced to take the fall for the real criminal.

Often, the criminal escapes, because he or she is smarter than law enforcement, some members of which seem to care less about justice than their selfish career advancement. Government often forces innocent citizens to deplete their savings on legal fees and lose their jobs, families, reputations, and hope—eventually to be housed in overcrowded jails where they are forced to survive in a real criminal environment. Or worse. Consider how many innocent people are put to death by those states with the death penalty. Your privacy should be the most important aspect of your life and, in fact, your life may depend on it.

EMINENT DOMAIN: GOVERNMENT'S EVICTION TOOL

Under a legal process known as eminent domain, government is seizing property held by homeowners for the purpose of generating more tax revenue from the construction of more-expensive new homes or commercial buildings.

The purpose of eminent domain is for the transference of private property ownership to government ownership for "the public's good." That is, when a private property is for the good of the public—as for the construction of a courthouse, a public road, or a school building—it can be purchased at fair market value by government.

If ever there was a reason for American property owners to wake up, it is during this era of increased government control through unfair property seizures that are occurring under eminent domain. The courts have ruled that not only can private property be taken for the public's good—a long-standing controversy based entirely on subjective opinion—but private property can now be seized for private use. The motivation for the government's seizure of a private property—allowing another private party or business to purchase it through eminent domain—is the increase in taxes generated by the new owner's construction project, of course.

EMINENT DOMAIN HITS A HOME RUN ON HOMEOWNERS

Do you trust your government to make decisions about when they have the right to throw you out of your own house? All for the "public's good," of course.

Consider the matter of Washington, D.C., residents who are being forced to leave their homes for construction of a ballpark. The D.C. government says residents living near the site of a proposed national baseball stadium must move out so that construction can begin on the ballpark. The city has seized the titles to the properties through eminent domain.

GOVERNMENT'S "FAIR MARKET VALUE" OF ONE CENT PER ACRE

A Texas man has been awarded $1 for his 105 acres of land seized by government through eminent domain. In May 2005, Glenn Seureau, a Pasadena landowner, lost his right to keep his property (which had been in his family for 150 years) in the court of Judge Lynn Bradshaw-Hull. The judge ruled that, having paid $1 to Seureau, the Port of Houston Authority now owns the property.

Seureau was previously paid $1.9 million by the Port and has been ordered to pay it back plus interest of 5.75 percent, as well as to pay the court costs of the Port of Houston Authority. Seureau, who believed that even the $1.9 million was less than the fair market value of his property, had planned to develop the 105 acres and has appealed the decision. (Source: Internet article, unspecified, 2005–2006.)

COP REALITY SHOWS AND SOLDIERS OF THE STATE

Beat cops and other law enforcement officers have become instant "action heroes," as Americans are shown the power of the state through reality television. The public is now entertained by a bombardment of reality shows portraying the police in action. Real footage is shown—then rerun and shown again—of police breaking down doors of suspected criminals' homes. Women posing as prostitutes lure potential Johns into hotel rooms, with hungry policemen and detectives waiting in the wings to cuff and transport the accused would-be buyers of sex to the nearest jailhouse.

People are stopped while driving their cars, for no obvious reason or for minor traffic infractions, and have their persons and cars searched by police. Kids buying small amounts of contraband substances are chased, roughed up in some cases, and taken away to jail by police. Taken away by those representatives of the tireless men and women in blue who risk life and limb to protect the public from recreational drug users, sex seekers, and speeders—as Big Bureaucrat spreads his wings throughout the community to provide safety to all.

Even livestock and pets are provided sanctuary from evil owners, who may not properly feed, house, or care for animals to the satisfaction of the badge-wearing, gun-toting experts known as the "animal police." Violators are arrested, tried, and sentenced, while their animals are confiscated and become property of the government. Meanwhile, MS13 gang members, Crips, Bloods, and other organized criminal gangs of all ethnicities continue to steal, rob, extort, and murder throughout all American states.

There are places in east and south-central Los Angeles where the police are afraid to patrol, let alone confront these criminals, whose numbers continue to grow. An estimated 5,000 to 10,000 illegal-alien Mexicans and others come into the country each day and line the streets, unlawfully solicit work, provide false Social Security numbers to employers, and avoid paying taxes on money earned.

An estimated 90 percent of the arrest warrants in Los Angeles County are for illegal aliens. Approximately 30 percent to 40 percent of the California prison population is composed of illegal aliens. Illegal-alien criminals are some of the leaders in identity theft, as they prowl our once-free land seeking the identities of legitimate citizens in order to illegally take what is not theirs for their own betterment.

Not even a wink or a nod is necessary anymore. Big Bureaucrat has clearly given the green light for illegal aliens to freely move about, holding up bank lines, fumbling through third-grade paperwork tasks, demanding free education from public schools in Spanish, as well as free medical care—while spreading third-world, nineteenth-century diseases throughout our once-great land.

Accused legal citizens, however—those dangerous sex seekers, casual drug users, and speeders—are not given such leniency. They become the real criminals to support the current police state and are brought into a system where detectives and vice cops write reports and fingerprint the accused—who are then taken to state and local jails that house them until they are able to pay their ransom to the state.

Once they make bail, the accused begin the tightrope walk through the legal system, hiring a defense attorney, fighting the charges, and making court appearances, where the charges are often beaten or dropped—providing the accused can afford a lawyer skilled enough to beat the government's prosecutor and impeach police or do whatever is necessary to free the client from the criminal system.

Citizens far too often have their human rights and freedoms abused and are forced to pay for Big Bureaucrat's abuse in the form of time, effort, and money to regain freedoms taken away by the very government that promised those freedoms. Prosecutors, defense attorneys, judges, court reporters, bailiffs, secretaries, clerks, and others are supplied with a steady stream of work during the process—whether the reason for the abduction of citizens is deemed just or not—all at the suspects' expense as they work their way through the American justice system.

FinCEN

FinCEN—the Financial Crimes Enforcement Network—is a network of databases and records maintained by the U.S. federal government. FinCEN—a branch of the U.S. Treasury Department—handles over 140 million computer files containing records from 21,000 depository institutions and an estimated 200,000 non-banking institutions.

The mission statement of the Financial Crimes Enforcement Network is to "safeguard the financial system from the abuses of financial crime, including terrorist financing, money laundering, and other illicit activity." FinCEN shares information with many government agencies, including the Bureau of Alcohol, Tobacco, and Firearms (ATF); the Drug Enforcement Administration (DEA); the Federal Bureau of Investigation (FBI); the U.S. Secret Service; the Internal Revenue Service (IRS), the Customs Service, and the U.S. Postal Inspection Service.

Authorized agents from these and other agencies investigate names, addresses, and Social Security numbers through FinCEN. State and local police have access to FinCEN as well. The FinCEN database allows government agents and police to investigate people rather than crime. Investigators may utilize FinCEN to tap into one's personal data for the purpose of accumulating information that may be unrelated to the business of solving a crime.

The powers afforded FinCEN and the agencies that use it should give the privacy seeker motivation to become anonymous. Now, do you really want your bank and brokerage accounts to be held under your real name, home address, and Social Security number?

BSA DIRECT

Think it is unfair and unconstitutional for the local traffic cop to learn where you keep your money by pressing a few buttons? At present, America's government is gaining even more information about her citizens through *BSA Direct*. The Bank Secrecy Act is administered by FinCEN and is the nation's most comprehensive anti–money-laundering law.

BSA Direct improves authorized users' access and ability to analyze BSA data. Data warehousing technology allows for the improved structure and storage of citizens' data and provides business intelligence and other tools to a user-friendly web portal. BSA Direct increases

FinCEN's ability to provide information to other agencies with an interest in subjects being investigated.

U.S. CUSTOMS

The U.S. Customs Service is the primary law enforcement agency responsible for protecting America's borders. Customs agents have nearly unlimited authority to search your person and property at will. Violate any laws or be suspected of such, and you will be detained until Customs is satisfied that you have done nothing illegal.

Expect the mail that you have forwarded back to you from your Western European mail drop to be opened on occasion by U.S. Customs agents, who may confiscate or open packages they believe may contain anything illegal. U.S. Customs is a huge thorn in the side of law-abiding citizens who want mail privacy and freedom.

Observe the many illegal aliens standing on your street corners as you fight traffic each day. Read the newspapers and view the photographs of long tunnels from the Mexican border into the United States. This is your U.S. government at work.

INTERPOL

The International Criminal Police Organization (INTERPOL) is the world's largest police organization, with a membership of 184 countries. INTERPOL, created in 1923, facilitates police cooperation among countries. The primary goal is to prevent and combat international crime. Their database is one you will want to stay out of, because once you are in it, there are few places to hide under your current true identity.

INTERNAL REVENUE SERVICE

This book is not about evading income taxes, although some make a good case for doing so. Literature is available that claims the payment of taxes to be "voluntary" and not required by law. Some of these "experts" make a compelling case as they advocate such systems as the formation of a Federal Contract Pure Trust Organization and individual sovereignty programs as a means of freedom from the IRS.

Although the Internal Revenue Service is not really a government agency but only a collection agency for the United States Treasury, few companies or quasi-government agencies are as feared by citizens as the IRS. If you know how to avoid paying taxes legally, then more power to you, and I wish you success. I do not. So I file my tax returns each year and take advantage of all the deductible expenses my accountant advises me to take. I prefer this to spending my life fighting the IRS in tax court, not to mention the time, effort, and expenses of such a legal battle.

Recently, a number of high-profile tax court cases have gone in favor of the defendant, taxpayer, or would-be taxpayer, as the case may be. In June, 2005, former IRS agent and CPA Joe Banister was found not guilty on all counts of alleged criminal tax fraud and conspiracy related to actions he took on behalf of a California business owner who had openly defied the IRS over several years by no longer withholding income and employment taxes from the paychecks of his workers.

So keep an open mind on the subject. The tax protestors may eventually have their day. Seek the advice of a competent attorney and certified public accountant, and do your own research

During a private conference, an attorney once advised me that when a Nevada Limited Partnership is used to hold assets, no one—not the government, courts, or the IRS—can confiscate the property held by this entity as a way to satisfy a judgment against a limited partner. Now, I am not saying that all who control a Nevada Limited Partnership should stop filing tax returns and believe they are home free, but legally, according to this veteran attorney, no one can seize the property interest of a limited partner held by this entity, when a limited partner is liable individually for a judgment.

Be advised that the law and the courts do not always favor those who are right. So just because another entity owns assets—including a Nevada Limited Partnership under your control—a U.S. court may still somehow force you to surrender these assets.

The same attorney who counseled me on the safety of the Nevada Limited Partnership further advised me that an additional safety layer, in the form of an offshore asset protection trust in a favorable foreign jurisdiction, would improve the chances of the unlikely seizure of a Nevada Limited Partnership from ever occurring. By having ownership of the Nevada Limited Partnership transferred to a trust based offshore, with the limited partner being the settlor and still in control of the assets, creditors from anywhere are forced to fight the battle of collecting the judgment outside U.S. borders.

A judgment from a U.S. court will not be recognized in the Cook

Islands, for example. Therefore, the plaintiff's attorney will be forced to try the case again in the Cook Islands. And that is an expensive and time-consuming process, giving the defendant and his attorney time to strategically plan to avoid seizure of assets owned by the offshore asset protection trust.

GUNS

According to the second amendment of the U.S. Constitution, Americans have the right to bear arms. I don't recall reading anything about government being able to require that guns be registered, ten-day waiting periods for buying pistols, or restrictions on the purchase of high-caliber firearms or ammunition. Your government sees it differently, however, and makes law-abiding citizens jump thorough hoops in order to exercise their second-amendment rights.

Those in the know tell me that government plans to disarm citizens eventually. Watch the cop action heroes during the reality TV shows some evening. See the slanted bias placed by police and the media on those "dangerous handguns." The public is being hypnotized into believing that gun ownership is the reason for violent crime, yet study after study demonstrates that crime decreases in communities where citizens are armed.

For example, in 1982, Kennesaw, Georgia, passed a law requiring heads of households to keep at least one firearm in their home, exempting those with criminal records or those who declined for religious reasons. Since 1982, there have been only three murders in the city. Crime against people has gone down and stayed low.

Gun owners who purchase their firearms at stores are required to provide their confidential information and identity documents. Concealed handgun-carrying permits, when they are issued, require even more scrutiny, plus a proficiency course supervised by a state-sponsored instructor.

Registration and carrying requirements vary from state to state, so check your laws in the event you wish to exercise your rights under the second amendment. By privately buying firearms, some gun enthusiasts escape the government paperwork and eliminate their names from Big Bureaucrat's watch lists. Those who are so inclined and have the necessary skills may purchase kits for firearms and assemble the weapons themselves, thereby eliminating serial numbers from their weapons. Make sure this is legal in your state before you do it.

American government is regulating citizens' ability to own guns and defend themselves by placing increasingly tight restrictions on their constitutional right to bear arms. Contrary to propaganda distributed by some media sources, America does not have the freedoms it is believed to have—especially concerning the possession of guns. Handgun ownership is prohibited in some jurisdictions. There is an ongoing battle over citizens' rights to own certain machine guns and high-caliber weapons.

Switzerland, on the other hand, mandates by law that every household head own a fully automatic machine gun and ammunition. The Swiss enjoy a very low crime rate. One excellent resource for educating yourself about firearms and survival tactics is radio host J.R. Moore, who may be heard on www.RepublicBroadcasting.com on Saturdays. Websites that provide information relevant to weapons and survival include:

1. www.TheLibertyman.com

2. www.FreezeDryGuy.com

3. www.e-gunparts.com

THE ILLEGAL-ALIEN MEXICAN PROBLEM

If you still don't believe American government is an "upside-down circus," attempt to drive in downtown Los Angeles. Or Phoenix. Or Las Vegas. In fact, you don't have to go to the Southwestern U.S. anymore to hear only Spanish being spoken and feel as if you are in third-world Mexico. Go to Georgia or Louisiana. Guess who is doing the clean-up work following Hurricane Katrina? Illegal aliens. Chicago was ranked number five in the nation among American cities where illegals live, in a recent study.

Go to any state and almost any city in our once-great country and watch government cater to the illegals, bending over backward to educate them in Spanish; give immediate citizenship to their newborn "anchor babies;" and provide food subsidies, housing, free medical care, and even worker's compensation benefits when they are hurt on the job while working in the country illegally.

How do illegal aliens affect your privacy? Ninety percent of the arrest warrants in Los Angeles are for illegal aliens. Guess which segment of the population is in the lead—or near it—for committing identity theft crimes against legal citizens? Illegal-alien Mexicans. Illegal-alien Mexicans and others are so expensive to you and me, the taxpayers who end up supporting them, that they not only rape our system, but inflate our prices. Simply through the law of supply and demand, the influx of illegal aliens into this country makes your bread, milk, meat, veggies, gas, and housing more expensive—as too many people compete for the available supply of these commodities and products, thus increasing their scarcity and driving prices higher.

Some years ago, your author became aware of the illegal alien problem and has listened to a number of people speak on the subject. Legendary radio talk show host George Putnam, of Los Angeles, began speaking out against these criminals forty years ago. Now, Terry Anderson, who can be heard worldwide via the Internet, hosts a weekly show on the illegal-alien problem. The Wake Up America Foundation, based in Las Vegas and founded by Mark Edwards, is also an active movement against these criminals. Some websites that may be of interest include:

1. www.TheTerryAndersonShow.com

2. www.TheWakeUpAmericaFoundation.com

3. www.RepublicBroadcasting.com

4. www.TheMinuteManProject.com

5. www.USBorderSecurity.org

6. www.MothersAgainstIllegalAliens.org

7. www.FrostyWooldridge.com

8. www.AmericanVoiceRadio.com

9. www.AmericanWorker.org

10. www.NumbersUSA.com

The Minute Man Project was founded by Jim Gilcrest. Modern-day "Minute Men" observe illegals crossing borders, alert Border Patrol, and actively promote the control of illegals crossing into the United States. Although these groups are well intended, sadly, there are more illegal aliens in this country today than ever before.

Government facilitates and allows this to happen in order to increase U.S. companies' corporate sales, decrease labor costs, and obtain more tax revenues to fund their operations. Also, the government gains instant access to ambitious young men and women who become soldiers to fight wars in faraway places—never mind whether these new soldiers are legal immigrants or have any allegiance to the United States of America.

Imagine the decrease in sales at Wal-mart, Costco, Sav-On, Home Depot, and other major discount stores if a raid on illegal aliens resulted in the deportation of every illegal alien in the United States of America, and no more were permitted to enter into the country. Imagine how many of the eighty-six hospitals bankrupted in California might be able to reopen their doors if all the illegals were booted out of the country.

How about the estimated 30 percent to 40 percent of illegal-alien prisoners in the California penal system? How much do they cost you, the law-abiding taxpayer? How much less would taxpayers pay each year if this nonsensical system was fixed? Wouldn't it be great to decrease identity theft—a crime committed frequently by these desperate, job-seeking, criminal illegal aliens?

But government, unlike you and me, does not have to act responsibly or balance its checkbooks. While corporate sales increase in America by revenues generated through sales of goods and services to everyone—including illegals—the costs of supporting them far outweigh the increases in sales from their purchases and the taxes they may or may not—and most often do not—pay. Even though the costs of supporting the illegals do not justify allowing them to remain in America from an economic standpoint, the federal government does not care.

You see, the income statement of all of corporate America—which is dependent upon total gross sales—is a separate account from the expense ledger which contains the tens of billions of dollars of expenses to fund illegals in America. So corporate America receives the benefit from the increases in sales, while the taxpayers pay for the government give-away programs to fund the illegal aliens.

In addition, politicians receive the benefit of additional humans—illegally here, of course—to fight their wars and vote for them on promises of give-away programs, amnesty for illegal-alien criminals, and many other benefits, as the illegal aliens do labor-intensive jobs at below market wages.

THE REAL I.D. ACT

On May 11, 2005, President Bush signed the Real I.D. Act into law. This act mandates that state driver's licenses or state I.D. cards cannot be used for any federal purpose unless they meet specific federal requirements.

Under the Real I.D. Act, non-compliant driver's licenses and state-issued I.D. cards cannot be used for identification to board federally regulated airplanes or to go into any federal facility. After May 2008, state driver's licenses or I.D. cards must meet Real I.D. Act compliance requirements.

As this is written, the deadline for compliance is nearly two years away. It is difficult to predict the future, but many expect the Real I.D. Act, when it goes into force, to be a deal-breaker, so to speak. Patriot radio station guests, hosts, and callers are outraged. Many see this as the lock on the gate to American freedom. Others have promised to ignore it—and these people include those who have not, until this time, protested loudly against what is now believed will be near-total government control over citizens.

Although the specifics of the card have not been published at this time, duplicates of some radio frequency identification (RFID) chips are expected to be the patterns from which the Real I.D. cards' chips will be modeled. Information on the chip within each card is expected to contain significant data on the various facets of your life which have heretofore been scattered around in various state and federal agency files or unavailable to government entirely.

Now, the plan is to make it easy, convenient, and cost effective for government agency employees to monitor U.S. citizens through one central locale, with one comprehensive, all-inclusive, national identification card. Cards and cardholders are expected to be located much like a cell phone when it is turned on. Already, equipment is being promoted which reportedly will be able to void out the signals used to track cardholders.

Once the card becomes enforceable and necessary to do your business, how will law-abiding citizens with a passion for privacy cope with their new "brands" placed in their pockets by Uncle Sam? Although any answer is strictly speculation, expect resistance to the intrusive Real I.D. card. Many protested driver's licenses when they became mandatory, and even today people live their lives without state-issued driver's licenses, U.S. passports, or any government-issued identification whatsoever.

The Real I.D.—a national identification card, to be sure—may become the proverbial line in the sand between big government and many citizens. The best defense against a controlling government has always been to keep abreast of the changes that occur, while making plans to sidestep all the privacy-invasive traps set for you as a citizen. As always, your goal should be to maintain your privacy—shielding it from everyone who does not need to know your business: government, investigators, stalkers, identity thieves and crooks of all kinds, and others who want to steal from you, harm you or a loved one, or make your life a nightmare.

Working within the limits of the current laws is always the best policy, and I believe the future restrictions that will be placed on American citizens and spawned from this legislation will contain loopholes that will allow innovative, privacy-conscious individuals to continue to manage their businesses and personal lives privately.

HOMELAND SECURITY AND THE PATRIOT ACT

Soon after 9/11/01, government began passing new laws designed to thwart the efforts of terrorists, who, they claim, are planning to invade the country and destroy us—unless, that is, we give Big Bureaucrat even more power over our lives.

The Patriot Acts I and II came along thereafter and are designed to destroy traditional American liberties while being promoted as laws against terrorist threats. Likewise with Homeland Security, the new giant agency saddled with protecting the U.S.A. in its war against one invisible, giant, terrorist leader believed to be hiding in Pakistan—and others whose bases are not known but who are spotted here and there around the world, with a few being occasionally picked off by our government.

Homeland Security works to screen and prevent would-be hijackers, terrorist criminals, and others from flying the "friendly skies." Since the Twin Towers disaster, two separate presidential appointees have manned the command post of the Homeland Security force now responsible for protecting the country from terrorists. Complete with danger-signal color codes, Homeland Security now broadcasts its warnings to citizens when terrorist dangers approach varying degrees of seriousness.

As of this publication, no additional attacks have been committed on American soil. The Patriot Act, perhaps the least understood of all modern legislation, is a kind of catch-all law. Essentially, it allows government to place just about any restriction imaginable on citizens—for the sake of the War on Terror, of course. Meanwhile, you and I, the good guys, are supposed to passively stand by and tolerate government agents monitoring phone conversations with Granny in Iran or Cousin Ali in Egypt. Or Hilda from Germany, Bill from Ireland, Bertha from Wisconsin—or the insurance man from down the street.

Government is restricting your privacy and freedoms unnecessarily, while claiming to be protecting this country. Observe your southern borders to verify the lie Big Bureaucrat is telling you. Some bankers will tell you that they need your Social Security number "because of the Patriot Act," in order to open a trust checking account—even when the trust has its own tax identification number.

Bankers and brokers may claim they must have your Social Security number, as well as the tax identification number, for the Nevada Limited Partnership account you plan to use to hold liquid assets due to the requirements placed on them by the Patriot Act. Yet, ahead of you in the bank's line are numerous illegal-alien Mexicans who are given the privilege of banking in your country without a Social Security number or a U.S. government identity document of any kind.

In fact, the Patriot Act requires banks and other financial institutions to "know their customer" and does not specifically state that all signers have to have their Social Security number on bank records. If, in fact, the goal of our government's new laws and its new agency is to protect us from terror, why does the U.S. have, essentially, an open border policy with Mexico? Why would any country desiring to eliminate terrorist threats allow 10,000 people to illegally cross its border daily without any identification screening whatsoever?

Meanwhile, legal citizens—taxpayers who have fully half of their earned gross income taken away by government taxes in one form or another—are being forced to give up their rights and freedoms at alarming rates and are being given few options but to comply with fascist-like dictatorial orders to show their papers, by a government with apparently one objective in mind—complete control over its citizenry.

REGAINING FREEDOM AND PRIVACY

In spite of your government's efforts to take freedom and privacy away from you, while telling you it is for national security, many are just not buying it. Much like property confiscation through eminent domain, government is abusing citizens' rights to privacy and freedom by passing comprehensive, all-intrusive laws designed to steal your privacy, while disguising its real motivation: control and tracking of you and your money.

There are those who proclaim they have nothing to hide and shout their support for the national I.D. card. These government supporters, at any cost of freedom, have no experience dealing with the demanding bureaucrats running the show or are simply mouthpieces for the administration itself.

Also, don't make the mistake of blaming Republicans or Democrats for any one particular ban on your freedoms. They are very similar in their beliefs at the highest levels of the parties, regardless of affiliation. In any case, real freedom and complete privacy of your affairs is never an easy or inexpensive task, so recognize that there will always be obstacles in your way to preserve your privacy, although there are generally lawful ways that provide privacy-minded citizens with the wherewithal to do their business without the world knowing about it—even under the current freedom obstacles we all face.

The time to begin your personal and business privacy plan is now, however, without further delay. Based on the newest revelations of government agencies monitoring citizens' telephone calls and computers, do you really want to have your cell telephone in your name, with a billing address leading to your door?

Perhaps you need to beef up your computer security and privacy. Standard firewalls will not protect your e-mail and IP addresses from being found, for those with the equipment, time, and money to monitor you as you use your computer for communication and your work. There are offshore proxy servers, secure methods of e-mail communication, and other privacy tactics you can employ if you desire to insulate yourself from nosey bureaucrats and other crooks out to steal your identity, money, and confidential information.

Do you now believe it may be prudent to title property—real and otherwise—in entities that have no traceable links to you? What about the car you drive? The chapter in this book on "Driving Secretly" includes proven methods for being unrecognizable as you travel. Read it again and think about how important it is to have the confidence of knowing that you are traveling anonymously while driving, unless you are forced to show your driver's license while you are operating a motor vehicle.

Certainly, we cannot avoid all of government's intrusions. We all have to fly on airplanes, pay our taxes, and present certain identity documents on occasion. Thus, we as privacy-minded people are still in the system but out of the loop. When the principles presented in this book are followed, citizens minimize their exposure to government in their business and personal lives.

Furthermore, even if government, an unsavory character, a private investigator, a stalker, an identity thief, or anyone else knows you exist, finding you can be a time-consuming and an expensive task. Unless you are really wanted and wanted badly, the costs to those doing the hunting will be prohibitive—both in terms of man hours necessary to accomplish the task, as well as the dollars expended for the satisfaction of coming face to face with the real you.

Of course, there will be some cases when the hunter has an unlimited budget—government, for example. Also, regardless of the budget or skill of the hunters, some rare individuals are so dedicated and so skilled and talented that they remain at large, no matter who hunts them or how much money is paid to find them.

An "official" address located offshore may be to your advantage, and this can be accomplished while sitting at your computer. An out-of-country base is a starting point for high-level security, as is the "verification" of such an address as evidenced by your statement in the "consumer statement" on your credit bureau reports.

When you receive creditors' bills and personal correspondences in another country, what is the world to think, but that you live there? Keeping credit bureau files locked up and "frozen" can be a good idea as well, thus keeping everyone ignorant of which banks extend you credit, as well as making all confidential, personal, and financial matters your secret.

Carefully review all sections of this book, while emphasizing those chapters under each part which will lead you toward accomplishing your business and personal privacy, based on your individual needs and goals—even during these uncertain, unprecedented times of government control over you. Become adaptable by study and experience, and welcome changes as new opportunities to increase your personal knowledge and develop new and better ways to make your life private.

SUMMARY

1. Citizens are abused by law enforcement in America today at alarming rates, as government strives to exercise control over all aspects of the lives of law-abiding people. Record numbers of innocent Americans are unlawfully incarcerated.

2. The American public passively allows government to steal their freedoms, while being brainwashed by a corporate-controlled mainstream media.

3. Eminent domain—the right of government to buy property from private owners at fair market value for the good of the public—is being abused by government. Private property owners are having their houses and other property seized by big government, which passes it on to other private sources for the purpose of generating increased tax revenues.

4. The television media is contributing to increased government power, as reality cop shows emphasize the need for more police power for misdemeanors and restrictions on the second-amendment rights of citizens, while felons— including repeat-offender illegal aliens—continue to cross American borders at a rate of an estimated ten thousand every day.

5. Abide by all U.S. customs laws and cross borders legally. Americans frequently have their mail opened by U.S. customs officials.

6. FinCEN, BSA Direct, and other government-controlled databases allow government to sneak into private financial affairs of citizens, who have their financial records available to be searched through these databases.

7. Interpol is a world police force designed to fight crime worldwide.

8. The Internal Revenue Service is one of the most feared quasi-government agencies in America. Americans are taxed based on monetary achievements by the I.R.S.

Certain entities, when structured properly—mainly the Nevada Limited Partnership, combined with an offshore asset protection trust in a favorable foreign jurisdiction—are reported to be judgment proof for claims and judgments from all, including the Internal Revenue Service.

9. Americans, despite their second-amendment rights, have lost freedoms associated with gun ownership. Armed countries, including Switzerland, and certain armed American communities, have low crime rates.

10. Illegal-alien Mexicans and others who unlawfully cross American borders are not pursued by law enforcement, and their ability to continue to invade the country is facilitated by greedy corporate businesses that pay them. The federal government facilitates the entry of illegal aliens and allows them to work illegally, without penalties. An open border policy with Mexico is against the constitution and the law, but the federal government overrides these laws and continues to allow this invasion at astronomical expense to citizen taxpayers.

11. The Real I.D. Act is scheduled to be enforceable in May 2008. All state-issued driver's licenses are ordered by the federal government to comply with Real I.D. Act requirements by 2008.

12. Homeland Security is responsible for the safety of U.S. citizens from terror.

13. The Patriot Acts provide government with unprecedented powers over United States citizens.

14. Privacy, though more difficult during the present time and into the future, can still be accomplished by those who have the information, skills, and dedication to make their personal and business lives private.

TWENTY-EIGHT

Your Individual Privacy Plan

"Success lies in the hour of decision."—Jesse Livermore

ASSESSMENT

Beginning to live a private lifestyle, with the freedom it will assure you, is best approached by making a decision to take an honest look at where you stand today, so far as your privacy is concerned. Consider your objectives and goals, as well. It is important to remember that not only does it take a period of time to gain high-level privacy, but skills and costs are involved, as well.

If you are currently living like most of the masses but desire to change to a more safe, secure, private style of living, congratulations on making the decision. It is doable. First, let's assume you are currently living as the average American man or woman but have had an awakening, whether through an event or simply through your own thought processes—either of which has given you significant motivation to make some changes.

Begin by considering what is most important to you, as well as establishing some short-term objectives that will enable you to make some progress toward a more private life. Like most, you probably own your own home. You may receive mail at home or at your office. Your money, investments, home, and automobile are probably held in your name or are owned jointly with a spouse.

You may work for an employer or have a business interest in your company—or be self-employed. You use your driver's license as your primary identification, may or may not have a U.S. passport, and have no alternate identity documents. Your telephones—both land-line and cell phone—are in your name, and the home telephone may be unlisted.

Recently, you have become aware of the potential dangers of having your life out in the open, and reading this book has increased your privacy awareness, so you now want to begin to form a plan to take the necessary steps to make your life private.

PRIVACY PRIORITIES

Perhaps the best place to start would be to begin to erase yourself on paper—to disappear. This can be arranged with some effort and over time, so let's establish some priorities—some simple solutions to solving the problem of your current availability to the entire world.

Let's begin the process of making you become invisible. You can "move" by establishing a mailing address/mail forwarding service with a reliable "nominee," as outlined in the "Communication" section of this book. A change of address with the post office will redirect all personal mail to your new "residence"—a big privacy step by itself.

However, you may want to bypass the post office entirely for privacy purposes, as it is best to have no record of your true name with the postal service. Instead of completing any government forms, simply notify everyone that you want to let know you have "moved." This is more private, completely breaks the paper trail from your previous address, and will eliminate numerous junk mailings.

In fact, every few years, it is a good quality control tactic to "move" and start fresh with a new address, to eliminate as many potential snoops as possible from learning where your mail is received. For snail mail, keep a list of all those that you want to be on your mailing list, and only add to it when receiving snail mail is absolutely necessary. Once this is done, you have taken a necessary and big step toward increasing your personal privacy.

Now, you can make arrangements to pick up your mail or have it forwarded a second time to a convenient location. And from this time forward, you will not use your home address to receive any mail or deliveries, whatsoever. Instead, you will utilize a mail-drop service for these purposes.

Your other priorities include your home and automobile. Guidelines in the "Travel" and "Home" sections of this book are offered, and you can customize them as needed to suit yourself.

Your money and investments, when held individually, provide an open book to your financial life for those resourceful and clever enough to find it. And someone may locate your assets, unless you hold personal money in the name of a trust, and investment assets in an LLC or limited partnership, depending on your requirements and as per the advice of your attorney. Also, it is important to title the accounts properly, including only the trust's name and business entity on the statements that are to be received by mail. All of these details are fully explained in the chapters in the appropriate sections of this book.

Rearranging your home ownership, utility account names, automobile title, and personal and investment accounts and assets requires time, thought, and financial commitment, so plan your strategies well, and seek out appropriate legal counsel when legal advice is needed.

Recognize that establishing a high level of personal and business privacy will require time and due diligence, so be prepared to take it one step at a time, while prioritizing your privacy program. Also, "maintenance" work will be required along the way to preserve your privacy, so keep abreast of important developments to make your life private.

EMERGENCY PLAN

No one ever wants a negative, lifestyle-changing type of emergency to occur. However, life has a way of throwing those crazy curve balls at us when we least expect them, and it behooves all of us to be prepared to handle whatever emergency should come our way. You don't drive your car without brakes or insurance, do you? Likewise, you should not be without an emergency plan in the event you are ever forced into living a very high-level privacy lifestyle.

Paramount to your preparation plan is the equivalent of your "safe house" or rented storage space covered in the "Home" section of this book. You must recognize that many people are faced with emergencies during their lives, and having an escape "stash" of supplies and money will ensure that, at the very least, you have time to think things through, with perhaps appropriate legal or other consultations for advice on a longer-term plan to deal with the problem(s) when this is appropriate.

So in addition to having an off-site storage space rented at all times, where valuables, tax records and receipts, documents, food and clothing, and other essential supplies and wares are stored, this facility should necessarily contain a knapsack of sorts—filled with supplies— which will easily fit in the trunk of your car if you ever have to make a speedy exit.

Alternate identity documents—with a matching debit card or a company debit card, with neither being reportable to any credit bureau and loaded with enough money for lodging and other essentials for a month—are also a good idea, according to successful, experienced privacy advocates. An equal amount of cash will enable you to purchase goods and services that will be untraceable when such a situation requires you to become invisible.

An automobile that is reliable and properly registered to a trust, an "anonymous car," for all practical purposes, as described in the "Travel" section, will enable you to travel secretly. Or you could use public transportation if your situation should warrant it.

Essential files and true identity documents, a laptop computer, office and mail supplies, safe deposit contents, medications, and individual preference items for travel, as well as a supply of emergency food, and luggage containing clothing and personal hygiene items, round out the list of what will be required to quickly pack your car and adopt a mobile living lifestyle, while keeping your basic home comforts intact.

If you have been fortunate and foresighted enough to have most everything in place prior to needing it, in order to enable you to make your life private, a mobile lifestyle will be most pleasant. If not, you will have to arrange for your privacy needs as you travel and are away from your normal domicile.

This is doable and will be the case for many privacy seekers, so utilize all that technology has to offer as you fax, e-mail, and phone your way to a high level of privacy, while utilizing professionals and nominees to provide you with guidance and privacy services.

Liquid financial assets enable the person requiring a mobile lifestyle to experience no discomfort or extra work, since all accounts can be conveniently accessed online as you travel about anonymously. When hard assets and real estate are held, some extra work and trusted employees or subcontractors will be necessary to handle your business.

As always, preparation and a willingness to adapt to whatever situation becomes necessary will enable the privacy advocate to live underneath privacy-invasive databases designed to track and control law-abiding citizens.

REVIEW OF THE PRIVACY DISCIPLINES

As previously mentioned, the more thoroughly prepared you are when an emergency presents itself, the more pleasant the experience of adaptation to the inconvenience. Becoming aware of the basic disciplines for your privacy program and taking whatever individual steps are necessary, based on your requirements and personal plan—combined with advice you receive from your selected attorneys and other advisors—will allow you to insulate yourself from those in the world who may want to interfere with your private life.

Let's review and summarize the privacy disciplines with which you must be familiar and which you may use, based on your particular lifestyle. Keep in mind that as life changes, so may requirements in regard to some of the disciplines.

1. IDENTITY THEFT

The fastest-growing crime in the United States, identity theft has made its mark as a concern for all Americans who desire their privacy and protection. Prevention is the answer. Do not expect "quick-fix" insurance-type packages currently being touted, to save you and your property from sophisticated thieves with hi-tech equipment.

Remember, privacy is always more expensive and time consuming than living like the masses. The trade-off is safety and peace of mind, so pay attention to the various sections of this book and study the applicable chapters under each section, in order to insulate yourself, your loved ones, and your property from those who have no business knowing your personal and business affairs.

2. IDENTIFICATION

Identification is key in today's world, and you will want to have an alternate/novelty identification available and at the ready to make a smooth transition to the "new you," as required for privacy. Few will require more than a good-quality foreign or novelty identity document, as described in the "Identification" section.

Never present identification other than your true government-issued identification to a government or law enforcement official. In the event you believe you may require a permanent identity change, you still have that option—and this can be legally accomplished during a time when it is not yet urgent that you make such a permanent change. If, however, an emergency arises, and you actually need a new identity now, it may be too late to legally change your name without serious repercussions.

Also, be certain that giving up your true identity is your best choice. If it really is your decision to become someone else, changing your name legally through a court or just by assuming a different name over time—when done to escape an obligation or when wanted for a crime or civil tort—will not be doable. This is because you will be required to state certain facts under oath, and your Social Security number will no doubt be "run" prior to being issued a new one, providing you are able to change your Social Security number—a difficult task indeed—along with your new name. Only in the rarest of cases—entering a witness-protection program, physical danger from an abusing spouse, for example—will a change of Social Security number be approved.

So recognize that while making permanent changes to your name and Social Security number on all permanent records can be accomplished in certain cases, making these changes is not a viable option when you are facing an emergency and need to "disappear" within a short period of time for privacy reasons.

For most, using an alternate name for privacy purposes is a good choice, while keeping one's true name for all official business. Remember the cardinal identification rule which applies in most states in the nation—one may go by whatever name he or she chooses, so long as using an alternate identity is not for the intention of defrauding another. Privacy seekers are advised to check all applicable laws in their given location prior to using alternate names and identity documents for any purpose.

3. COMMUNICATION

Privacy seekers who establish high-level telephone privacy, establish a cell telephone in an alternate name, or use a cell phone company such as Tracfone or Net 10, which have no name registration requirements.

A prepaid plan is a good idea, though more expensive than those popular one- and two-year contract deals—though these come with their own drawbacks, including lengthy contractual obligations, a credit check, and regular reporting to the credit bureaus. This is a private investigator's dream, and most people buy these privacy-invasive plans, while supplying the telephone company with their actual home address as well.

Successful privacy advocates never buy a cell telephone in their own name or give out their Social Security number to a telephone company.

They opt for the more-expensive, no-contract, prepaid cell telephones, which allow them to pay for minutes in cash at a store or anonymously by using their prepaid debit card held in their alternate name or company name. Voicemail, pay telephones, and telephone cards further assist them in their quest for a secure, confidential, telephone communication system.

Mail privacy—an important component of making your life private—is best accomplished while using nominees in a distant state and in a foreign country to receive your mail and then forward it back to you at the time and location you request. Your mail nominee can also handle remailing letters for you as well, to create an illusion of you being far away from your actual location. Independent nominees are more private and generally provide a better quality of service, in my experience, when compared to the commercial mail-receiving agencies, which typically hire entry-level, low-wage employees.

Also, these companies are regulated by their competition—the U.S. Postal Service. I have always been curious about that fact. When I have had occasion to ask why these companies put up with this and allow their own competition to require them to have customers complete those government forms and have the option of disallowing them to service certain customers, most have no explanation or answer to this question.

Avoid them. Use independent nominees to handle your mail. Your communication system will be complete when you establish certain security measures to ensure that your e-mail and your computer are not easily traced back to you. With enough motivation, suitable equipment, and a budget to support their efforts, identity thieves, investigators, or others cannot only find your city but your Internet service provider and actual location.

Your computer has its own unique IP ("Internal Protocol") address that reveals your actual geographic location. But through the use of certain kinds of "proxy servers," it is possible to hide your IP address and gain a degree of anonymity. Other supporting software or hardware can be used as needed, depending on your individual needs.

E-mail, another tell-tale give-away identifier unless you are careful, can be made anonymous by remailing e-mail or by using complete software programs that will assist you in making all of your computer operations private. A number of programs and additional items of equipment on the market will assist you in your computer and internet privacy goals.

4. HOME

Concealing your home location will offer the most challenges, particularly when you live as most Americans who own their own homes, while purchasing them and recording the ownership in their own names.

Once this is done, a simple solution which may be effective is to arrange a "dummy sale" and sell the home to a trust to create a new owner, thereby eliminating the previous owner's name from the county database as the legal owner.

Traditional mortgages will not enable one to live anonymously. A creative home financing option will need to be arranged in lieu of obtaining a loan from a mortgage company.

Utility account records provide an easy and convenient way of locating people, and in order to keep yourself from being found by Gumshoe or others, use the services of an independent nominee to obtain your accounts and maintain them with the various utility companies. Disconnecting the utilities held in your name and having a nominee obtain them again while you "move" may work, but I would opt to really move if I were inclined toward a privacy lifestyle.

Reviewing the options for ultimate privacy living in the "Home" section of this book will expose you to your options and requirements of each anonymous style of living. You must realize that ownership of your residence, while preserving your privacy, is the most complicated form of privacy living, and you may want to consider the other available choices when privacy becomes a top priority.

Mobile-style living, whether in a hotel, motel, extended-stay hotel, or recreational vehicle offers one the most privacy and fewest complications, due to the use of third-party services and utilities, as well as the capability of being able to change locations on short notice. Consider mobile-style living when you are under pressure to relocate in a hurry, for any number of reasons.

Traditional renting arrangements enable one and his family to move on short notice as well, usually while giving one month's notice, although a six-month lease or longer may be required initially to occupy the property.

Renting an off-site storage space with good security is essential for storing supplies, records, and valuables that are best stored away from one's home or office. Emergency equipment and supplies may be stored there as well. In all cases, when occupying your home and when privacy is a priority, establishment of an alternate name with no link whatsoever to your true name is essential for privacy purposes, according to a number of privacy seekers.

Family members will have to be educated about privacy tactics and family privacy policies in order for your plan to be successful. All utilities and services necessary for the operation of the home will need to be obtained in the names of third-party nominees to preserve anonymity, in most cases.

5. TRAVEL

Serious privacy seekers will have their car properly registered to a trust. I say "properly registered," as special attention to detail to ensure that no ties to you exist on the registration is an important consideration. Also, no mailings concerning the registration should have your name as trustee on the paperwork. Review the "Travel" section for specific, detailed travel information.

Trusts are the preferred entity for holding titles to automobiles and enable one to enjoy more privacy than does any other form of ownership.

Few forms of transportation will provide one with an anonymous means of traveling. Airlines and trains will want to see government-issued identity documents prior to allowing you on board. Ships will check for the same identification. Traveling with another driver or by bus will allow you to go anywhere in the continental United States without any identification requirements. Whenever you cross borders, a passport will be required.

Five to ten thousand illegal aliens cross into the United States from Mexico every day without anyone stopping them to check their identification. Illegal border crossings are accomplished by people riding in cars and trucks as well as by pedestrians.

6. FINANCES

Anonymous bill paying, through the use money orders, cash, and debit cards held in alternate names, enables one to keep business and personal liquid assets concealed. Privacy banking can be accomplished through the use of trust accounts for personal money and limited partnerships and LLCs and other entities for business and liquid investments. Consult your attorney for the best plan for you, based on your circumstances.

Real estate may require creative financing for privacy purposes. Investment real estate and other illiquid assets should be held in separate entities for asset protection and privacy. Review the "Finances" section for information on how to structure registration of investments for privacy purposes. In all cases, entities will provide legal privacy layers for anonymous registrations, when registrations are required for legal entity status.

Credit bureaus are the equivalent of corporate big brothers and will require your attention to ensure that your credit bureau reports reflect accurate, current information. Freezing your credit bureau reports may be warranted. Credit is a wonderful leverage tool when it is used properly at attractive interest rates. Carefully attend to your credit bureau reports in order to have the advantage of available credit, while keeping your credit history and personal credit report private and confidential.

7. BUSINESS

Preparation for a job, business, skill, or profession begins during the education process. Public schools provide state-sponsored educational curricula as well as their own trained personnel, from elementary levels through doctoral programs. With these curricula come the philosophical influences of government that are forced upon students as they progress toward preparation for careers. Private schools—especially online schools—have accreditation standards that are equal to the state's public schools and may be less privacy invasive.

Home schooling and correspondence education programs also allow students to obtain education credentials from kindergarten through high school graduation. Independent-study programs, combined with credit for life and work experiences, enable one to obtain bachelors and masters degrees at certain universities and colleges.

Business people who found companies may register the business entity without revealing themselves as having any connection to the company whatsoever, when privacy guidelines are utilized as emphasized under the "Business" section. Trusts and administrative trustees, combined with a business friendly state such as Nevada for the company registration, enable anyone to operate privately, while following all legal and compliance guidelines. Consult your business attorney and tax advisor for professional advice on all business matters specific to your individual requirements.

Individuals who work for an employer as a traditional employee have the least ability to privatize their work affairs. Registries, unions, independent contractors, and employment arrangements, wherein the employee works for a trust or LLC he/she has created—an entity which is then "hired" by the employer—will enable the employee to remain private as an employee, since the "employee" on record will be the trust or LLC, with its own tax identification number.

Competent people skills, combined with a demand for one's professional and/or business or technology skills, will allow one to secure such an employment arrangement. Non-government employers will be the most amenable to contracting with an LLC or a trust for services.

Professional and technical employees have the greatest chances of working under the umbrella of a trust or LLC as their "employer." In all cases, one's business should not have a name related to his or her true name when privacy is a strong consideration.

8. BEHAVIOR

The "Behavior" section is the most important part of this book. Developing the communication and behavioral skills necessary to handle the privacy lifestyle is paramount to your success.

Many times, one's ability to relate to a government employee or a quasi-government business such as a bank or brokerage company will be the deciding factor in the receipt of the business or personal consideration required to make your life private. Practice all communication skills, and refer often to the "Behavior" section of this volume.

Through proper speaking and writing communication, you will not get everything you want every time you want it, but your batting average will improve substantially when you operate from a positive frame of reference, with polished communication skills. Living a high-level privacy lifestyle creates stress, and you should recognize that few people can be trusted with your secrets. Self-reliance and a privacy plan will enable you to make your way anonymously through the world as an invisible man or woman, if you desire such a high level of secrecy.

Virtually all aspects of privacy are included in this book. Privacy advocates have utilized the principles herein to successfully live a private life, while being law abiding citizens. So can you. Nominees are used for those services that require a stand-in or substitute person in place of the actual person receiving the services. Carefully select your nominees by using professionals by referral when possible, and form a contract for these important services.

Government agencies of all kinds may present barriers to your privacy plan. Above all, abide by the laws of the land, while creating privacy layers to enable you to be invisible to government and others for privacy purposes. Study and an increased awareness of changes as they occur will allow you to live your life as privately as is necessary.

Those privacy seekers who want high-level security and privacy can stay within the limits of state and federal laws. Creating an invisible you who has essentially disappeared on paper is the greatest defense you have for avoiding the government nonsense which plagues the United States of America today. Use the system with your creative genius for your privacy benefits, while being careful to obey the laws.

With the right resources, as outlined in the various chapters under the privacy sections of this book, one can live a life of anonymity. Realize that obtaining a high level of privacy takes time, effort, and money, not to mention the professional advice and individual planning specific to your own lifestyle.

Start with an honest, accurate assessment, make a plan which begins with the basics as described in this chapter, and plan your additional privacy measures as you so desire. Prioritize and establish the most important privacy aspects first to give you an immediate level of privacy.

This book will serve as your reference for years to come, and you will be successful when you adopt the principles and methods as they are presented. Laws and governments change from time to time, so you must be adaptable and flexible and create an open-minded awareness to make the proper life adjustments as you continue to live anonymously.

SUMMARY

1. An accurate assessment of your current level of privacy, both in your personal and business life, will serve as a starting point for establishing priorities and objectives for increasing privacy and security.

2. Basic privacy can be accomplished with a simplified plan of not associating your true name with your home, automobile, or communication system. Additional privacy measures can be accomplished as per your individual needs and requirements.

3. An emergency plan to disappear, complete with a "stash house" or private storage space will enable one to relocate, with time to receive professional consultations and make plans to cope with any given emergencies or catastrophe which may occur.

4. A number of privacy disciplines are included in the sections of this book. Chapters applicable to these disciplines are written under each section. Carefully review these parts and chapters to make an individual plan for privacy as you make your life private.

Glossary

ADMINISTRATIVE TRUSTEE: A person designated on Trust documents to perform limited and specific duties as a Trustee.

ALIAS: *See* Alternate Name.

ALTERNATE IDENTIFICATION: Identity documents issued in an alternate or Assumed Name by private sources for non-official use. Also known as Novelty Identification.

ALTERNATE NAME: A name used for anonymity and security. Also called an Assumed Name or an Alias.

ALTERNATE PRIMARY IDENTIFICATION: Alternate identification documents issued by private sources for non-official use. Examples are foreign country passports, identification cards, and driver's licenses issued in an alternate name. Also called Novelty Identification cards.

ALTERNATE SECONDARY IDENTIFICATION: Supporting identification documents issued by private sources for non-official use and that are secondary to Primary Alternate Identification. Examples are debit cards, school and work I.D., and insurance cards issued in an alternate name.

ANONYMOUS CREDIT/DEBIT CARDS: Credit and debit cards issued in an Alternate Name or without a name for privacy purposes.

ARTICLES OF ORGANIZATION: The founding documents and controlling provisions of a Limited Liability Company (LLC) which are filed with the secretary of state.

ASSET SEARCH: Privacy-invasive search for all classes of assets held by a person under investigation.

ASSUMED NAME: *See* Alternate Name. Also known as an Alias.

AUTOMATIC CLEARING HOUSE (ACH): Electronic transfer of currency for bank deposit or payment of bills.

BANKING PASSPORT: Unofficial passport manufactured in the names of defunct governments and countries, the names of which have since changed. Reportedly used by some privacy advocates for foreign banking and alternate identification.

BIG BUREAUCRAT: Any government agent, official, or agency.

BSA DIRECT: Bank Secrecy Act "direct access," which will improve users' ability to analyze BSA data and increase FinCEN's ability to provide information to other agencies with an interest in subjects being investigated.

CHEXSYSTEMS: An association of financial institutions that network together for the purpose of developing and maintaining a database that stores the records of customers considered undesirable by banks.

CLUE REPORT (COMPREHENSIVE LOSS UNDERWRITING REPORT): Database of consumer information and claims history created by ChoicePoint, which insurance companies can access during the underwriting process.

COMMERCIAL MAIL-RECEIVING AGENCIES (CMRAs): Companies that offer mail receiving and related services to businesses and individuals and are regulated to some extent by their competition, the United States Post Office.

DUAL TRUST ACCOUNT PRINCIPLE: The practice of using two non–interest-bearing checking accounts held by one or two different Trusts with two separate banks for the purpose of increasing personal financial privacy. The accounts are designated as a "Public Trust Account" and a "Private Trust Account."

DUMMY SALE: A sale arranged to change titles to property, while the original owner(s) continue to maintain control over the property through a separate entity.
Example: Christopher and Debra Freedomlover own an automobile in their names.
They "sell" the car to the Jack Frost Snowflake Irrevocable Trust, register it in the name of the Trust—of which they are the Trustees— and continue driving the Trust-owned automobile, which is under their control but not associated with their True Names on any government registration records.

EMPLOYER IDENTIFICATION NUMBER (EIN): A taxpayer identification number assigned by the Internal Revenue Service to Limited Partnerships, Limited Liability Companies, Trusts and other entities.

FAMILY LIMITED PARTNERSHIP: *See* Nevada Limited Partnership.

FICTITIOUS BUSINESS NAME: The assumed name of a business "doing business as" (DBA)—a particular name for business purposes.

FinCEN: The Financial Crimes Enforcement Network is a network of databases with over 140 million computer files containing records from 21,000 depository institutions and an estimated 200,000 non-banking institutions.

FREEZE CREDIT REPORTS: The process of locking up or "freezing" one's credit bureau files for privacy purposes.

FRAUD ALERT: A notice placed on a financial account or confidential information report to enhance privacy and security.

GENERAL PARTNER: A partner with unlimited legal responsibility for the debts and liabilities of a partnership.

GRANTOR: A person who creates a Trust.

IDENTITY THEFT: Fraudulent assumption of another's identity by means of stealing crucial personal information.

IRREVOCABLE TRUST: A Trust that, once formed, cannot be changed.

KEYLOGGER: Software programs that monitor a user's keystrokes and send the information back to the party attempting to gain information about the target.

LIMITED LIABILITY COMPANY (LLC): A hybrid legal entity that has characteristics of a corporation and a partnership.

LIMITED PARTNER: Partner in a Limited Partnership, having little or no voice in the management of the entity and not legally responsible for the debts and liabilities of the Limited Partnership.

MAIL COVER OPERATION: The monitoring and/or theft of citizens' mail by government agents, private investigators, postal service employees, or others when information is sought.

MEDICAL INFORMATION BUREAU (MIB): A membership organization of insurance companies which stores and exchanges confidential medical and personal information on policy holders and prospective policy holders. Address: Medical Information Bureau, P.O. Box 105, Essex Station, Boston, Mass., 02112. Telephone: (617) 426-3660.

NEVADA LIMITED PARTNERSHIP: A business entity registered with the Nevada secretary of state. A General Partner controls the partnership and has unlimited liability. Limited Partner(s) have limited liability and have little or no control of the partnership.

NOMINEE: A person who stands in or substitutes for another and is under agreement to provide services which may include receiving mail, signing documents, obtaining utility services, and other services for the privacy advocate.

"NOVELTY" IDENTIFICATION: *See* Alternate Identification.

OFFICIAL IDENTIFICATION: True birth or "given" name. Refers to Primary Identification government-issued documents.

OFFSHORE ADDRESS: An address located in a foreign country used for the purpose of receiving mail only. Also known as an "offshore mail drop."

OFFSHORE ASSET PROTECTION TRUST: A form of Irrevocable Trust created for the principal purposes of preserving and protecting one's wealth against creditors.

OPERATING AGREEMENT: Establishes the rules regarding the operation of an LLC and the rights and obligations of the members.

PARTNERSHIP AGREEMENT: A written agreement among the partners that spells out the terms and conditions and conduct of the partnership

PHISHING: A practice often used to steal identity documents and information about one's property and money through false claims of legitimate business solicitation through e-mail.

PRELOADED DEBIT CARDS: MasterCard and Visa cards which require cash to be deposited at participating stores prior to purchasing goods and services or making cash withdrawals. Also called "stored-value cards."

PRIMARY IDENTIFICATION: Government-issued identification which may be a passport, state-issued driver's license, state-issued identification card, or a birth certificate.

PRIVACY ADVOCATE: One who desires to live anonymously and takes steps to make his or her life private. Also known as a "privacy seeker."

PRIVATE TRUST ACCOUNT CONCEPT: A non–interest-bearing bank checking account held in the name of a Trust and maintained for the purpose of privately storing personal money. The Private Trust

Account is the inactive account of the Dual Trust Account Principle. Deposit only non-traceable money orders and cash into this account. Make cash withdrawals only from the Private Trust Account.

PUBLIC TRUST ACCOUNT CONCEPT: A non–interest-bearing bank checking account held in the name of a Trust and maintained for the purpose of clearing checks and storing personal money. The Public Trust Account is the active account of the Dual Trust Account Principle. Deposit checks and any negotiable instruments—and withdraw and receive funds at will while using this account. Keep the account balance low.

RESIDENT AGENT: An individual or entity designated by a Limited Liability Company (LLC), Limited Partnership, or other entity to accept official documents on behalf of the company.

REMAILING: Privacy tactic used to disguise the location from which a letter, bill or other item has been mailed by the use of a third party, who receives the original mailing in an enclosed envelope from the sender at a distant location. The remailing is done by the third party at a ruse location, which creates a location illusion for the sender of the mail.

REVOCABLE TRUST: A Trust that, once formed, may be altered or changed during the Grantor's lifetime.

RESIDENCE MAIL DROP: A home mailing address provided by a Nominee standing in to receive mail correspondence on behalf of a Privacy Advocate.

SECONDARY IDENTIFICATION: All identity documents not included under Primary Identification, including school identification, Visa and MasterCards, insurance cards, library cards, work identification cards, and all other identification cards.

SELF-INSURANCE: The process whereby a person or a business insures against possible future loss of property, life, health, or other losses by setting aside money which would normally be paid in premiums to third-party insurers for such coverages.

SETTLOR: A person or entity who forms a Trust and settles his assets into the Trust. *See* Grantor.

SIGNER: The authorized signatory on a bank account. Trustee(s) may be the signers on Trust checking accounts. Managers may be the signers on a Nevada Limited Partnership account.

STATE-ISSUED IDENTIFICATION: Driver's licenses and state identification cards.

STRUCTURING: Term used by government to charge citizens with "unlawful" cash deposits and withdrawals deemed to have been "structured" just below $10,000. Citizens may be charged for depositing and withdrawing money they own or control.

TRUE NAME: A person's birth name.

TRUST: An entity established to empower someone else to manage and care for property. A Trust must have three essential elements: property, Trustee(s), and beneficiaries.

TRUST CHECKING ACCOUNT: A liquid non–interest-bearing checking account held in the name of a Trust. Negotiable instruments may be made payable to the Trust or to any signer/Trustee individually.

TRUST MANAGER PRINCIPLE: A Trust which is registered as the "manager" of a registered business entity. A Trust may be the "manager" of record on secretary of state records for a Nevada Limited Liability Company (LLC), for example. A Trust manager can be the only company contact on public records with the State of Nevada, except for the Resident Agent, and can be located anywhere in the world.

TRUSTEE: Company or individual(s) named to make decisions on behalf of the Trust.

TRUSTOR: The individual who provides property and forms a Trust.

Index

Mail nominee 32, 36, 41, 57, 87, 154, 361

MasterCard 2, 21, 24, 26, 46, 47, 50, 53, 69, 110, 161, 187, 188, 207–209, 226, 227, 255
See also Credit cards, major

Medeco locks 77, 89

Medical Information Bureau (MIB) 27, 372

Merchant account 228, 230

Minute Man Project 345

Mobile lifestyle 54–56, 58, 358

MoneyGram 113, 203, 210

Money orders 95, 109, 117, 136, 155, 158, 161, 174, 187–189, 194, 201–203, 206, 222, 236, 262, 304, 320, 363, 374

Mortgage companies 84, 85

Motor homes 54, 55

Movers 54, 71, 80, 96

Multiple mail drops 134

N

"Novelty" identification 373

National identification card 347, 350

National Rifle Association 55

National Security Agency 14

Net-10 54, 150, 156, 360
See also Prepaid cell phone

Nevada, State of
Advantages for privacy and business 216

Nevada Family Limited Partnership 217, 218, 220, 229

Nevada Limited Liability Company 13, 173, 174, 217, 238, 273, 275, 277, 280, 282, 283, 375

Nevada Limited Partnership 13, 86, 97, 99, 137, 219–221, 223–225, 229, 232, 235, 236, 238, 253, 273, 276, 277–280, 282, 283, 311, 342, 349, 353, 371, 372, 375

Nevada secretary of state 218, 234, 238, 273, 275, 279, 372

Nevis 46, 227, 276, 282

Nominees 13, 14, 32, 34–36, 41, 57, 59, 66, 67, 69–72, 74, 79, 82, 87, 91, 140, 147, 154, 155, 158, 161, 174, 175, 185, 186, 194, 197, 202, 251, 254, 258, 280, 288, 301–308, 356, 358, 361, 362–365, 373
As bank account holders 301
Friends or family as 304

Nominee services
Retaining 306

Nominee theory for privacy 301

Notary public 84

Novelty I.D. 24, 25, 26, 29, 68

NSA 7, 14
See also National Security Agency

Privacy advocates 26, 28, 32, 34–36, 41, 51, 67, 71, 72, 82, 83, 89, 109, 120, 133, 134, 140, 203, 308, 358, 360, 370, 374

Privacy disciplines 358–368

Private domain name registration 173

Private investigators 7, 23–25, 39, 41, 57, 73, 86, 95, 102, 104, 133, 136, 143, 173, 185, 249, 251, 253, 273, 302, 307, 351, 360, 372

Private trust account 188, 206, 222, 223, 262, 374
See also Dual trust account principle

Professional Coin Grading Service (PCGS 235

Property taxes 63, 64, 79, 90, 285

Proxy servers 166, 175, 350, 361

Public computers
See Third-part computers, use of

Public trust account 188, 205, 206, 222, 223, 262, 268, 271, 374
See also Dual trust account principle

R

Radar, living beneath the 7, 16, 24, 41, 47, 61, 62, 69, 132, 135, 297, 319, 326

Radio frequency identification (RFID) chips 347

Rare coins 97, 232, 234–238

Real estate 64, 82, 83, 85–87, 90, 216, 231–234, 238, 278, 280, 282, 289, 331, 358, 364

Real I.D. Act 346, 347, 353

Recreational vehicles 54, 56, 59

Remailing 132, 134, 136, 138, 140, 201, 202, 210, 361, 374

Rental cars 110

Renter's insurance 55

Renting 13, 50, 55, 62–64, 66, 68, 69, 72, 76–78, 90, 95, 149, 172, 257, 362
Advantages of 62

Residence mail drop 32, 36, 374

Resident agent 219, 225, 278, 280, 374

Retirement accounts 265, 271

Retirement plans 265–267, 271
Types of 266

Reverse reference phone searches 143

Revocable living trust 276

Revocable trust 83, 91, 178, 276, 374

Roommate, living with 72–74, 80

RV 54–56, 59
See also Recreational vehicles

S

"Safe room" or "Safe house" 89, 91, 357

"Spoofing" 164